Outcome Measures for

Child Welfare Services

THEORY AND APPLICATIONS

Stephen Magura

Beth Silverman Moses

Child Welfare League of America, Inc.
Washington, D.C.

Child Welfare League of America
440 First Street N.W., Washington, D.C. 20001

Current printing (last digit)
10 9 8 7 6 5 4 3

Jacket design by Anita Crouch
Book design by Rose Jacobowitz

Printed in the United States of America

Library of Congress Cataloging in Publication Data

Magura, Stephen, 1947–
    Outcome measures for child welfare services.

    Bibliography: p.
    1. Child welfare—United States—Administration—
Evaluation.   2. Social work with children—United
States—Administration—Evaluation.   3. Sociometry.
I. Moses, Beth S., 1953–   .   II. Title.
HV741.M335 1986   362.7'042   86-4248
ISBN 0-87868-224-4

"That, Sir, is the good of counting. It brings everything to a certainty, which before floated in the Mind indefinitely."

—Samuel Johnson
(Boswell's *Life of Samuel Johnson*, 1791)

About The Authors

Stephen Magura holds a Ph.D. in Sociology from Rutgers University and a B.S. in Physics from Clarkson University. He has experience in evaluation research, social service program development, operations analysis, productivity improvement, statistics and computer applications. He has directed national and statewide research and evaluation projects at the New Jersey Division of Youth and Family Services, the Child Welfare League of America, Inc. and Narcotic and Drug Research, Inc., and has served as a consultant to many human services organizations. Dr. Magura has published widely in social work and social research journals. His current interests are family preservation services and drug abuse treatment.

Beth Silverman Moses received an M.S.W. from Fordham University and a B.A. in Sociology from the City University of New York. She has worked in the public and voluntary sectors conducting program evaluations involving criminal and juvenile justice, services to the elderly and single parents, and community-based coordinated services. Ms. Moses has two books forthcoming on child welfare issues from the Child Welfare League. Currently she is evaluating intensive crisis intervention projects designed to prevent child placement.

Contents

List of Illustrations

List of Tables

Acknowledgments

A study of this scope and complexity could not have been conducted without the support of many people, for which we are deeply appreciative.

The following agencies and then-current administrators collaborated on the field-testing of the Child Well-Being Scales and the Parent Outcome Interview:

Agency	Individuals
Baltimore County Department of Social Services, Towson, Maryland	Camille B. Wheeler, Director
	Mildred Taylor, Deputy Director
City of Baltimore Department of Social Services, Baltimore, Maryland	Ernestine Jones, Assistant Director, Family and Child Services
	Regina Bernard, Chief, Protective Services
Hennepin County Community Service Department, Minneapolis, Minnesota	Michael W. Weber, Director
	Rick Dettloff, Supervisor
	Charles Hogan, Supervisor
	Raymond Ahrens, Supervisor
	James Christiansen, Supervisor
Metropolitan Dade County Department of Youth and Family Development, Miami, Florida	James J. Mooney, Director of Professional Services
	Florence N. Parnell, Director Community Outreach
	Miguel A. Reyes, Assistant Director

Texas Department of Human Resources, Austin, Texas

Merle E. Springer, Deputy Commissioner, Financial and Social Programs

Gayle Owens, Administrator, Research and Evaluation

Beverly Archer, Research and Evaluation Liaison

Loren Nyer, Director, Impact Evaluation Project

Cynthia McKenzie, Regional Director for Families and Children's Services, Dallas, Texas

Margaret Maxwell, Regional Director for Families and Children's Services, Nacogdoches, Texas

The New York Foundling Hospital, Project Basement, New York, New York

Anne Grizzle, Prevention Social Worker

Spence-Chapin Services to Families and Children, Mother Infant Program, New York, New York

Martin Frommer, Project Director

We thank project coordinators and field interviewers at each agency for their diligence in implementing the study. We are especially indebted to all of the agency caseworkers who completed the Child Well-Being Scales and the clients who consented to be interviewed.

Providing valuable consultation to the study were Professor Alfred Kadushin, Professor Norman Polansky, Professor Elmer Struening, and Dr. Ann Shyne. We were also aided by the advice and comments of many colleagues and professionals during the course of the study. They have improved our work, but we are responsible for any shortcomings.

The national survey of professionals, reported in chapter 4, could not have been conducted without the kind cooperation of nearly 800 caseworkers, supervisors, and administrators.

Dr. Mary Ann Jones, coauthor of the grant proposal and Director of Research at the Child Welfare League, provided administrative and intellectual support as well as indispensable encouragement for this study.

Secretarial duties were ably carried out by Julia Giordano and Anne Moore. Alicia Biederman was a capable research assistant. Shelby Miller contributed to the grant proposal. The unstinting assistance of many additional League staff during the course of this study is gratefully acknowledged.

At the U.S. Children's Bureau, this study was well supported by Dr. Charles Gershenson, Director, Program Development and Innovation Division, and by our project officers, E. Dollie Wolverton (1979–81) and Alice Fusillo (1982–83). The value of their assistance and encouragement cannot be overestimated.

Finally, we express appreciation for the funding provided by Grant No. 90-CW-2041 from the Administration for Children, Youth and Families, Office of Human Development, Department of Health and Human Services, Washington, D.C.

July 1984

STEPHEN MAGURA
BETH SILVERMAN MOSES

1

Defining
and Measuring
Case Outcomes

Introduction

Need for Outcome Evaluation

The present "Age of Accountability" poses difficult and as yet unmet challenges to the child welfare field. Weary of relying on faith in well-intentioned but often unavailing programs, society is asking social workers to prove that their work is worth supporting. "It is not a generous or forgiving age. It is an age when little or nothing will be taken for granted" (Briar 1973:2).

How well have child welfare services been able to respond to this continuing "crisis of accountability" (Neuman and Turem 1974)? An examination of the nation's child welfare system in 1976 by the U.S. General Accounting Office concluded that:

> We found no means being used or proposed for assessing, at specified intervals, the extent of change in and adequacy of a child's situation. . . . The evaluations by

local child welfare officials were primarily concerned with areas such as maintenance of case files, service planning, and service delivery. . . . We believe that
the effectiveness of any assistance program must be expressed in terms relative to
the well-being of the program's target population (USDHEW 1976:6,12,64).

As pressures for accountability have increased, many child welfare agencies have tried to
identify service objectives and to develop accurate measures of progress toward them. Unfortunately, consensus on objectives has been hard to attain, and precise measurement of a
child's well-being and the suitability of the child's care have faced formidable conceptual and
technical obstacles. Despite several decades of effort, the child welfare field still lacks generally
agreed-upon, valid, useful, and readily obtainable client outcome measures (Shyne 1976).

This situation was documented by two nationwide surveys of its member agencies
conducted by the Child Welfare League of America in 1974 and 1979. On both occasions a
majority of respondents indicated reliance wholly on global staff assessments of an informal,
nonsystematic nature, to measure case outcomes. A considerable number of agencies had
attempted "in-house" instrument development, but the results were rarely disseminated to the
field as a whole for needed critique and refinement. Turnover of outcome measures at agencies
was rapid between 1974 and 1979, and considerable ambivalence was reported about the
value of the measures used. The outcome measures were criticized most frequently for being
overly subjective; too general or simplistic; insensitive to case progress or changes over time;
and of undetermined reliability and validity (Magura and Moses 1980).

Social welfare programs are currently undergoing a painful period of retrenchment.
Clearly, shifts in social values or the political climate are beyond the influence of program
evaluation. Nevertheless, by documenting program results for clients, evaluative research can
help prevent further erosion of funding for the maintenance and improvement of essential
services to nearly two million children and their families.[1] The purpose of this book is to
provide improved tools for assessing the effectiveness of child welfare services.

Child Welfare Services Defined

The field of child welfare may be defined as "the broad range of activities designed to
benefit children, promote their well-being, and strengthen or assure provision for meeting
their physical, social, emotional, educational and moral needs" (Kadushin 1978:4). Child
welfare *services* are more specifically defined as those social services designed to "ensure that
children will have the care, protection, and treatment they need when their parents, for any
of a variety of reasons, are not able to provide these essentials" (Reid 1979:15). This excludes
health, nutritional, educational, and recreational services that also contribute to the welfare
of children but do not focus on "the problems of the child that result when the needs which
parents are ordinarily expected to meet are either unmet or inadequately met" (Hagan
1957:1). Child welfare services are offered through at least 4,000 specialized and multiservice
public and voluntary agencies in the United States (Kahn 1977:103).[2]

There is no standard typology of child welfare services. Distinctions have been made in
several ways, such as the level of intervention (supportive, supplementary, or substitute care),
the purpose of the service (protective, preventive, custodial), the type of problem (abuse,
neglect, dependency, child behavior), or the specific service modality. The most common
modality, past and present, may be defined as social casework with families and children.
Briefly stated, this involves both direct counseling of clients and the arrangement of other

services within the context of a supportive relationship. The specific services provided as part of casework may or may not be "child welfare services." For example, day care, homemaker, and foster placement are commonly defined as child welfare services, while mental health treatment, medical care, and educational services are not.[3]

The practice philosophy of child welfare services today is the preservation of family life. "Our perceptions of families—their strengths and weaknesses in coping with problems that create risks to family stability—shape the content of child welfare programs" (Stein 1981:3). The emphasis of child welfare services has been shifting dramatically from protecting children using foster care to protecting them at home; this practice philosophy is reflected in new terms such as "home-based services," "family-centered practice," "permanency planning," and "preventive services." Although not always attainable, the goal always is to ensure the well-being of children by maintaining or restoring adequate parental care and family stability.

Program Evaluation in Child Welfare

Program evaluation may be defined briefly as the use of scientific methods to describe a program and to determine its effects. A general model for program evaluation, consistent with most current terminology, is presented in Figure 1-1.

Program objectives are statements of what a program is trying to accomplish. These statements may refer to processes (for example, improving efficiency of service delivery) or outcomes (such as improving service effectiveness).

Program inputs are resources used in the course of program operations to produce outputs. Resources are typically measured in terms of money, facilities, staffing, equipment, and materials.

Program operation variables are the structural arrangements of the agency and the procedures followed by practitioners that facilitate the provision of services. They determine the process by which resources are converted into program outputs. For instance, in the case of child protective services, a structural variable would be the existence of a specialized, 24-hour intake unit, and a procedural variable would be the set of instructions for social workers regarding the initial family contact. Desirable program operation characteristics in social work are often termed "best practices." Best practice recommendations for the entire range of child welfare services may be found in standards adopted by the Child Welfare League of America and in agency self-assessment manuals developed by the Urban Institute (Sundel et al. 1978).

Program outputs are the direct products of the system, usually represented by unit of service measures such as number of intake studies completed, hours of counseling provided, days of day care arranged, and so forth. The United Way (1976) has made the most notable attempt to standardize service units for the social services, including child welfare services. Several state and local agencies have also made efforts in this area, usually in conjunction with the development of computerized management information systems (Bowers and Bowers 1976). There is as yet, however, no generally accepted unit of service classification for most social services.

Goal Variables		Process Variables			Outcome Variables	
Program Objectives	→	Program Inputs	Program Operation	Program Outputs	→ Client Outcomes	Social Impacts

Figure 1-1   Program Evaluation Model

A client outcome is a change (or lack of change) in the condition, functioning, or problems of a client that can be attributed to the program. Client outcomes of greatest interest are those related to program goals or objectives; that is, statements of what a program is trying to accomplish for its client population. The goals of child welfare services are usually stated in such terms as protecting children from abuse and neglect or ensuring that they have permanent and secure homes. Client outcomes for child welfare services thus involve determining, for example, whether child maltreatment has recurred in a family, or whether parents have improved their capacity to meet their children's physical and emotional needs.

Of course, clients may experience outcomes unrelated to or even antithetical to program objectives. For instance, a program may inadvertently foster dependency on services even as it helps clients solve problems in living. In addition to formal, manifest objectives, latent or displaced program objectives may exist that also affect outcomes for clients (Deutscher 1976). One can suggest that highly visible child protective services, such as hot lines and abuse investigations, often receive funding priority to convince the public and legislators that "something is being done" about child maltreatment, while less dramatic preventive and in-home services are underfunded despite their objective of reducing the incidence of maltreatment. Actual evaluations of service must be aware of these possibilities. This book, however, considers only the development of client outcome measures for predetermined, stated program objectives for child welfare services.

Social impacts may be defined as the consequences of individual client outcomes for the wider community. To have social impact, client outcomes must be stable over time and pertain to social goals. For example, enrolling truant or delinquent children in alternative schools may have social impact in two ways: in the short term, it may reduce the community crime rate, and in the long term, it may produce additional self-supporting members of the community. In this sense, social impacts are the returns of the child welfare system to society in exchange for resources invested.

Two concepts are commonly used to assess program performance: effectiveness and efficiency. Program effectiveness can be defined as the ratio of units of client outcome to some standard unit; this standard may represent the maximum improvement or deterioration possible in any given problem area or may represent some minimal level of adequacy as legally or culturally defined. Efficiency can be defined as the ratio of units of client outcome either to units of program output or to units of resource input. Program output would be used in the definition when interest is focused on the relationship between work accomplished and client outcomes. Resource input would be used when interest is focused on the relationship between the amount of money spent for services and client outcomes (Hatry 1978).

A program evaluation design may be defined as a plan dictating "*when and from whom* measurements will be gathered during the course of an evaluation" (Fitz-Gibbon and Morris 1978:9). A design is a strategy for gathering comparative information so that inferences can be drawn about the influence of program operations (processes) on program results (outcomes). There now exists a substantial specialized literature on evaluative research that this book will not attempt to summarize.[4] The elements of good program evaluation design are the same for child welfare services as for other human services, and a familiarity with the basic concepts is assumed.

Fundamental to any evaluation are the methods chosen or developed to measure the client outcome constructs. The availability of suitable measures often dictates the form of the evaluation design itself, sometimes even determining whether evaluation will take place at all. It is fair to say that evaluation of child welfare services has been seriously retarded both by ambiguity in defining the content of desirable outcomes and by uncertainty about the best methods of measuring that content. To make further progress toward the resolution of these issues is the concern of this book.

Types of Outcome Variables

Three main types of case outcome variables appear in evaluations of child welfare services. These types can be termed "case status," "client status," and "client satisfaction" variables. "Case status" variables are changes in the stage or phase of a case, in a client's service status or legal status. For children, this includes such events as movement to and from foster care, freeing for adoption, case closing, case reopening, and so on. In relation to the general program evaluation model in Figure 1-1, these events are best defined as "program outputs." "Client status" variables are defined as changes in a client's (child's or parent's) behavior, motives, knowledge, or resources; this includes measuring changes in presenting problems, family functioning, and so forth. "Client satisfaction" variables measure the degree to which services have fulfilled the client's subjective needs, expectations, or wishes.

Case status variables have been used as proxy indicators of client status when more direct measures of the latter are unavailable. For instance, foster placement is taken to indicate the unsuitability of a child's home situation. Case status variables are also used as what can be termed "performance indicators" for child welfare services. For example, given a service mandate to select the "least restrictive alternative" for children, then one indicator of successful service is a low foster care placement rate. Child welfare agencies have tended to emphasize the performance indicator approach in their evaluations, largely because such data seem objective and readily obtainable. Although performance indicators are an important part of service evaluation, they are no substitute for true client outcome measures. More detailed discussion of these issues follows.

Case Status Variables

We have suggested that case status variables may be interpreted in two ways: as proxy indicators of client outcomes and as performance indicators for the service system. Whether expressed as agency "objectives" or service "outcomes," these two usages are rarely distinguished clearly in the child welfare literature. Probably the case status variable used most frequently in child welfare service evaluation is "foster care placement." The meaning of this term as an outcome variable thus bears closer examination.

Separating children from their families is rightly regarded today as the least desirable method of providing children with needed protection and care. Among the most important reasons for this view are the risk of emotional damage to both parents and children, the difficulty of effecting reunion, and the cost of placement. Consequently, preventing or curtailing the necessity for foster care has assumed particular importance as a criterion of success for child welfare services (Magura 1981).

Evaluations have generally not directly measured "the necessity for foster care." Such measurement would entail determining whether there was unacceptable risk of harm to children if they were to remain at home, or if they were to return home, despite the provision of in-home services to the family. Instead, actual placement has been used as a proxy measure of this concept; that is, the very fact of placement is taken to indicate the unsuitability of the home situation for a child.

This method is tenuous because of the many sources of variability in determining who gets placed and who does not. Standards for child placement are not uniform (Mnookin 1973); individual social workers do not agree highly on placement decisions (Phillips et al. 1971); nor are alternative services equally available to all families.[5] Thus the fact that a child was placed may not be a good indicator of his or her family situation.

In general, it is not wise to use a service event or decision, such as foster placement, return home, or case closing as a proxy measure of family functioning. Client outcomes should be defined independently of services provided so that outcome data can help to inform service decisions and to assess their quality. It is clearly possible for agency practice to shift so that service statistics will change without any concomitant change in client situations or problems having occurred.

Even taking case status measures at face value, as proxies for client outcomes, yields rather crude evaluation. Case status measures are usually insensitive to degrees of client improvement; for example, a case may be closed following a certain amount of improvement, but lesser though significant improvements that do not result in a major case decision will not be identified. In addition, case status measures usually do not specify what types of client improvement have occurred.

Case status variables have assumed an important part in agency accountability as performance indicators. Perhaps the single greatest priority of child welfare services in the last decade has been to reduce the scope of the foster care system. There have been important moves to change the way in which child welfare agencies deal with families, away from what has been perceived as an overreliance on foster care and toward intensive work with parents and children in their own homes. Consequently, decreased rates of foster placement, reduced lengths of stay in care, and increased rates of adoption for children who need new homes are defined as desirable case outcomes. There is no difficulty here as long as these variables are interpreted as indicators of *system change*; that is, a transformation in the way clients are being served by the child welfare system. These results may be excellent indicators of the effects of new practice philosophies and case management techniques, such as permanency planning and independent case review.

One must be careful not to conclude, however, that changes in such performance indicators necessarily connote changes in client situations. For example, children may be returning home from foster care more rapidly because of more realistic agency standards or worker attitudes for recommending return home, more frequent assessments of parental capacity for successful reunion, or increased availability of aftercare services to enable adequate monitoring after return. These reasons may all be considered desirable system changes that are suitably reflected in a case status variable such as length of time in foster care, yet the actual home situation at the time of return need not have changed—only the agency's and community's response to it may have changed.

Client Status Variables

Considerable consensus exists on the types of client problems germane to child welfare services. These problems are usually conceptualized as types of actual or potential unmet needs of the child or types of actual or potential harm to the child. Examples include such problems as physical, sexual, or emotional abuse; physical neglect, such as lack of food, shelter, and clothing; educational neglect; need for medical or psychological treatment; inadequate supervision; economic exploitation; and parental absence (CWLA 1973; Kadushin 1980). In addition, an inadequate nurturing environment may lead a child to function or behave poorly. Problems may include delinquency, incorrigibility, and school refusal, as well as symptomatic or neurotic behavior.[6]

One cannot proceed further without noting that the terms "child abuse" and "child neglect" have been roundly criticized for their ambiguity by, for example, Giovannoni and Bacerra (1979). Sometimes the terms serve as labels to denote any child protection situation, whatever the etiology; at other times their use conforms more nearly to statutory definitions of assaultive or negligent parental conduct. A national study (USDHHS 1981) indicated that only 44.5% of substantiated protective service cases met definitional criteria of maltreatment based primarily on statutory definitions of child abuse and neglect. The criteria required evidence of "purposive acts" or "marked inattention" to the child's needs by the parent, resulting in "foreseeable and avoidable injury" or an "unreasonable prolongation or worsening of an existing injury." The implication for client outcome measurement is that, if legal criteria of abuse and neglect are used to define problems and desired outcomes, then most of the cases accepted today by child protective service agencies would fall outside the scope of the definitions. Excluded would be many cases where the issue is prevention of imminent or predictable harm, and cases where a parent could not reasonably be held responsible for a child's unmet need or injury. Such exclusions would not serve children's interests.

The admittedly remedial or "deficit" orientation of child welfare services focuses concern on whether children's needs are met in relation to some minimum standard, as defined by community norms or legal statutes. The distinction between protection from actual or potential harm and protection from abuse or neglect is again pertinent. Parents may well meet a legal standard of caring for their children in good faith and to the best of their ability with available resources, yet still not meet the community norm for adequate child care; economically deprived or mentally retarded parents are examples. The degree of irresponsibility (with its connotation of blame) shown by parents is certainly an important aspect of outcome measurement for child welfare, but it would seem wise to keep its measurement separate from that of actual or potential harm to children, of which irresponsibility is only one among many possible causes.

Inadequate role performance by parents may have a variety of sources, as outlined by Kadushin (1980). A parent may be impaired, physically or mentally; may reject the caretaking role; may be affected by role conflicts; may be subject to excessive demands by a handicapped or disturbed child; may lack access to adequate opportunities and community resources; or may be absent altogether. The cause of the problem matters little from the child's point of view. Successful outcomes may be said to occur when the conditions inimical to the child's well-being are improved or remedied.

These considerations suggest that client outcomes for child welfare services may be typologized as follows:

1. Parental role performance, defined as the direct, interpersonal activities performed by adults in their caretaking and socialization role as parents

2. Familial capacities for caretaking, defined as the parents' attributes, as well as other family resources, that facilitate or inhibit satisfactory parental role performance

3. Child role performance, defined as the child's age-appropriate interpersonal and task behaviors in various social contexts (home, school, and community)

4. Child capacities for performance, defined as the child's personal attributes that facilitate or hinder satisfactory role performance

This typology will be used in chapter 2 to classify a set of research instruments recommended for client outcome evaluation. There is certainly no single "correct" way of conceptualizing client outcome domains for child welfare services. The main point is that in selecting or developing outcome measures more attention must be given to identifying what domains are being addressed, especially since different domains may be pertinent to different services or client groups.[7]

Client Satisfaction

A client satisfaction measure may be conceptualized in two ways: as a proxy measure for case outcomes that are not directly measured or as a desired end product of service in itself. Most evaluations that use client self-reports have included some information on satisfaction with services. Clients are asked a general or global satisfaction question, or specific questions on different aspects of the service process.

The rationale for using client satisfaction as a proxy measure of case outcome is that, if services have benefitted the client in the ways intended, the client should be pleased (satisfied) with those services. In other words, satisfaction is taken to be a consequence of successful service, service that has achieved its objectives and helped the client. Finding that a client is satisfied with the service received is thus interpreted as evidence for service effectiveness; effectiveness as perceived by the client determines satisfaction.

In the other approach, service effectiveness and satisfaction with services are regarded as two separate concepts not necessarily highly related to each other. A client may be satisfied with the service process or service provider, irrespective of whether the client's status has changed. The basis of client satisfaction may be the sincerity of the provider, the competence with which services are provided, gratitude for the attempt at help, or other factors aside from actual service results. From this perspective, service effectiveness is only one factor associated with satisfaction and may not be the most important one. It can be argued that there is value in ascertaining client satisfaction with the service process, since service should always be offered with compassion, concern for individual dignity, professional competence, and the like characteristics. Accordingly, client satisfaction should be ascertained, as well as actual client problem resolution.

Whether client satisfaction is determined entirely or predominantly by service effectiveness would seem to be an empirical question. Studies thus far have shown relatively high correlations between client reports of service effectiveness and satisfaction with services (for example, Magura 1982). These findings, however, must be interpreted with caution. Indicators of service effectiveness are often global questions about the "helpfulness" of the service provider. Often more specific questions about service results are not asked. Indeed, using client satisfaction as a proxy measure of service effectiveness seems a poor substitute for asking clients directly whether beneficial changes in specific, relevant areas of their lives have occurred.

From Concept to Measurement

Stated most generally, the measurement of a concept means specifying observable indicators of the concept. Observations are classified according to a standardized procedure to indicate the presence, absence, or degree of the given conceptual attribute.[8] Measurement is much more difficult for the client status domains than for the case status variables. Measuring client outcomes requires rules for making inferences about knowledge, attributes, or motives; or systematic procedures for classifying observed behavior or reports of behavior. The entire array of concerns about instrument reliability and validity becomes relevant. Measuring case status, in contrast, is mostly a matter of definitional consensus and recording accuracy; the concept is more or less identical with the recorded case event. For instance, once the definition of a "foster home placement" is agreed upon and an agency information system accurately records placement data, nothing problematic remains in the measurement process. This is not to say that the two preceding conditions are always easy to meet, but the difficulties are practical rather than methodological.

Sources of Outcome Information

The nature of child welfare services is such that usually only the service providers and the clients themselves have access to sufficient knowledge about a family to enable determination of outcomes. Use of case records by an evaluator is simply a form of reliance on worker-provided information. Direct observations of family life or individual behavior by evaluators are usually not feasible, nor could this observation be intense or nonintrusive enough to yield satisfactory information. Thus the measurement problem reduces to developing the best procedures for systematizing the informant's (worker's or client's) knowledge of the family, or structuring the informant's direct observations of the family, a point made years ago by Blenkner (1950). The evaluator's task, then, is to use the worker and/or the client as intermediaries in collecting data about the family and its members. Opportunities for validating their reports either through third parties or records of other institutions will usually be very limited.

It is not possible to answer conclusively the question of who the preferred source of information might be. Social workers are certainly capable of participating in more sophisticated data collection procedures, including instrumentation and evaluation design, than are clients. Clients in principle have more complete and direct access to factual information about themselves than do workers, and they are the only reasonable source of satisfaction measures. The questions are whether clients are reflective enough to register that information and unbiased and articulate enough to report it accurately. The issue of bias is, of course, pertinent to social workers too, especially if their responses for a service evaluation are unwisely linked to sanctions for their work performance.

These considerations suggest that a multiple indicator approach to client outcome measurement, or what has been termed "triangulation" (Denzin 1978), would be desirable. As a general rule, the credibility of findings is increased if consistent results are obtained using different methods of measurement. Client outcome indicators obtained independently from both social workers and clients are one way to seek more valid measurement.[9]

Service outcome information in child welfare has usually been derived directly from service providers or from their case records, because these sources are more accessible than clients and may offer more methodological options. This preference is reflected by Kadushin's (1980) comprehensive review of protective services outcome studies that were conducted during the 1970s. Because clients have been little used thus far as informants in child welfare evaluation, and because they are such an important potential resource, we will summarize the state of the art in this area.

Status of Client-Based Evaluation

Only a handful of published studies in the child and family services field, most of recent date, have used client feedback for outcome evaluation (Magura and Moses 1984; Chess et al. 1982; Magura 1982; Lahti 1982; Horowitz and Wolock 1981; Pelton 1981; Jones 1981; Shapiro 1979; Rubenstein and Bloch 1978; Jenkins and Norman 1975; Maluccio 1979; Beck and Jones 1973). In contrast, client self-reporting has been much more widely used in the evaluation of other human services. For example, Ware et al. (1978) identified 111 studies on patient satisfaction with health and medical services published between 1950 and 1976. Ellsworth (1975) has reviewed the mental health field's extensive experience with client self-reports for measuring effectiveness.

Although not especially visible in the published child welfare evaluation literature, client feedback seems of considerable interest to individual agencies. The national survey conducted by the authors (Magura and Moses 1980) identified a relatively high level of in-house experimentation with client self-reporting of outcomes. Forty-one percent of all identified outcome measures were client self-report instruments, and 54% of those child welfare agencies using any measures employed at least one client self-report instrument. It is noteworthy, however, that none of the state-level agencies responding used client self-reports for routine evaluation of any major child welfare service.

The survey also asked agencies whether they would "find useful a procedure to assess case progress based on structured client interviews or questionnaires"; that is, a client self-report measure. Sixty-nine percent of the agencies replied affirmatively and 28% replied they were "not sure"; only 3% dismissed the concept. These responses, together with the frequent appearance of client self-report instruments in the survey, suggest that agencies are generally interested in obtaining direct client feedback about service outcomes and satisfaction with services.

Unfortunately, individual agencies rarely have the resources to develop an evaluation method to the point where it is validated, can be generalized, and is therefore suitable for dissemination. Client self-report measures are particularly difficult to design, test, and implement. The development of adequate, well-documented client self-report measures in the human services is usually a lengthy process requiring special funding.

Several published client self-report instruments are pertinent to child welfare evaluation and also are adequately documented; two are reviewed in chapter 2 (Beck and Jones 1980; Koss et al. 1979). The client self-report schedules used in most child welfare studies are unpublished and otherwise unavailable, and reliability/validity issues are dealt with but rarely. These facts practically ensure that each study will develop its instruments *de novo*, and that methodological progress in this area will be retarded.

Certainly there are many methodological concerns in obtaining service outcome information directly from child welfare clients. To some extent the problems are the same as those encountered in asking anyone "sensitive" questions or in interviewing "deviant" persons. The available evidence for the validity of responses obtained from parents in child welfare cases is largely impressionistic, since there is often no practical way to verify self-reports of parental behaviors or family situations. Most of the studies cited earlier found that parents voluntarily disclose at least some negative or embarrassing information about themselves or their families. Presumably this disclosure is attributable to the promise of confidentiality, adequate rapport with the researcher, and a basic desire to be honest. The authors' formal assessment of the reliability and validity of a new parent interview is presented in chapter 7.

Additional methodological difficulties in client-based evaluation are response rates and preserving privacy and confidentiality. Previous studies have managed to obtain responses from anywhere from one-third to two-thirds of the client samples. Evaluations should incorporate tests for possible nonresponse bias whenever possible, for example, by comparing respondents and non-respondents on presenting problems and/or on alternative measures of outcome.

Client confidentiality is a particular problem in child welfare service evaluation, because state child abuse and neglect reporting laws may make it impossible to promise blanket confidentiality, as is usually done in other research studies involving deviance (Legal Action Center 1983–84). In addition, there may be ethical dilemmas when an evaluator observes, or receives a report of, a condition harmful to a child. It is difficult to specify a uniform and always acceptable way of addressing these issues.

Dimensions of Instrument Structure

Instruments for obtaining client outcome information may be structured in a variety of ways. Awareness of the major dimensions can help in understanding the advantages and disadvantages of different client outcome measures encountered in evaluative research. Although for convenience the dimensions are discussed as dichotomies, each one should usually be viewed as a matter of degree.

Two of the three scale dimensions discussed by Coulton and Solomon (1977)—"global vs. specific" and "generalized vs. individualized"—are also presented below. Their third dimension, "anchored vs. unanchored," does not seem as fundamental. For instance, scale points may be anchored with inferential rather than factual criteria, which may be said to defeat the purpose of anchoring.

The five dimensions described below pertain not only to "rating scales," but to any measurement instrument. These dimensions do not exhaust the ways instruments could be described, though we have found them particularly helpful in analyzing outcome measurement methods. Where a certain structure seems more generally useful than another for outcome evaluation, we note it.

Descriptive versus Inferential Measures

It has been quite common to solicit the informant's (social worker's, client's) inferences about the level of case outcome. This method has many variations, such as asking the informant whether the situation is "good," "fair," or "poor"; "adequate" or "inadequate";

whether "problems are resolved" or "not resolved"; or are "better," "the same," or "worse." The defining feature of this approach is that a summary judgment, opinion, or prediction is solicited from the informant, without documenting the basis of the judgment. Alternatively, informants can be asked to describe aspects of a family's situation or a family member's functioning, focusing on what is factual and directly observable. The informant is not asked to interpret the facts; rather, this interpretation is done independently against certain standards or norms. For example, a child's school absences can be documented over a given time period and compared with known average or "acceptable" attendance.

Reliance on inferences in measuring client outcomes tends to beg the question of measurement; it shifts the burden of measurement from the evaluator to the informant without giving the informant any assistance in categorizing client behaviors or situations. Nevertheless, it is not always easy to distinguish between the descriptive and the inferential, since every particular observation involves some degree of judgment in classification. A thorough discussion of this issue is given in Shyne (1959). (See also Conners 1979).

Global versus Specific Measures

Global measures require a simultaneous score on multiple dimensions or areas of client outcome, while specific measures allow individual scores on separate dimensions. The latter procedure recognizes that a service outcome may be a complex phenomenon, and that different components of an outcome may respond differently to intervention. Global outcome measures, which have the obvious advantage of yielding a single score for a case, have been criticized as inherently ambiguous because of the inability to know how much each component of the measure is contributing to the total score (Coulton and Solomon 1977).

Generalized versus Individualized Measures

Generalized measures of client outcome are applicable to all clients with similar problems; individualized measures are tailored to a particular client and his or her presumably unique problems. Generalized measures are most commonly used in evaluative research, while individualized measures have achieved some popularity in mental health evaluation (Davis 1973). True individualization includes the inherent drawback that the outcome measures are not comparable across different clients and programs, making them of limited use for program evaluation purposes—there is no valid way to aggregate the results.

Goal Attainment Scaling, proposed by Kiresuk and Sherman (1968), is a specific individualized outcome measurement technique that has been used in many evaluation studies, though rarely in child welfare (an exception is Benedict 1978). Seaberg and Gillespie (1977) identified serious problems with Goal Attainment Scaling and its application in four areas: conceptual, prediction statement definition, computational, and evaluation design. Kiresuk and Sherman's defence (1977) did not resolve most of these problems. (For another critique, see Cytrynbaum et al. 1979).

Helping professionals may be attracted to Goal Attainment Scaling because of its surface similarity to the case management methods of "Problem-" or "Person-Oriented Recording" (Hartman and Wickey 1978; Martens and Holmstrup 1974) or the "Task-Centered System" (Reid 1978). Although these latter methods rightly encourage the setting of behavioral objectives and succinct documentation of case progress, the data generated remain narrative, particularistic, and unstandardized. The evaluator's task must be to organize and classify such raw data, so that comparisons between cases and groups of cases can be made. Goal Attainment Scaling as it has developed provides little assistance with this phase of evaluation.

Associanistic versus Holistic Measurement

Associanistic measurement means that outcome scores are determined by summing individual indicators. Holistic measurement implies that outcome scores are obtained by considering the relationships among various indicators; that is, by integrating or synthesizing individual elements of information to form a score. An index score formed by adding scores of individual items on a checklist (for example, an index like "number of child-rearing problems") constitutes associanistic measurement. Alternatively, a rating of "adequacy of child rearing," based on examples of good, fair, or poor child rearing as criteria, would be more in accord with holistic measurement. The rater is asked to consider the child-rearing situation "as a whole" and in context. To make the latter measurement less global, more specific components of child rearing could be identified to be rated. (This method is in fact the approach used in developing the Child Well-Being Scales, presented in chapter 3.)

Sequential versus Retrospective Measurement

Sequential measurement techniques determine change by comparing measurements obtained at several points in time; for example, "before" and "after" measurements on a given outcome variable. In contrast, retrospective techniques "reconstruct" change on the basis of a single measurement: for example, self-reports of change obtained during a follow-up interview.

Sequential methods are usually preferable for measuring outcomes, if only because accuracy is likely to be greater at the time of the situation or event being measured. The issue is not clear-cut when self-report measures are involved, however. Howard (1980) has shown that traditional, sequential pretest/posttest ratings may be contaminated by "response-shift bias." This bias arises when a treatment intervention changes the informant's standard with regard to the variable measured by the self-report instrument. Recommended to eliminate the bias are retrospective pretest and posttest ratings. (This approach is used for the authors' Parent Outcome Interview, described in chapter 6.)

Current Outcome Measurement Implementation

State-Level Capabilities

Computerized Information Systems

A national survey of state-level child welfare information system capabilities was conducted in 1980 (Westat 1980). Almost all states were found to have automated information systems for their major child welfare services. About half of the systems included an item (data element) completed by the social worker at case closing, indicating whether "the case goal was achieved" (or similar language). This sort of phrasing is about as close as these systems have come to defining a true client outcome measure.

This type of item is extremely limited for several reasons. It is entirely judgmental; the criteria used by individual social workers to rate achievement are unknown, and consequently the degree of consistency among workers in their ratings is also unknown. The item is usually global, in that the case goals (or alternatively, the presenting problems) referred to tend to be phrased in vague and general terms (for example, "to raise family functioning to level where children are not at risk"). Lastly, the fixed responses to this type of item are usually dichotomous ("yes-no") and thus not sensitive to *degrees* of goal achievement or problem resolution.

Computerization is certainly an important aid in program evaluation and may be essential for successful large-scale and/or routine client outcome measurement. Computerization does not improve the conceptualization or validity of the outcome measures, but it can contribute significantly to efficient information collection, data analysis, and dissemination of results to decision makers. The present generation of computer systems places no practical limitations on the amount and form of evaluation data that may be stored and processed at a reasonable expense. Nevertheless the child welfare field is still struggling with the complexities of designing multipurpose, computerized management information systems that, among other desired properties, include valid client outcome measures.

Types of Measures in Routine Use

The Child Welfare League's recent national survey included determining what measures (tests, scales, questionnaires, interviews) were in routine use by state social services departments to measure client outcomes for child welfare services (Magura and Moses 1980). Of the 32 state departments responding, only six reported any attempts to measure client outcomes that went beyond the simple global, judgmental ratings described above. Some of these were behavior problem measures limited to the institutional or residential treatment populations (for instance, Pinckney and Shears 1981). Several of the measures designed for child protective or foster care services and used in pilot studies have since been discontinued by the agencies; these include INCADEX in Texas (Coombes et al. 1978a,b) and a family-functioning scale developed for the Muskegan Model County Project in Michigan (Kremer 1980).

An indepth study of seven states was conducted in 1982 to determine the criteria and means used to measure the efficiency and effectiveness of the states' social service programs. The study found that effectiveness information, such as "change in client status," "is neither readily available nor is it easily understood once collected" (Majchrzak et al. 1982:3–14). There was a high level of interest in all seven states in improving their outcome assessment capabilities, however, and several of the states had active projects under way.

Some noteworthy progress has been made recently in state-level implementation of case status measurement (performance indicators). Several coherent, representative systems for child welfare services are the Integrated Performance Management Reporting System in Illinois (Stringer and Marth 1982) and the Voluntary Cooperative Information System (American Public Welfare Association 1982). These systems typically use measures such as "permanency goal achievement," with goals defined in terms of child placement status— "remain at home, returning home, adoption, placement/foster, placement/relative, independence, long-term care, family goal" (Stringer and Marth 1982).

There is little doubt that agencies believe client status variables are equally important and would like to measure them. An increasing number of state departments are defining service objectives explicitly in client outcome terms. For example, Michigan's Department of Social Services (1980) has phrased "desired program results" for family preventive services as "improvement in the functional level of the family in areas associated with abuse and neglect at the time of closure" (and similarly for other child welfare services). As another example, the Minnesota Department of Public Welfare (1984) defines program effectiveness as "percent with no further abuse or neglect following the program."

The weakness enters at the point of developing actual instrumentation and evaluation methodology. As many agencies have discovered, specifying objectives for clients is not identical to measuring the extent that objectives are achieved. Most social service departments have a file drawer filled with discarded "quick and dirty" instrumentation. Progress will occur only when states recognize this reality and resolve to devote more resources to strengthening evaluative methodologies.

Selected Examples of Outcome Studies

The state of the art in child welfare outcome evaluation can be illustrated by discussing several major evaluations of protective services. The works selected are Berkeley Planning Associates' (1977) national evaluation, a subsequent Berkeley Planning Associates' study in Michigan (Collignon et al. 1981) and the Coombes et al. (1978a,b) evaluation in Texas. All are unquestionably above average, well-documented efforts that feature a variety of typical approaches to measuring changes in client status, rather than solely changes in case status. Our objective is to present a methodological critique of these studies to help indicate the kinds of outcome evaluation difficulties continuing to confront the child welfare field.[10]

Berkeley Planning Associates' (BPA) Evaluation of Protective Services

BPA (1977) evaluated the effectiveness of 11 child abuse/neglect treatment projects throughout the United States with information collected on 1724 cases. The primary outcome measures for parents were abuse/neglect "reincidence while in treatment," "improvement in select areas of child functioning," and "reduced propensity for future abuse or neglect." All information was obtained from the clients' social workers through self-administered questionnaires.

Abuse/neglect reincidence was measured by asking whether any of the following occurred during the service period (questions were put at intake and at monthly or quarterly intervals until case closing):

- Death of child, due to abuse
- Severe physical abuse
- Moderate physical abuse
- Mild physical abuse
- Sexual abuse
- Emotional abuse
- Death of child, due to neglect

- Severe physical neglect
- Moderate physical neglect
- Mild physical neglect
- Failure to thrive
- Emotional neglect

This typology makes some broad distinctions (abuse vs. neglect, physical vs. emotional), but nevertheless constitutes relatively global outcome measurement. This has disadvantages for evaluation purposes. For example, "physical neglect" is usually recognized as a multifaceted concept; it is useful to know what kind of physical neglect has occurred or recurred. It is also important to be able to determine the effects of particular services on specific physical neglect problems.

The evaluators did attempt to measure the seriousness of physical abuse and neglect. One-sentence definitions were provided for each term in the typology. Inspection indicates, however, little difference between the definitions of "severe" vs. "moderate" physical abuse and of degrees of physical neglect.[11] These observations are supported by the results of the reliability test conducted by the evaluators on the items; workers were unable to rate case histories consistently on "severe," "moderate," and "mild" abuse and neglect (BPA 1977:D.3, D.9).

This raises the important question of what constitutes an appropriate reliability test for such outcome measures. The evaluators constructed three written case summaries and had project social workers complete outcome items on them. It should be clear that this procedure is far removed from the actual evaluation task that workers were asked to perform; that is, to complete the outcome items based on direct knowledge of their own cases.

Finding high inter-rater reliability when coding obvious written statements may be irrelevant. On the one hand, BPA(1977:D.9) found that 80% of the workers rated physical abuse as having recurred, upon reading the following description: "Mrs. L. reports to slapping Laura and telling her 'to wait until we get home'."[12] On the other hand, case records may not have enough detail in a certain area to allow reliable coding of well-defined behaviors and situations. But this need not imply that workers are unable to make such distinctions when rating their own cases, rather than facsimile case records. Consequently, a different approach to testing the reliability of social worker ratings is probably required.[13]

The second type of outcome measure used by BPA (1977) is a set of 13 parent-functioning ratings that were completed at case intake and termination. These involve relatively specific areas, primarily of emotional functioning (for example, "stress caused by living situation," "understanding of self"). Each area is rated on a five-point index, with the end points of each index defined by factual, descriptive anchors.[14] The main problem here is that these are only partly anchored scales. Like all such measures, the meaning of movement from one point to another—for instance, from "2" to "3"—is ambiguous. The reliability of the ratings, again examined by having workers rate facsimile case records, is subject to the same objections discussed above.

The third outcome measure used by BPA (1977) is a social worker's rating of "potential for future abuse" and "potential for future neglect." The ratings were made on a five-point index at case intake and termination, and ratings were compared to determine whether there was a "reduced propensity" for abuse or neglect.[15] Again, the ratings were only anchored at the end points; for example, abuse "very likely" vs. "very unlikely" in the absence of service. These ratings constitute judgmental predictions of client behavior on global constructs, quite tenuous in our view.

Michigan Follow-Up Study of Protective Services

A later study by BPA (Collignon et al. 1981) examined the validity of the parent-functioning and potential-for-abuse/neglect ratings described above. Three hundred protective services families in Michigan were followed up 18 months after the conclusion of services. The predictive validity of these measures was tested by correlating them with abuse/neglect reincidence at follow-up. Reincidence was measured both by re-reports on the state registry and by follow-up ratings made by social workers, the latter based on direct contacts with former clients or with agencies serving former clients.

The results were as follows. The correlations between potential abuse/neglect and registry re-reports were .05 or less. Potential for neglect and potential for abuse correlated .13 ($p \leq .05$) and .04, respectively, with workers' follow-up ratings of abuse/neglect. Correlations between the functioning items at closure, and at change from intake to closure, also appeared to be low and negligible.

Although there was a small, statistically significant association between the workers' potential for neglect rating at closure and abuse/neglect rating at follow-up—something the Collignon et al. (1981) report stresses—the likelihood of artifact must be recognized. Workers doing the client follow-ups were given no guidelines or methods to determine whether abuse or neglect had recurred in a family. How did they decide on this?[16] Possibly the same judgments that led workers to conclude a family had a high potential for maltreatment at closure also led them to conclude that maltreatment had recurred since closure.[17] This could easily account for the single statistically significant correlation found. In any event, the potential-for-neglect item cannot be considered valid, since it failed to correlate at all with registry re-reports, an independently obtained reincidence measure.

The INCADEX ("Indicator/Index") System

The INCADEX instrument consists of 134 checklist items defined as "indicators of abuse and neglect" (Coombes et al. 1978a,b). The instrument, completed from case records, was used in several child protective services evaluation studies at the Texas Department of Human Resources. The items are grouped into 18 categories; five of these categories with examples of items are:

- Medically Diagnosed Injuries (skin damage, history of prior fractures)
- Lack of Physical Necessities (appropriate clothing; nutritious food)
- Punishment (excessive punishment; bizarre punishment)
- Lack of Supervision (child regularly unsupervised for short periods; child locked in or out of house)
- Parental Behavior Toward Child (parent ignoring child; child held responsible for family problems)

The instrument is intended to be completed at least twice, at the "intake/investigation stage" and at a follow-up time such as case termination. Outcomes are measured by computing summary indices of abuse, neglect, and sexual abuse at the two times and subtracting follow-up scores from initial scores.

A salutory feature of INCADEX is the attempt to provide descriptive and factual definitions for the individual items.[18] This is not done consistently, however, leaving some very judgmental items undefined (for example, "child pre-delinquent"; "parent ignores child").

The main problem with INCADEX is its extremely associanistic method of index construction which fails to deal adequately with validity issues. Each item is scored dichotomously (present-absent), and the total number of items present represents the score for each index; however, the seriousness of the checklist items summed varies greatly. For example, taking Medically Diagnosed Injuries, seriousness ranges from "skin damage" or "old scars" to "dismemberment" or "brain damage." One must conclude that total, unweighted, composite scores for such items are not useful either for one-time case assessment or for measuring case change.[19]

It is entirely possible in principle to assess and track cases on individual items rather than on such arbitrarily formed indices. Coombes et al. (1978a) report some findings for individual items indicative of predictive validity. For instance, children placed in foster care more often had parents with poor parenting skills and "unstable parent behavior" than children remaining at home. Unfortunately, practicality demands that some way be found to summarize the information contained in 134 very different items. Dichotomous response items also tend to be insensitive to change. Many of the items would be far better measured on a continuum of relative adequacy. In brief, simply counting up the number of items "present" at different times is clearly no indication of change in the seriousness or severity of a child protective services case.

The INCADEX work, despite its limitations, does represent an important attempt to become more specific, factual, and comprehensive about the measurement of child abuse and neglect.

Conclusion

Outcome evaluation research in child welfare services has not yet sorted out the issues discussed in this chapter. There is no "common core" of client outcome measures that possess credibility among professionals in the field. Evaluations have emphasized case status variables as proxy measures of client outcome. True client outcome measures do not appear often, and when they do, they tend to be rather primitive methodologically and, usually, inadequately examined for reliability and validity. In chapter 2 there appear reviews of existing research instruments that can be recommended to measure client outcomes for a broad range of child welfare services. Chapters 3 and 6 describe two new instruments, tailored to the needs of child welfare outcome measurement, that attempt to ameliorate at least some of the methodological problems discussed in this chapter. Validation and field test results for the new instruments are presented in chapters 4, 5, and 7.

Notes

1. A national survey in 1977 found that 1.8 million children were receiving publicly funded social services (Shyne 1980; Shyne and Schroeder 1978).

2. This apparently includes only organizations identifying themselves as "child welfare agencies." Child welfare services may also be delivered through a wide variety of agencies or programs with

different identities: community mental health agencies, hospital-based programs, child guidance clinics, family service agencies, youth service agencies, maternity homes, parent education programs, and family therapy programs. Services to aid parents in their parenting role, or to deal with the emotional and behavioral consequences of poor parent-child relationships, may be available in any of these contexts.

3. Family income maintenance is often discussed as a child welfare service (Kadushin 1980; Frederiksen and Mulligan 1972), yet it is usually administered separately by public welfare departments. Head Start has a developmental and educational purpose and is not usually classified as a child welfare service.

4. For a recent introduction, see Rossi, Freeman, and Wright (1979). For advanced designs, see Cook and Campbell (1979).

5. One telling fact is that states have greatly different child placement rates, although there is no reason to believe that there exist correspondingly great differences in the types and severities of child welfare problems.

6. Residential treatment services for children have traditionally dealt with child behavior problems, but recently the child protective system has increasingly been expected to provide in-home services as well, under the assumption that the parent-child relationship and/or the social environment is usually the locus of the child's difficulty.

7. Millar and Millar (1981:27–28) make a distinction between "critical events" and "client functioning and problem levels" as types of case outcomes. Critical events "reflect an undesirable occurrence that an agency is trying to prevent, or a desirable occurrence that the agency is attempting to achieve." The actual examples of critical events given usually, but not always, refer to what we are calling case status variables, and it is this concept Millar and Millar probably have in mind. Their general definition of critical events could, however, also logically include changes in client functioning, and their dimensions of client functioning often include what they are calling critical events. For instance, a critical event is a "client becoming employed and no longer in need of services," and the client-functioning dimension of "economic self-support and security" includes the "extent to which employable clients are employed." We suggest that our distinction between case status and client status outcome variables is more clear-cut.

8. "Strict" definitions limit the meaning of measurement to assigning true numbers to observational units, according to a rule. Though social science research deals primarily with categorization of observed events, the types of problems encountered in both processes are analogous. The important thing is to be clear about the rules that are being followed and the limitations of the results.

9. Scheirer (1978) argues that perceptions of all program participants, including staff, clients, and evaluators affiliated with the program, are invariably positively biased. If this proposition were taken literally, objective evaluation of child welfare services would be impossible or impracticable. Fortunately, this proposition seems too extreme; it is altogether possible to obtain negative results in child welfare evaluation! Seriously, we believe bias can be minimized by remaining aware of its possibility and using appropriate methodologies—for example, by requiring descriptive rather than inferential reporting by participants (see next section).

10. The discussion of these studies will be limited to the adequacy of the outcome measures employed. No critique of the overall research design or description of the substantive findings will be undertaken, unless it has some bearing on that issue.

11. The BPA (1977:C.18) definitions of degrees of physical neglect are as follows:

> *Severely neglected.* Child found severely malnourished, excessively ill-clad, provided with grossly inadequate hygienic care, without proper shelter or sleeping arrangements and/or left unattended, unsupervised for long periods of time to the point of extreme danger to child's life.
>
> *Moderately neglected.* Child moderately malnourished, ill-clad, dirty, without proper shelter or sleeping arrangements, left for short periods of time without supervision and/or

exposed to unwholesome or demoralizing circumstances with danger to physical and mental health.

Mildly (slightly) neglected. Child ill-clad, dirty, poorly supervised and/or exposed to unwholesome circumstances with no immediate danger to physical and mental health.

Note the tendency toward tautological definition; that is, "severe" and "moderate" appear both in the terms to be defined and in their definitions. The presence or absence of several other judgmental adjectives is used to distinguish between levels. For example, "*excessively* ill-clad" vs. just "ill-clad"; "*extreme* danger to child's life" vs. just "danger to physical and mental health." Different ways of phrasing what seem to be identical concepts are also used, for example, "grossly inadequate hygienic care" vs. "dirty"; "left for short periods of time without supervision" vs. "poorly supervised." The same problems tend to appear in all three categories. As a result, this attempt to differentiate degrees of physical neglect is not very successful, in our view.

12. We do not know what the other 20% thought. To complicate the issue, adhering strictly to BPA's (1977:47) definitions, the behavior described is not clearly abuse! "Mild physical abuse" was defined as "child showing superficial, light bruises, few in number." Actually, the "progress" and "termination" sections of the case history never mention any physical marks on the child.

13. The reliability studies of the Child Well-Being Scales reported in chapter 5 illustrate several more suitable approaches.

14. An example of the index definitions is as follows (BPA 1977: C.25):

Stress Caused by Living Situation
A client's living situation refers to the household in which the client is living and more specifically the relationship between the different members of the household. Stress refers to the degree of tension or compatibility between household members. This may be caused as much by the physical set-up of the living situation as by the actual responses family members have to each other. A low rating would imply that the client experiences a great deal of stress or tension from his/her living situation. A high rating implies that the client experiences little or no tension or stress from his/her living situation. Questions to think about prior to rating clients include: Who is living in the household? Are there problems within the household which make life difficult or pressured for the client? Is life relatively pleasant? If the client has a mate, is the relationship filled with constant argument, conflict, or tension? If the client is single, how much stress is caused either by being the only adult in the household or by the many temporary relationships the client might have with other adults?

The rating format is:

1	2	3	4	5
Stressful				Unstressful

This discursive style of definition, with the meaning of "low" and "high" ratings embedded in it, is not especially convenient. The normal format for anchoring an index would simply be to define the desired rating points.

15. The rating criteria for future abuse were:

Potential for Future Abuse   This indicator refers to your judgment of how likely it is that the client will abuse his/her child. Use your own definition of potential or propensity. Consider all aspects of child abuse, both physical and emotional as well as sexual. When making this rating, assume that the client will be receiving no services. Ask the question: how likely is it that this client will abuse his/her child if no (additional) services are offered? A low rating would indicate that it is *very likely.* A high rating would indicate that it is *very unlikely*. Think about other clients you have worked with or situations you've seen in which abuse re-occurred before rating client on this scale.

16. Collignon et al. (1981:78–80) present evidence that social workers were confused about what to do during the follow-up or about how to obtain accurate information. Indeed, obtaining the sort of information asked for in any direct manner might be considered unrealistic. For instance, for "abuse," workers were asked to indicate the occurrence (and severity) of the following events during an 18-month period on the basis of a single follow-up contact with the former client or contact with another agency or collateral: "physical injury, congenital drug addiction, rape, incest, molestation, exploitation, unnatural acts." We also wonder how follow-up information could be readily obtained from other agencies, given both legal and professional confidentiality requirements.

17. Collignon et al. (1981:79–80) report testimony from social workers that they used changes on the parent-functioning measures—Reactions to Crises, Understanding of Self, for example—as one basis for making their "potential for abuse/neglect" judgments. In addition, "any reincidence during treatment was believed by workers to be correlated to stressful events," and "abusive or neglectful events that were part of a long-established pattern were considered likely to reoccur." It is not so difficult to imagine a worker contacting a former client and, upon finding a somewhat distressed parent who is known to have a history of problems, guessing that child maltreatment had recurred in that family; but should such an inference be relied on?

18. For example:

> *Inappropriate Punishment*   Child punished in a "non-traditional" manner. Examples: beaten with an electric cord, locked in a closet for prolonged periods, beaten with a club, hit with an iron.
> *Family Socially Isolated*   The family has few or no contacts outside school or work. There are few friends or supportive relatives. The mother who is a housewife may be especially isolated with no regular contacts outside her children and husband (if he is in the home).

19. Apparently this problem of ambiguous index scores is the main reason the INCADEX procedure has been discontinued in Texas (personal communication from agency administrator). For research purposes, though, correlational analysis of the INCADEX items has yielded some pertinent findings (Coombes et al. 1978a).

2

Selected Existing
Client Outcome Measures

Introduction

This chapter presents detailed assessment of 13 instruments selected from the existing research literature as potentially useful in client outcome measurement for child welfare services.

Domains of Client Outcomes

Following the typology developed in chapter 1, client outcomes for child welfare services are seen to encompass four broad domains, each with several subareas:

1. Parental Role Performance

This involves the common, direct, interpersonal activities that are performed by adults in their nurturing and socialization role as parents. Five main subareas can be distinguished: physical care and supervision; emotional care; discipline; education and stimulation; and providing guidance and security.

2. Familial Capacities for Caretaking

This involves the personal attributes, as well as other family resources, that facilitate or hinder satisfactory parental role performance. Four relevant parental attributes may be distinguished: parenting abilities (knowledge, attitudes, and motivation); physical health; emotional health; and social role enactment. Other family resources include elements such as income and social supports.

3. Child Role Performance

This involves age-appropriate role performance in various contexts (home, school, and the community). Role performance may be subclassified as relational behavior (conduct toward others) and task behavior (most important, academic achievement).

4. Child Capacities for Performance

This involves attributes of the child that facilitate or hinder satisfactory role performance. Four subareas may be distinguished: physical health and development; emotional health; mental abilities; and commitments (attitudes and motivations).

Criteria for Instrument Selection

1. Content

Preference was given to multidimensional instruments that were comprehensive in at least one of the outcome domains as previously defined or that spanned several of the domains. This was done for several reasons. First, child welfare casework is often intended to produce a variety of outcomes; it is also difficult to predict where a given type of result will occur. Second, child welfare agencies cannot under any circumstances be expected to apply routinely a large number of special-purpose instruments. Third, program evaluation is facilitated if common instruments are used for all clients; instruments with a wide scope of content seem essential, given the generic nature of child welfare casework and the practical necessities of agency evaluation.

2. Administration

Instruments were acceptable if they could be completed in at least one of four ways: by the social worker directly; by the parent, through interview or self-administration; by a researcher working with available records.

Instruments designed to be completed by a worker should not require special educational background or a lengthy period of training. No more than about 2 hours of instruction or training should be necessary to prepare for initial completion in a field setting (although real proficiency with the instrument may of course come only with additional experience). The instrument must be adapted to completion in a "naturalistic" setting or from existing knowledge of the family, rather than requiring special laboratory conditions, physical testing of subjects, imposition of structured observation, and so on.

Client interview schedules must use easily understood language (preferably eighth-grade level), be as matter-of-fact and nonthreatening as possible, and be as standardized as possible, to facilitate both the interview process and the subsequent analysis. Self-administered instruments should have all the preceding characteristics as well as requiring no more than about 30 minutes to complete.

3. Quality

The instrument must demonstrate superior characteristics in as many of the following areas as possible: reliability, validity, sensitivity to change, availability of normative data, ease of scoring, completeness of information, prior usage in evaluation studies, and accessibility of documentation (cf. next section).

4. Overall Balance

Instruments were selected with a view to covering all domains fairly equally and to provide alternatives for the source of outcome information (agency vs. client).

Sources of Instrumentation

Existing instrumentation in the following fields was identified and screened for relevance: child welfare research, social services evaluation, family research, child development, mental health evaluation, and behavioral assessment. The search process was aided by using several existing reviews of instruments for various fields: Millar et al. (1977) and American Public Welfare Association (1980) for social service outcome evaluation; U.S. DHEW (1973), Hargreaves et al. (1975) and Ciarlo et al. (1981) for mental health evaluation; Straus and Brown (1978) for family research; Johnson (1976) and Walker (1973) for child development; Haynes and Wilson (1979) for behavioral assessment. Unpublished internal agency evaluation studies and current evaluation projects were identified through abstracts compiled by Project Share (1979), Eric (1975–79), and U.S. DHEW-ACYF (1977–1979). In addition, agency-developed instruments were identified through a national survey conducted by the authors (Magura and Moses 1980).

Copies of about 200 instruments (with documentation) were obtained for inspection. Of these, 13 were finally considered suitable for detailed critical review and inclusion in this book. Each of the instruments represents in its own way the state of the art in outcome measurement and can be recommended for agency use. None of the instruments, however, including the new ones developed by the authors, is perfect. Evaluation research may be improved by locating and using the best available instrumentation, but this should not lead to complacency. There continues to be a need for improved outcome measurement methods in child welfare.

Description of Measures

Overview of the Instruments

Figure 2-1 relates the content of the instruments reviewed in this chapter to the classification of outcome domains. (The two new outcome measures developed for this book,

Figure 2-1 Client Outcome Measurement

Domains for Selected Measures	HOME Inventory	Childhood Level of Living Scale	Family Functioning Scale	Parenting Stress Index	FSA Questionnaire	Client Outcome Questionnaire	Knowledge of Child Development	Pre-school Behavior Rating Scale	Developmental Profile II	Child Behavior Checklist	Behavior Problem Checklist	Children's Pathology Index	HIS Child Health Status Measures	Child Well-Being Scales (Chapter 3)	Parent Outcome Interview (Chapter 6)
1. Parental Role Performance															
1. Physical care/supervision	X	X	X			X								X	X
2. Physical discipline	X	X	X											X	X
3. Emotional care	X	X	X											X	X
4. Guidance/security														X	X
5. Education stimulation	X	X		X	X									X	
6. General/global															
2. Familial Capacities for Caretaking															
1. Parenting abilities		X	X	X		X	X								X
2. Physical health		X	X	X	X									X	
3. Emotional health		X	X	X	X										X
4. Role enactment														X	
5. General/global		X	X	X	X										
6. Other family resources															
3. Child Role Performance															
1. Relational behavior		X	X	X	X	X		X	X	X	X	X	X	X	X
2. Task behavior		X	X	X					X	X		X		X	X
3. General/global										X					
4. Child Capacities for Performance															
1. Physical health/development								X	X	X	X	X	X		
2. Emotional health/development								X	X	X	X	X	X		
3. Mental development/abilities								X	X	X	X				
4. Commitments															
5. General/global															
Mode of Administration															
1. Provider—Self-Administered	X	X	X					X	X	X	X	X		X	
2. Parent—Self Administered				X					X	X		X	X		
3. Parent—Interview					X	X	X								X

the Child Well-Being Scales and the Parent Outcome Interview, are included for comparison purposes.) Except for the Knowledge Scale, all measures are multidimensional according to our classification. The measures tend to focus either on the parent (1 and 2) or the child (3 and 4) domains, though several are broader in content. The four outcome domains are represented about equally within this group of measures.

The "general/global" specification indicates that an instrument includes the domain, but does not measure its constituent dimensions in any detail. Single-item measures of individual dimensions, or of the entire domain, would be of this type. This may not be unsatisfactory within the context of a particular instrument, but it does help indicate the emphasis of the instrument. Conversely, an instrument is defined to measure a dimension in detail if there are multiple items that may be combined into indices or scales. In any event, Figure 2-1 is only a rough guide to the content of the measures, and should not be used to select or reject instruments. Some instruments also measure other variables such as client satisfaction, services received, and environmental factors that are not reflected in Figure 2-1 but may be of interest to the user. Thus, reference to the subsequent reviews of the instruments is essential.

It was more difficult to locate suitable measures in the parent than the child domains. Measures of parenting role performance, knowledge of parenting, and attitudes toward parenting are rare indeed. Most of the measures in these areas were in fact developed in response to the lack of adequate existing instrumentation.

An exception is the area of adult emotional or mental health, where a large research literature exists. Instruments in this area, which include psychiatric rating scales and mental health questionnaires, were considered for inclusion in this book. It was decided not to include any because of the highly specific content of the instruments and the specialized education or training required to complete or administer most of them properly. These instruments were developed for use in assessing adult psychiatric or psychological services; although child welfare agencies sometimes arrange such services for parents, extensive or detailed evaluation of mental health services is beyond the agencies' scope. Yet since some indication of parents' emotional health may be helpful, instruments that include this as one dimension are represented here. For example, the Client Outcome Questionnaire includes a 10-item Mental Distress index drawn from the Denver Community Mental Health Questionnaire (Ciarlo and Reihman 1974), and the Parenting Stress Index includes a nine-item subscale for Mother Depression. Several good compilations of adult mental health measures are available for those who wish to investigate them in greater detail (Hargreaves et al. 1975; Ciarlo et al. 1981; USDHEW 1973).

The literature revealed much to choose from in the areas of child role performance and child emotional health. A great number of "behavior checklists" and similar instruments have been developed and tested. The measures selected for inclusion here [Child Behavior Checklist (CBC), Problem Behavior Checklist (PBC)] were judged to be superior overall to others of similar content, given the evaluation needs of child welfare agencies, though some of the others would also be acceptable. (For a review, see Achenbach and Edelbrock 1978.) The two measures selected have a particular advantage in being applicable to children of a wide age range.

An effort was made to avoid redundancy in selecting the "behavior checklist" measures. One distinction between the PBC and the CBC is that the former measures only deviance, while the latter, a longer instrument, measures conventional behavior ("social competency") as well. (The Children's Pathology Index uses a rating scale format and is specifically intended to measure the child's behavior and adjustment in a treatment setting.) There are also other differences between the instruments; consequently, potential users may select the instrument most compatible with their evaluation needs and desired emphasis.

Figure 2-1 also shows the administration method(s) for each instrument. About half the measures are intended to be completed directly by a social worker, and the other half are designed for parent interviews or self-administration. The literature search could not locate suitable measures expressly designed for completion by using case records or other available documentation. Studies of social casework outcomes have been done on the basis of case records, but the instruments used generally have not been examined for reliability or validity, have usually relied on relatively unstructured items for outcome assessment, and have rarely been used in more than one study. Thus, such instruments are relatively undeveloped. In addition, of course, it is doubtful whether a generally applicable instrument could be developed in view of the diversity and lack of standardization in case recording practices.

One advantage of most of the instruments selected is that their content has a modular format or consists of individual rating scales or several subscales, thus making it possible to use only portions of the instruments. Potential users should remain aware of this possibility, and not eliminate an instrument from consideration simply because not every part is regarded as equally good, pertinent, or useful.

Format of the Reviews

The instruments are discussed under the following headings:

1. Title
2. Author(s)
3. Content: Briefly indicates what the instrument measures.
4. Subject: Indicates on whom the instrument is completed.
5. Description: Describes in some detail the purpose of the instrument, its theoretical orientation (if any), and its internal structure and content. Examples of items are given for the various content areas.
6. Scoring: Outlines the procedures for deriving sources on the instrument.
7. Administration: Indicates who is to complete the instrument, how and when this should be done, the length of time required, and whether there is an instruction manual available.
8. Reliability: Measure of a construct that is stable and consistent, yielding the same results under a variety of circumstances, is said to be reliable. Some readers may be aided by the following brief definitions of terms that will be encountered in subsequent discussions of reliability:

> • Stability: Involves comparing measurements made by the same observer at two or more points in time (test-retest method).
> • Equivalence: Involves comparing measurements made by different observers at the same point in time (inter-rater reliability), or comparing measurements using two or more sets of items drawn from the same domain (internal consistency).

Typical coefficients or techniques used to assess equivalence are:

• Split-halves: This technique involves dividing the items in half (for example, even-numbered vs. odd-numbered items) and computing a measure of association between the two sets of scores.

• Alpha coefficient: Essentially the average correlation between all possible split-halves of an instrument.

• Kuder-Richardson (KR)-20 coefficient: Analogous to alpha for dichotomously scored items (Nunnally 1978: 233).

• Alternate forms: A presumably equivalent form of the instrument is constructed by varying the content or format of the items, and measurements by the original and alternate forms are compared.

Other coefficients and techniques used in the analysis of reliability (as well as validity) are:

• Pearson product-moment correlation (r): A measure of covariation between two interval-level variables (Blalock 1972: 361).

• Intraclass correlation: Essentially a product-moment correlation within classes of a categorical variable, and sometimes used to measure response agreement between paired, interval-level measurements at different times (stability), or for different observers (inter-rater reliability) (Blalock 1972: 354; Andreasen et al. 1981).

• Kappa coefficient: A measure of response agreement for categorical variables (Cohen 1960; Light 1975).

• Reliability coefficient: Any summary statistic (like those above) used to estimate a measure's reliability.

• Factor analysis: A statistical procedure for deriving a smaller set of variables, or "factors," that account for observed patterns of item intercorrelations. Derived factors are often used as a basis for scale construction, because the relatively high average correlation among items "loading" on a factor implies a relatively high internal consistency for those items.

9. Validity: A measure that reflects true differences on the construct of interest is said to be valid. Validity has been classified in many ways; the following terms are consistent with common usage and will be used in the reviews of the instruments:

• Content validity: Concerns how adequately or representatively the measure incorporates or samples the desired conceptual domain. Establishing content validity may involve comparing the measure to definitions or examples of the conceptual domain as specified in the literature, by experts, or by intended users of the measure.

• Criterion-related validity: Involves comparing the measure to another whose validity has been demonstrated, or using the measure to distinguish among groups known to differ on the given construct. Two types of criterion-related validity are sometimes defined as (1) Concurrent validity—Involves comparison with a criterion measure obtained at the current time, or distinguishing between groups on the basis of their present status; and (2) Predictive validity—Involves comparison with a criterion variable obtained in the future.

• Convergent validity: Involves determining whether different measures of the construct yield the same results (neither is assumed to be a criterion). The greater the variation in methods, the more credible the test.

• Discriminant (or trait) validity: Assumes that indicators of the same construct (trait) have higher correlations with each other than with indicators of different constructs. Common statistical methods used are factor analysis and Likert item analysis. Trait validation may be done on an exploratory basis, but results are more credible if done on a confirmatory (hypothesis-testing) basis. (The latter involves specifying the presumed indicators of different constructs in advance of the analysis.)

• Construct (nomological) validity: Involves determining whether the measure is associated with measures of other constructs according to theoretical expectations. The credibility of the analysis depends on the truth-value of the theory.

10. Sensitivity to Change: Discusses any findings relating changes on the measure to other variables (for example, program or treatment variables); this may be thought of as examining the construct validity of changes on the measure.

11. Completeness/Response Rates: Discusses experience with the instrument regarding missing data. Completeness refers to the frequency of satisfactory completion of individual items or the availability of sufficient information to compute summary scores for the measure. Response rate refers to any kind of sample attrition (interview completion rates, return rates, staff participation rates, and so forth, as applicable).

12. Norms: Indicates the types of samples, for which score distributions are available, that may aid in the interpretation of new studies using the measure.

13. Discussion and Recommendations: This section notes particular advantages or disadvantages of the measure, extent of its previous use for evaluation, the types of child welfare evaluation for which it appears most suitable, and any modifications of it that child welfare agencies might wish to consider.

TITLE: *Home Observation for Measurement of the Environment (HOME) Inventory*
AUTHORS: *Bettye M. Caldwell and Robert H. Bradley*
CONTENT: *Quality and quantity of cognitive, social, and emotional support available to children at home.*
SUBJECT: *Children aged birth to 6.*

Description

The HOME Inventory is intended to measure the stimulation potential of a child's early developmental environment. It was developed to substitute for reliance on social class or socioeconomic status as indices of the adequacy of a child's home environment. The inventory has two age-graded versions, Birth to Three and Three to Six (Preschool).

The six subscales of the Birth to Three version, and examples of items for each, are (45 items total):

1. Emotional and Verbal Responsivity of Mother [11 items; e.g., "Mother spontaneously vocalizes to child at least twice during visit (exclude scolding)"].

2. Avoidance of Restriction and Punishment (8 items; e.g., "Mother does not shout at child during visit").

3. Organization of Physical and Temporal Environment (6 items; e.g., "When mother is away, care is provided by one of three regular substitutes").

4. Provision of Appropriate Play Materials (9 items; e.g., "Child has push or pull toy").

5. Maternal Involvement with Child (6 items; e.g., "Mother tends to help child within visual range and to look at him often").

6. Opportunities for Variety in Daily Stimulation (5 items; e.g., "Father provides some caretaking every day").

The eight subscales of the Preschool version and examples of items for each are (55 items total):

1. Stimulation Through Toys, Games, and Reading Materials [11 items; e.g., "Toys or game facilitating learning numbers (blocks with numbers, books about numbers, games with numbers, etc.)"].

2. Language Stimulation [7 items; e.g., "Parent teaches child some simple manners—to say, 'Please,' 'Thank you,' 'I'm sorry'"].

3. Physical Environment Safe, Clean, and Conducive to Development (7 items; e.g., "There is at least 100 square feet of living space per person in the home").

4. Pride, Affection, and Warmth (7 items; e.g., "Parent holds child close ten to fifteen minutes per day, e.g., during TV, story time, visiting").

5. Stimulation of Academic Behavior (5 items; e.g., "Child is encouraged to learn colors").

6. Modeling and Encouragement of Social Maturity (5 items; e.g., "Some delay of food gratification is demanded of the child, e.g., not to whine or demand unless within ½ hour of meal time").

7. Variety of Stimulation (9 items; e.g., "Family members have taken child on one outing—picnic, shopping excursion—at least every other week").

8. Physical Punishment (4 items; e.g., "Mother neither slaps nor spanks child during visit").

Scoring

Each item is scored "yes" (= 1) or "no" (= 0). Summed scores for each subscale and a total score are computed.

Administration

The HOME Inventory is to be completed by a person who goes to the home when the child is awake and can be observed in interaction with the mother or primary caretaker. The authors state that "in order to cover certain important transactions not likely to occur during the visit, it was necessary to base about one-third of the items upon parental report" (Caldwell and Bradley 1978:11).

The authors recommend limiting measurement to one child in the family at a time. The target child must be present and awake so that he or she "can be observed in his or her normal routine for that day. . . . No assumption is made that the presence of another person in this home will not in some way distort the parent-child interaction" (Caldwell and Bradley 1978: 88). The user must decide whether this assumption is tenable, since the need to interview the mother may cause distraction.

The manual provides additional clarification for completing each individual item. This is helpful, yet it is difficult to see how many of the items could be satisfactorily observed without provision for a relatively unstructured free observation period during the home visit. The feasibility of this is uncertain.

The authors avoid giving standardized interview questions, but do give guidelines and examples of probes for the questioning. This material would require some study and bears out the authors' requirement of "good interviews" to administer the HOME.

The authors report that the entire procedure takes about one hour. A manual (Caldwell and Bradley 1978) details the development of the HOME Inventory, provides instructions for the rater, and includes copies of the forms.

Reliability

Reliability data for the Birth to Three HOME came from a sample of 174 ethnically and socioeconomically diverse families residing in Little Rock, Arkansas. Internal consistency (KR-20 coefficient) was .89 for the total HOME, and averaged .70 for the six subscales. HOME data were available for children in 91 families when the children were 6, 12, and 24 months of age. Intraclass correlations, computed as a measure of stability for total HOME scores, were .57 for 6 versus 12 months and .76 for 12 versus 24 months. Since these time intervals are longer than usual for test-retest analysis, the degree of stability over time is impressive. (Low correlations could as easily have been attributed to actual changes in home environments as to instability in HOME scores.) There was a slight tendency for mean scores to increase over time (11% between 6 and 24 months).

A factor analysis of the Birth to Three HOME found low to moderate intercorrelations among the subscales, indicating that the subscales measure identifiably different, but not independent, dimensions. Individual items were always more highly correlated with their subscale score than with the total HOME score, as should be expected on the basis of the factor analysis.

Reliability results for the Preschool HOME, using a previous 80-item version completed on 238 families, are similar to those summarized for the Birth to Three HOME.

The issue of inter-rater reliability was not examined in detail. The authors state "it is easy to obtain high levels (90% or better) of inter-observer agreement after fairly brief periods of training" (pp. 11–12). Evidently this statement refers to agreement on individual items. Conditions contributing to agreement are the dichotomous nature of the ratings (as the authors indicate) and the low "difficulty" (proportion of families rated "no") of many items. To know how much agreement on ratings beyond that expected by chance actually exists, however, it would have been necessary to compute a coefficient such as Cohen's (1960) kappa.

Validity

The HOME Inventory is intended to be a more valid measure of a child's developmental environment than is family socioeconomic status (SES). Nevertheless, the two measures should be related to some extent, since higher SES households have greater access to resources that contribute to environmental adequacy. With few exceptions the HOME subscales for both versions correlate moderately (.3–.5) with such SES measures as parents' education and occupation, father's presence, and home crowding. The authors point out that high correlations with SES would decrease the utility of the HOME (p. 62).

The HOME Inventory, particularly the Birth to Three version, has been extensively used in studies of the cognitive development of children. Both versions correlate well with I.Q. scores, and the version for younger children appears to be a better predictor of I.Q. than a combination of SES measures. The HOME has also been found to correlate as predicted with such variables as language scores, clinical malnutrition, and school competence. A complete review of studies relating to the HOME's predictive and construct validity may be found in Caldwell and Bradley (1978).

There appears to be no information on the HOME's convergent validity; that is, its association with alternative measures of mother-child interaction, such as other observational coding systems, perhaps over longer periods of time, or measures based entirely on parental self-reports. A potential problem with the instrument is that observations during a single visit may not be a representative sampling of family interaction.

Sensitivity to Change

The average difficulty of the items, as measured by the proportion of the normative sample "failing," was fairly low (.30). The authors suggest that items of low difficulty help make the HOME sensitive to change from an environment that offers almost no support for a child's cognitive growth to one that offers adequate support (Caldwell and Bradley 1978: 20, 27). It might also have been desirable to have the same range of difficulty in items selected for each subscale. This was apparently not a criterion for scale construction, as some subscales are disproportionately loaded with either low- or high-difficulty items.

Hamilton (1972) used a previous 63-item version of the Birth to Three HOME to evaluate the effects of an early intervention program. The program included developmental day care, child care training, and other educational and support activities. HOME scores increased substantially after 6 months of participation, and changes in HOME scores also correlated with children's gains on the Denver Developmental Screening Test.

Norms

Means and standard deviations for the Birth to Three version are available for children aged 6, 12, and 24 months (N = 174). On the Preschool version, statistics are available for children aged 36–42 months and 48–57 months (N = 238). The normative samples are about two-thirds black, and two-thirds of the families are non-welfare (Caldwell and Bradley 1978).

Completeness/Response Rates

No information has been given on the proportion of items that can typically be completed satisfactorily by a rater. The addition of an explicit "unknown" category for the user might be helpful. Of course, whether home visits can be made at all always depends on the cooperation of the study population.

Discussion and Recommendations

The HOME Inventory attempts direct, relatively standardized measurement of environmental and interaction factors believed to be associated with adequate child development. This makes it highly appropriate for the evaluation of child welfare services. It has been refined over a 15-year period and used by many investigators.

Although the HOME Inventory was designed as a screening instrument, there seems to be no inherent reason why it could not serve as an outcome measurement device as well (experience with it as such is still limited). Completing it adequately in the space of an hour without previous knowledge of the family could, however, be a formidable task. Only experienced interviewers able to handle rather complex dual tasks of semistructured questioning and observation should attempt it. Social workers at social service agencies should find it feasible, since they could base it on multiple visits to a family, if need be, and may have other sources of information as well.

SOURCE: *Caldwell and Bradley (1978).*

Available from: Bettye M. Caldwell, Center for Child Development and Education, University of Arkansas at Little Rock, 33rd and University, Little Rock, Arkansas 72204

TITLE: *Childhood Level of Living Scale (Urban Version)*
AUTHORS: *Norman A. Polansky, Mary Ann Chalmers, Elizabeth Buttenwieser, and David Williams*
CONTENT: *Quality of parenting behavior and adequacy of child's home environment*
SUBJECT: *Child aged 4 to 7.*

Description

The Child Level of Living Scale (CLL) includes a wide range of specific conditions of child caring from unacceptable to optimal. The CLL was developed originally as a measure of child neglect and marginal child care in a study of maternal behaviors in rural Appalachia. It was revised to be applicable in an urban setting and the study replicated on samples of neglecting and non-neglecting families in Philadelphia.

The CLL consists of 99 items divided into two parts, Physical Care and Emotional/Cognitive Care, within which there are nine subscales. The subscales, and examples of items from each, are as follows:

I. Physical Care

1. General Positive Child Care (15 items, e.g., "Mother uses good judgment about leaving child alone in the house"; "Bedtime for the child is set by the parent(s) for about the same time each night").

2. State of Repair of House (10 times, e.g., "Storm sashes or equivalent are present").

3. Negligence (7 items, e.g., "There are food scraps on the floor and furniture").

4. Quality of Household Maintenance (8 items, e.g., "There are leaky faucets").

5. Quality of Health Care and Grooming (7 items, e.g., "Mother has encouraged child to wash hands before meals").

II. Emotional/Cognitive Care

1. Encouraging Competence (20 items; e.g., "Planned overnight vacation trip has been taken by family"; "There are magazines available").

2. Inconsistency of Discipline and Coldness (14 items; e.g., "Mother seems not to follow through on rewards"; "The child is often pushed aside when he shows need for love").

3. Encouraging Superego Development (14 items; e.g., "Parents guard language in front of children").

4. Material Giving (4 items; e.g., "Crayons are made available to the child").

Scoring

The CLL items are to be answered either "yes" or "no." There are both positively and negatively valued items, and scoring always assigns a "1" to the desirable response. The items are not weighted, and the maximum score is 99. If information is not available to complete all items, the authors suggest computing an adjusted score based on the proportion of total number of items rated.

Administration

The CLL is intended to be completed by a service provider or social work researcher "who knows the family well." Responses are to be based on all information available from direct home observations and interviews with the child's mother. A single visit to the home would not seem sufficient. The focus is to be a "target" child aged 4 to 7.

In one study, an average of 15 minutes was required by social workers to complete the scale (Magura and DeRubeis 1980).

Reliability

Polansky et al. (1978) used the scale with 124 white, low-income families in Philadelphia; 46 had been referred to agencies for child neglect, and 79 were presumed non-neglecting families ("controls") recruited in various ways. Evidence for the internal consistency of the CLL is as follows: The authors report that there were "moderate to moderately high intercorrelations" among the subscale scores. In addition, the correlation between the Physical and Emotional/Cognitive parts was .81.

A separate factor analysis was conducted of items in the Physical Care and Emotional/Cognitive Care areas. The General Positive Child Care items accounted for 53% of the [common?] variance of Physical Care items, and the Encouraging Competence items accounted for 49% of the variance of the Emotional/Cognitive Care items (Polansky et al. 1981:70). This suggests the possibility of a shortened CLL based on these two subscales.

The authors have attempted to ensure the reliability of the CLL by restricting it to "reports on limited, concrete issues, items as specific and unsusceptible to distortion as possible" (Polansky et al. 1981:67). Actually, the scale seems to consist both of specific, potentially observable behaviors, and of relatively abstract items requiring considerable synthesis of available information by the rater. The latter is particularly true for items on the Emotional/Cognitive part (for example, "Mother is tuned into child's indirect emotional signals").

Validity

Concurrent validity was examined in the Philadelphia study by determining the scale's ability to distinguish families referred to agencies for neglect from the "control" families. The mean score (proportion of all items "passed") was .47 for the neglect group and .81 for the control group ($p < .001$). The point biserial correlation between the CLL score and referral for neglect was .74 (Polansky et al. 1981:75).

Construct validity of the CLL is indicated by its observed correlations with several theoretically predicted variables: mother's general maturity, verbal accessibility, and relatedness (positive) (Polansky et al. 1981:113); withdrawal tendencies in children (negative) (Polansky et al. 1970); and children's nutritional state, physically measured (positive) (Hepner and Maiden 1971). Magura and DeRubeis (1980) reported that changes over 6 months on the subscales of Geismar's (1980) Family Functioning Scale were correlated with changes in the total CLL scores for 22 families receiving child protective services.

Content validity of the CLL items has been addressed by examining whether agreement exists between social workers and parents on the meaning of quality child care. A total of 439 mothers, representing six demographic subgroups—white/black, urban/rural, and working/middle class, were asked to respond to each CLL item on a six-point, Likert-type scale ranging from "report" (to child welfare agency) to "excellent." Responses were grouped as "bad," "doesn't matter," and "good." The result was that on 92 out of 99 items all parent subgroups agreed with the social workers' categorization. The authors state that the seven items showing disagreement (four concerning physical child care, three emotional) should not be used in evaluating the level of child care. In general, the authors conclude that the high degree of consensus among the diverse groups included in this study provides encouraging evidence of the existence of a large, culture-free pool of items with which the worker may assess adequate and inadequate child care (Polansky et al. 1983).

A more specific content validity question is, to what extent is the CLL relevant for its practical, intended purpose of helping a protective services worker to decide "to what extent his concern about a home is justified" or to help a judge decide "whether or not a child is to be removed" (Polansky et al. 1978)? There are many items that clearly do not describe situations falling below minimum community standards of child care—that is, those items classified as "doesn't matter" or "good" by the respondents described above. It is important to recognize that it would be wrong to assume that the reversal of a "good" item would be rated by respondents as "bad." For example, though "floors swept every day" and "prayer before bedtime" were rated "good," it is not obvious that their reversal would be rated "bad." In addition, there seem to be few if any items that most respondents considered detrimental enough to warrant reporting. (Publication of the ratings for all items would be helpful to potential users.)

Sensitivity to Change

The large number of scale items are advantageous for attempting to measure change. The yes/no format of the items, however, may render the scale insensitive to change in some areas; certain items involve concepts that would be better measured on a continuum (for example, "Child is often ignored when he tries to tell mother something").

Two social work intervention evaluations reported statistically significant changes in CLL scores, though these were primarily due to improvements in the Emotional/Cognitive area (Polansky et al. 1983).

Norms

Polansky et al. (1983) have reported distributions of CLL scores from four separate studies, involving low-income neglecting families, multiproblem families, and families with children at risk of placement.

Completeness/Response Rates

There is no information available on the proportion of items that typically can be completed by a rater. There is no choice of "unknown," so that in the absence of explicit instructions, raters might respond "no" to an item when the information is in fact unknown. (Users should consider adding "unknown" as a response choice.)

Discussion and Recommendations

The CLL is one of the few instruments that have attempted to define the quality of child care in concrete, behavioral terms. Defining nine conceptually distinct dimensions of child care potentially allows a better assessment of where problems exist and where change has taken place. In protective service agencies, users should identify those items consistent with their working definition of child neglect and their standards for intervention. Change on such items could then be tracked separately. For example, one study chose the 50 items (some revised) from the CLL judged most relevant for the service population (Jones 1981:132, passim).

The precoded response format allows the scale to be easily scored and scores to be computerized. Thus the scale could be integrated into an overall management information system.

Field experience with the CLL has been limited, but with suitable adaptation it certainly has potential value for child welfare agencies.

SOURCE: *Polansky et al. (1981) and Polansky et al. (1978).*

Single copies and more information also available from: Norman A. Polansky, School of Social Work, University of Georgia, Athens, Georgia 30602

TITLE: *Family Functioning Scale*
AUTHOR: *Ludwig L. Geismar*
CONTENT: *Assessment of family social functioning and individual adjustment of family members.*
SUBJECT: *Family system and family members.*

Description

The Family Functioning Scale was developed to help evaluate social work intervention projects and has been used in several major studies over a 25-year period.

The scale is based on a structural-functional conceptualization of the family. The family is viewed as a social system with the goals of autonomy (existence as an independent unit), integration (interdependence and unification of constituent elements), and viability (capacity for problem solving and survival). The scale organizes the functional prerequisites necessary to achieve these general goals by nine Main Areas of functioning:

Construct I. Mainly Intrafamilial Relationships
   1. Family Relationships and Unity
   2. Care and Training of Children
Construct II. Mainly Extrafamilial Relationships
   1. Social Activities
   2. Use of Community Resources
   3. Relationship to Social Worker
Construct III. Mainly Instrumental Behavior
   1. Economic Practices
   2. Health Practices
   3. Home and Household Practices
Construct IV. Individual Adjustment and Behavior

Constructs I, II, and III represent descriptions of role clusters that may involve several family members; the concern is the adequacy with which the family as a unit performs these functions or tasks. These three constructs include eight "Main Areas" of family functioning. Construct IV, which is also the ninth Main Area, represents role sets of individual family members; the concern here is the adequacy with which each member contributes to various family functions as defined in Constructs I, II, and III. Each Main Area is composed of several subareas (a total of 26). For example, Family Relationships and Unity has five subareas: Marital Relationship, Relationship Between Parents and Children, Sibling Relationships, Family Solidarity, and Relationships with Other Household Members.

The 26 subareas of functioning are rated on partially anchored, seven-point scales, as follows: 1, inadequate; 2, near inadequate; 3, below marginal; 4, marginal; 5, above marginal; 6, near adequate; 7, adequate. Three levels of functioning—inadequate, marginal, and adequate—are always explicitly defined, the others are not. The general rating criterion is that "adequate" represents functioning "in line with community expectations," "inadequate" indicates functioning so "damaging to the family and/or society as to entitle the community to intervene," and "marginal" indicates functioning that is "potentially problematic but not sufficiently harmful to justify intervention on legal grounds." An example of specific rating criteria for a subarea is as follows:

> Family Relationships and Unity—Relationship Between Parents and Children
> (1) Inadequate
> No affection is shown between parents and children. There is great indif-ference or marked rejection of children. No respect is shown for one another. No approval, recognition, or encouragement is shown to children. If any concern is shown at all by parents, it takes the form of frank discrimination in favor of a few against the rest. Parent-child conflict is extremely severe. (Above so serious as to constitute neglect or abuse as legally defined, warranting community interven-tion.)
> (4) Marginal
> Affection between parents and children is intermittent, or weak, or obscured by conflict. Parents' anger is unpredictable and unrelated to specific conduct of children. Family members are played off against each other. There is marked favoritism with no attempt to compensate disadvantaged children. There is little mutual respect or concern for each other. Parents and children are frequently in conflict. Parents of very young children are indifferent in handling or assuming responsibility for them. (Danger to children is potential not actual.)
> (7) Adequate
> Affection is shown between parents and children. Parents try always to be consistent in treatment of children. Children have sense of belonging, emotional security. Children and parents show respect for each other, mutual concern. Parent-child conflict is minimal or restricted by consistent attention, free com-munication, and desire for harmony. Parents of very young children derive satisfaction from caring for them, and assume major role in their care.

The latest publication of the Family Functioning Scale (Geismar 1980) also includes a new, additional set of scales to rate individual child functioning in detail. (No field experience with this new set of scales has been reported as of this writing.)

Scoring

Ratings for the subareas within each Main Area are summed to yield nine Main Area scores. A total scale score rarely has been used.

Administration

There are two alternative procedures for completion, the original and a later, simplified method.

The original method is first to write a narrative "Profile" of the family and then rate each subarea. Information for the profile is obtained either by an indepth parent interview or from available data such as case records. An Outline for Profiling Family Functioning provides guidance for conducting a semistructured interview or for organizing available data. The scale ratings need not be done by the same person who wrote the profile.

The simplified method uses precoded categories for each subarea to profile the family, from which the scale ratings are then made. According to the author, this method "is less useful for diagnostic purposes but much more economical" (personal communication). The correlation between postcoded profiles in the original method and precoded ones in the simplified method is .77 (Geismar 1980: 177).

With either method, Geismar (1980) recommends that collecting and organizing the information for the ratings be done by a researcher or practitioner with "prior experience in handling family data in a conceptual manner" and who is skilled at interviewing (if available data are not used). Practitioners may be able to collect the required information efficiently in conjunction with their regular casework interviewing.

Although the profile of family functioning can conceivably be written or coded from available records, adequate completeness of information seems to require a family interview lasting from 2–3 hours (Geismar et al. 1972). Additional time is required to write the narrative, which ran 10–12 pages in one study (Wallace 1967), and to assign the ratings. Magura and DeRubeis (1980) found caseworkers spent an average of 4½ hours per family in writing and rating; updating every 6 months took an average of 2 hours. Use of the simplified, precoded method of organizing information would reduce this time considerably.

A manual has been published describing the development of the scale and giving detailed instructions (with a complete example) for its use (Geismar 1980).

Reliability

Inter-rater reliability was investigated in two studies. Geismar and Krisberg (1967) had three independent judges rate the initial levels of family functioning in the nine Main Areas for 30 intensive service cases. All three judges agreed on the scale position (1 through 7) for 29% of the ratings, and two judges agreed while the third checked an adjacent scale position for 58% of the ratings. When follow-up ratings were done from agreed-upon initial positions, the corresponding percentages were 54% and 43%, respectively. The scale's authors regard these as acceptable levels of reliability in rating initial functioning and movement. Wallace and Smith (1968) had two independent teams of judges rate scale movement (change) for 100 multiproblem families assigned to treatment and control groups. The discrepancy in rating aggregate average movement for the groups was about one-quarter scale point. On an individual case basis, 40% of the Main Area scores assigned by the independent raters were identical, and in another 40% the differences were no greater than one scale point.

Data from a study of 150 socially disorganized families were analyzed to determine whether Guttman (cumulative) scaling requirements were met (Geismar et al. 1962). The coefficient of reproducibility was .88 and the coefficient of scalability was .69, which are on the borderline of acceptability (Edwards 1982). Scores from the study of 555 families did not meet Guttman scaling criteria, but Pearson correlations between Main Area scores ranged from .38 to .81; most were above .50 (Geismar et al. 1972). These findings constitute some evidence for the internal consistency of the Main Area categories.

The reliability of profile writing, or the "degree to which different people who read the same case material conceptualize and profile the material in the same way," has also been examined with reportedly favorable results, though no details are given (Geismar 1980:168).

Some cause for concern about the scale's reliability comes from the fact that descriptive anchors are given for only three of the seven scale points on each dimension. For example, no specific guidance is given the raters to help distinguish between "below marginal" and "near inadequate" situations. Although problems attributable to this lack have apparently not been encountered, Geismar (1980) does recommend that each new study try to verify the reliability of the scale for its team of coders and study population.

Validity

Factor analysis was conducted on the Main Area scores obtained for 555 young urban families (Geismar 1973). The five factors that emerged showed some resemblance to the conceptual scheme on which the scale was based.

Several studies have investigated the convergent validity of the scale. Geismar et al. (1972) compared client and caseworker responses to a structured questionnaire with items based on eight Main Areas of family functioning (excluding Relationship to Social Worker). Respondents were asked whether each situation was better, worse, or the same. Agreement for 157 worker-client pairs was highest on Economic Practices (85%), lowest on Social Activities (65%), and in-between on Care and Training of Children (73%).

Change as measured by evaluators' before-after scale ratings was compared with change as assessed by clients and workers on the structured questionnaire. The overall correlations between the two measures were gamma = .35 and .33 for the workers and clients, respectively. In the category Care and Training of Children, there was no relationship between change on scale ratings and client assessment of change. The authors suggest two reasons for the low to negligible correlations between the two ways of assessing change. First, "fairly substantial" changes would have to occur for a scale rating to be raised or lowered whereas "relatively minor alterations" in family functioning could result in assessments of "better" or "worse." Second, scale ratings may be subject to ceiling effects, in that a rating of "adequate" cannot be improved, even though "adequate" is not intended to denote "problem-free." Of course, the discrepancies could also be due to true differences of opinion.

Wallace and Smith (1968) compared changes in Family Functioning Scale ratings with independently scored changes in Hunt-Kogan Movement Scale ratings. Project cases as a group were rated slightly higher than control cases on both measures. This was not the strongest possible test of convergent validity, since case-by-case comparisons of ratings on the two measures were not reported. Moreover, the two measures are quite similar methodologically.

Geismar (1973) reported that scale ratings of husbands' and wives' independent interviews were significantly correlated.

It is important to recognize that the scale ratings cannot validly be used to make decisions about intervention in a family, since the seriousness of family dysfunctioning in any area is defined partially in terms of the perceived necessity for intervention (see item example in Description). The rating of a family is consequently affected by the community standards for intervention that are implicitly applied.

Sensitivity to Change

The scale has been used primarily in evaluations of casework effectiveness. Evidence of the reliability and validity of case movement as measured by before and after scale ratings has already been reviewed above.

The Main Area scores seem capable of registering differential change. One study found no significant overall differences in scale movement between intervention and control groups but did find significant differences on three Main Area scores that seemed attributable to differential service emphasis (Geismar et al. 1972).

There is some indication that the scale is most sensitive to differences in dysfunctional families (Geismar and LaSorte 1964; Geismar and Krisberg 1967; Magura 1981); least sensitive with more typical families (Geismar 1973; Geismar and Geismar 1979).

Norms

Frequency distributions of total scale scores and Main Area scores are available for a sample of 555 young urban families drawn from a register of first births to mothers under the age of 30 in 1964–65. The total scores are also subclassified by ethnicity, socioeconomic status, and marital status (Geismar et al. 1972).

Scores for several smaller samples of low-income, multiproblem families selected for intensive projects have been published (Geismar et al. 1962; Geismar and Krisberg 1967; Wallace 1967; or Wallace and Smith 1968).

Completeness Response Rates

Obtaining sufficient information for the scale ratings has not been identified as a major problem. All studies cited, however, have relied primarily on client interviews rather than on available data such as case records. It has been pointed out that the information available to practitioners may depend both on the areas emphasized during service and on intrinsic difficulties in identifying certain types of problems, especially problems in expressive functioning (Geismar et al. 1972:102).

Discussion and Recommendations

The Family Functioning Scale is a standardized procedure for writing and rating what is essentially a "psychosocial history" of a family. It seems to be the most highly developed instrument of its kind and has been used in numerous outcome studies. It has a particular advantage in being potentially useful to practitioners for individual case assessment purposes, though for this it does require a considerable investment of staff time and training for profile writing. For program evaluation purposes alone, the simplified, precoded method of organizing material seems preferable and more feasible; it has been used successfully in recent work (Geismar and Geismar 1979; Phillips 1981). The scale is most suitable for studies requiring a broad and comprehensive description and follow-up of a family.

SOURCE: *Geismar (1980).*

For additional information: Ludwig L. Geismar, Graduate School of Social Work, Rutgers University, New Brunswick, New Jersey 08903

TITLE: *Parenting Stress Index*
AUTHORS: *Richard R. Abidin and William T. Burke*
CONTENT: *Child care demands and parental coping capacity.*
SUBJECT: *Parent-child relationship, for children birth to age 10.*

Description

The Parenting Stress Index (PSI) was developed to identify stress factors in parent-child interaction that may be associated with unsatisfactory caretaking and/or problems in child development. The instrument assumes that stress is multidimensional, that it has multiple sources, and that stress factors are additive in effect. The PSI was designed for use as a screening and diagnostic tool in pediatric practice.

The PSI consists of 101 items grouped in two domains, under which are included a total of 13 subscales. (Older versions consisted of 150 items grouped in three domains.) The domains, their subscales, and examples of items, are:

I. Child Characteristics Domain
  1. Child Adaptability/Plasticity (11 items; e.g., "My child gets upset over the smallest thing").
  2. Acceptability of Child to Mother (7 items; e.g., "My child doesn't seem to learn as quickly as most children").
  3. Child Demandingness/Degree of Bother (9 items; e.g., "My child is always hanging on me").
  4. Child Mood (5 items).
  5. Child Distractibility/Activity (9 items).
  6. Child Reinforces Mother (6 items).
II. Mother Characteristics Domain
  1. Mother's Depression, Unhappiness, Guilt (9 items; e.g., "There are quite a few things that bother me about my life").
  2. Mother's Sense of Competence (13 items; e.g., "Being a parent is harder than I thought").
  3. Mother's Attachment (7 items; e.g., "It takes a long time for parents to develop close, warm feelings for their children").
  4. Restrictions Imposed by Parenting Role (7 items).

5. Social Isolation (6 items).
6. Relationship with Spouse (7 items).
7. Parental Health (5 items).

Two-thirds of the items, including the examples above, ask the parent to respond as follows: "Strongly agree, Agree, Not sure, Disagree, Strongly disagree." The remaining items have a variety of multiple-choice formats.

Scoring

The scoring procedure assigns numbers (usually 1 to 5) to the multiple-choice response categories, and then sums the numbers for sets of items to obtain total, domain, and subscale scores. High scores indicate high stress, low scores low stress. The guideline offered for what total score might engender clinical concern is one in the 85th–90th percentile of the normative sample. The domain and subscale scores could then be used to help identify specific sources of stress (Abidin 1982a).

Several subscales of earlier versions of the PSI contained duplicate items. In the current version, each subscale is independent of the others (personal communication).

Administration

The PSI is designed to be self-administered by the parent. In field tests among low SES parents it "was readily understood by all the parents who completed the sixth grade" (Abidin 1979).

Since the PSI is self-administered, costs will depend on whether subjects are paid for completing it and whether assistance in completing it may be needed by some subjects. Completion time is between 20 and 30 minutes (Abidin 1979).

The PSI schedule is accompanied by a printed, well-designed, self-scoring answer sheet that allows efficient tallying of subscale, domain, and total scores. There is a manual explaining the administration procedures and suggested clinical interpretation of scores for each subscale.

Reliability

Three-week test-retest correlations and internal consistency coefficients (Cronbach alphas) have been obtained for the PSI total and domain scores on samples of mothers with children in a pediatric clinic:

	Test-retest, N = 15 (Burke and Abidin 1978)	Test-retest, N = 45 (Abidin 1979)	Alpha, N = 534 (Abidin, personal communication)
Total Score	.82	.96	.95
Mother Domain	.71	.91	.93
Child Domain	.84	.63	.90

Items defining a situational/demographic domain, which appeared on earlier versions of the PSI, were eliminated in the current version due to unsatisfactory reliability.

Validity

The initial PSI item pool was developed by reviewing the clinical and research literature on stress, parenting, and child development, with the result that 95% of the items were directly related to specific research findings that a given variable is related to stress in the parent-child system. Final item content was based on recommendations of a panel of six professional judges and experiences from pilot testing (Burke and Abidin 1978).

Trait validity of the PSI was examined by factor analysis. Factor analysis of 16 subscale scales from an earlier version resulted in a three-factor structure that accounted for 58% of the common variance. The first two factors supported the clinically defined mother and child domains. The third factor was inconclusive. The first two factors accounted for 51% of the variance.

Factor analysis of the 50 items in the child domain yielded an eight-factor structure, accounting for 44% of the variance of the items. Four of the clinically defined subscales were supported by the factor structure.

Factor analysis of the 55 items in the mother domain yielded an eight-factor structure accounting for 45% of the item variance. Five of these factors clearly supported five of the clinically defined subscales (personal communication).

Several studies have examined criterion-related validity by comparing PSI scores for groups presumed to differ in stress factors. PSI scores of mothers of cerebral palsy children ($N = 20$) were higher on average than for mothers of control children ($N = 30$), with most of the difference located in the Child Domain (Zimmerman 1979, cited in Abidin n.d.). Sixty percent of the PSI scores for a clinic-referred population ($N = 40$) were at the 90th PSI percentile versus none of a normal matched group ($N = 30$) (Lafiosca 1981, cited in Abidin n.d.). Mash and Johnston (1983) report higher scores on most subscales in the Child and Mother Domains for mothers of diagnosed hyperactive ($N = 40$) versus normal children ($N = 51$). Mothers of physically abused children who were referred for services were found to have higher scores in all three PSI Domains than mothers of nonabused children (Mash et al. 1982).

Very low PSI scores may not be valid. Abidin (1982a) states that "there is some evidence from both our research and clinical experience that extremely low scores (below 250) may be related to dysfunction in the mother-child system. The mothers who earned extremely low scores tended to be very defensive, fearful, and mildly paranoid." This apparent bias might help account for the finding in a study of medical utilization rates that higher incidence of visits for child injuries occurred in families reporting either high or low stress on the PSI (Abidin 1982b). Abidin (1979:6) has indicated the possibility of developing a "correction factor for defensiveness and denial" based on particular patterns of responses on the PSI found associated with dissimulation.

In a sample of 206 mothers in a pediatric clinic, physicians' global stress rating had a low, though statistically significant, correlation ($r = .15$) with total PSI scores. The physicians appeared unable or unwilling, however, to make the requisite distinctions among levels of stress during routine medical appointments, so that this may not be an adequate test of convergent validity (Abidin 1979).

Some findings related to the PSI's construct validity are also available. An observational study of 18 abusive mothers and their children found that PSI scores were positively related to maternal nonresponding behavior and negatively related to mothers' use of praise during interaction sessions (Mash et al. 1982). Positive correlations have been found between scores on the PSI Child Domain and behavior rating scales, such as the Child Behavior Checklist (Mash and Johnston 1983) and the Behavior Problem Checklist (Lafiosca 1981, cited in Abidin n.d.:6).

Sensitivity to Change

The PSI was used as a pre-post measure to evaluate the effects of parent education groups in a psychiatric hospital for children and adolescents. Nine statistically significant changes were found out of 14 predicted changes on subscales in the Child and Mother Domains (Lafferty et al. 1980). Total PSI scores were found to be reduced following brief parent counseling (1–8 sessions) in a pediatric practice (Abidin n.d.). This suggests that the PSI is capable of measuring typical program effects.

Norms

The PSI has been normed on a sample of 534 mothers with "target" children between the ages of 1 month and 10 years, drawn from a private group pediatrics practice in a small Virginia city (Abidin n.d.). A chart is available showing the percentile ranks of total, domain, and subscale raw scores for this sample.

There is some indication that PSI scores of mothers with younger children are generally higher than those with older children: thus, age-specific norms may be made available in the future (Abidin 1982a).

It is not clear whether low SES or minority persons are adequately represented in the sample, or whether these characteristics are related to PSI scores.

Completeness/Response Rates

No information is available.

Discussion and Recommendations

The PSI meets a need in the child welfare field for a structured instrument designed to measure parenting difficulties. It has a potential application in a wide range of child welfare services and may be particularly useful in preventive services; however, its ability to predict child maltreatment in the absence of intervention has not yet been determined. The instrument is currently being used in at least 23 basic and evaluative research projects, so that more information about its utility in various contexts should soon be forthcoming. Its experience as an evaluation instrument has been favorable thus far.

SOURCE: *Richard R. Abidin, Institute of Clinical Psychology, University of Virginia, Charlottesville, Virginia 22903*
   or
Pediatric Psychology Press, 2915 Idlewood Drive, Charlottesville, Virginia 22901

TITLE: *Family Service Association Follow-up Questionnaire*
AUTHORS: *Dorothy Fahs Beck and Mary Ann Jones*
CONTENT: *Changes in family's problems, contribution of service to changes, and client's satisfaction with agency and counselor.*
SUBJECT: *The "primary client" and other family members.*

Description

Family Service America (FSA) has developed a methodology for conducting routine follow-ups of service outcomes for clients served by local agencies. Two versions of a client questionnaire have been developed, a "long form" and a "short form." The long form consists of 22 structured, multipart questions in the following areas (partial listing):

- Most important presenting problem and help desired
- Direct services or referrals received
- Satisfaction with counselor and with service process
- Changes in status of specific presenting problems
- Family's neighborhood and environmental situation
- Changes in family dynamics
- Changes in personal coping capacities of family members
- Contributions to problem change of agency services vs. other external influences

One key set of items on the long form requests the client to check the problems present in the family at application and to mark each one as "much better," "somewhat better," "the same," "somewhat worse," or "much worse." Some of the 25 specific problems listed are:

- "Problems between husband and wife"
- "Raising children, taking care of their needs, training, discipline, etc."
- "Not enough money for basic family needs"
- "Doing poorly at work or having trouble holding a job"
- "Trouble handling emotions or behavior"

The short form consists of 11 questions focusing on clients' perceptions of overall change in problems and on satisfaction with the agency. Changes in specific problems such as those above are not included.

Both questionnaire versions contain the following example of a "satisfaction" question:

"In general, how did you feel about the services of the agency? (*Possible responses:* "Very satisfied; satisfied; somewhat dissatisfied; very dissatisfied; no particular feelings one way or the other.")

Scoring

Both forms yield a composite client "change score" for the family (rather than for individual family members). The authors recommend deriving this by subtracting a weighted sum of "better" ratings from a weighted sum of "worse" ratings on selected items, and then dividing by the total number of items rated. Also recommended is a method of calculating a composite client satisfaction score, based on responses to five satisfaction questions and following analogous logic. Responses to all items may of course also be examined individually (Beck and Jones 1980).

FSA has also developed a procedure for adjusting change scores according to different agency rates of client nonresponse. The adjustment corrects local averages to take account of the percentage return achieved before local findings are compared with national norms. This correction is based on a regression equation that reflects the relation between percentage return and the extent and direction of the agency average deviation from expected change scores for 36 agency follow-up studies reported in detail to FSA ($r = -.36$). Local/national comparisons also routinely take account of (1) four different client characteristics for each case in the sample; (2) the proportion of returns received by mail, personal contact, or phone; and (3) the size of the city where the agency is located. Agencies must be members of FSA to have their questionnaire results adjusted with this procedure (personal communication).

Administration

The respondent is to be the "primary client" as defined by the agency. The questionnaires are suitable for mail self-administration, or for telephone or in-person interviewing. In selecting interviewers for the long form, "agencies have reported success with active and retired caseworkers, case aides, board members, students, and volunteers" (Beck and Jones 1980:19). It is not recommnded that caseworkers interview their own clients (p. 91).

To minimize costs, the instrument authors recommend beginning with a mail approach and following up with telephone or in-person contacts to encourage submission of the questionnaire or to arrange a personal interview. Mail questionnaires are not advised for clients who have minimal education or read poorly (Beck and Jones 1980:8–9,88). Consequently, in agencies serving primarily clients of lower socioeconomic status, some personal or telephone interviewing may be necessary.

To enable its use with non–English-speaking clients, the short form has been translated into Spanish and French (personal communication).

The authors report that adequate time and cost estimates are not available, but they do term these "substantial." Personal interviews using the long form take an average of one-half hour. The authors indicate costs have been kept down through volunteer help and cooperative arrangements with universities (Beck and Jones 1980:8,93). Millar and Millar (1981) include cost estimates for client follow-up studies that do not assume use of free help.

A manual is available giving instructions for planning a client follow-up study, for conducting it, and for analyzing and presenting the results (Beck and Jones 1980). The manual can serve as a valuable tool, even if the FSA questionnaires themselves are not used; it offers much useful and practical information. Unfortunately, the current publication consists of the original 1974 manual and two supplements, which means the reader must often refer to three sources to obtain information on a given topic. A rewritten, consolidated manual would be preferable.

Reliability

Except where other samples are described, reliability and validity information comes from a national follow-up study of 1906 clients who had been served by 266 FSA agencies in the U.S.; the long form was used (Beck and Jones 1973).

Stability of the change score was determined by comparing duplicate mail questionnaires obtained about 3 weeks apart from 31 clients; the Pearson r was .93 (Beck and Jones 1974: 594; 1980:102).

The internal consistency of the change score was determined by correlating it with subscores for four component areas—changes in presenting problems (.79), in problem coping (.81), in family relationships (.82), and in individual family relationships (.78) (Beck and Jones 1980:102).

To examine the equivalence of change scores computed from the long and the short forms, both methods were used to compute change scores on 111 randomly selected FSA clients at a Boston agency that completed long forms. (The long form contains all questions used to compute short form change scores, but not vice versa.)

Although averages for the two scores were originally believed to be similar (Beck and Jones 1980:116), further analysis has shown that scores on the short form tended to be higher, perhaps because omission of detailed questioning encourages the client to be guided in his or her ratings primarily by major impressions for change of the principal problem (personal communication).

Validity

In the national study, convergent validity was examined by having counselors complete questionnaires on their own clients at case closing. Change scores were calculated from both client- and counselor-completed forms and compared; the correlation was $r = .34$. Change scores based on client responses were found to correlate $r = .27$ with counselors' global ratings of outcomes for their clients (Beck and Jones 1980:103). In addition, for the total sample average change scores based on client response were considerably higher than those based on counselor ratings (Beck and Jones 1973:60).

This low consistency between counselors and clients might be attributable to several factors: clients and counselors not completing the questionnaires at the same time, differences in client and counselor interpretations of the questions, differences in access to pertinent information, or differences in the valuation of the same information. The authors, in fact, found that descrepancies in change scores increased with length of delay in contacting the client after closing and with decreases in the adequacy of information available to the counselor (Beck and Jones 1973:104–105). The influences of substantive factors, such as dissatisfaction in the client-counselor relationship, were also explored (Beck and Jones 1973:130–131). One explanation not fully examined was the degree of disagreement between counselors and clients on case problem definition. Published analysis indicates agreement on problem improvement in about two out of three cases, for those areas defined as a problem by *both* caseworker and client (Beck and Jones 1973:96–97). Since there was apparently considerable disagreement on problem definitions, the discrepancies in change scores may partially reflect differences in the specific problems chosen to be rated by counselors and their clients.

A small study ($N = 40$) by Korte, cited by Beck and Jones (1980:103), compared client ratings of change in family relationships and in problem coping with the counselor's assessment of whether treatment goals had been met; the correlation was $r = .46$.

Correlations among various alternative measures of change in client-completed questionnaires have also been examined. In the national study, client change score correlated .74 with client's global rating of outcome (global rating was not used in computing the change score) (Beck and Jones 1973). Four individual studies by Korte, Wattie, Macon, and Clark compared several relevant components of the change score with changes on other family and marital standardized self-report measures. Moderate correlations (.3–.5) were obtained (cited by Beck and Jones 1980:103).

Change scores seem to be modestly affected by the follow-up method, with mail responses, telephone interviews, and in-person interviews yielding increasingly favorable results in that order (Beck and Jones 1973:106,161). The authors conclude that "clients feel somewhat freer about expressing negatives when the contact is indirect" (Beck and Jones 1980:92). Interagency comparisons processed by FSA now include a correction for this factor (personal communication).

There is an interesting published exchange on the validity of the client change score (Schuerman 1975; Beck and Jones 1976). Other useful commentaries on the questionnaire appear in Beck (1979), Millar and Millar (1981), Millar et al. (1977), and Reid and Smith (1981).

Sensitivity to Change

The national study found statistically significant correlations between client change scores and such variables as counselor-client relationship, total number of interviews, influence of non-agency service factors (all positive), severity of problem situation, and number of neighborhood and community problems (both negative) (Beck and Jones 1973:168).

Completeness/Response Rates

Follow-up questionnaires were received on 53% of the eligible sample in the national study. According to the authors, the response rate is lowered by the inclusion in the base of agencies who undertook no follow-up at all (Beck and Jones 1980:91–92). The interview approach, used in three-quarters of the cases by agency choice, yielded a 72% response rate, while the mail approach had a 56% return (base of these percentages excludes cases where no follow-up was attempted or the client could not be located). These return rates were obtained with an average time lapse of 3 months between the date of last service and questionnaire follow-up. Reasons for nonresponse were client could not be located (44%), client unwilling to participate (33%), agency believed follow-up contraindicated (5%), and other (18%) (Beck and Jones 1973:106–107).

Of the questionnaires completed in the national study, 11% overall did not have enough information to enable calculation of change scores, reducing the effective response rate from

53% to 47% (Beck and Jones 1980:91). Also, 22% of the mail questionnaires, but only 9% of the interviews, did not permit change scores to be computed.

Current experience with the short form at agencies indicates that only about 7% of the mail questionnaires do not permit computation of a change score (personal communication).

Experience indicates that single mailings of questionnaires without further follow-up efforts are likely to result in return rates below 30%. With several additional mailings and phone or personal interviews when necessary, response rates have often reached 60% to 70% (Beck and Jones 1980:92). Achieving response rates about 45% has usually required completing some questionnaires through phone interviews. The response rate is also substantially eroded by long delays, such as a year or more, between the closing interview and the initial mailing (personal communication).

The maximum return rate obtained by any agency to date with the long form has been 76% (Beck and Jones 1980:92). The maximum with the short form has been 80% (personal communication).

A test has now been made of the difference between the response rates for the long and the short forms. Using systematic random assignment to short and long form, only a negligible increase in response rate was found with use of the short form as compared with the long form (Greenblatt and Bruder 1982).

Norms

Only its member agencies may purchase from the FSA an analysis of their questionnaire returns that includes comparisons with recent national normative data.

There are data published on change scores and individual item frequencies for the national study (Beck and Jones 1973). These norms, however, are no longer directly comparable with results from the revised forms currently in use, although the same variations by demographic and service characteristics still hold true. Caution should also be exercised in comparing the national data with results based on low response rates, since change scores have been found related to response rate (personal communication).

Discussion and Recommendations

The FSA Questionnaire is currently the most widely used instrument for soliciting client feedback on family service outcomes. The forms have been extensively used by individual FSA agencies since 1974. In addition, the authors report usage by mental health clinics, community counseling centers, and local United Ways. Agency-university cooperation is a frequent characteristic of these studies and has helped to improve local study procedures and interpretations.

Reliability and validity information is limited, largely due to inherent difficulties in developing such tests for client follow-up interviews. Differences between client- and counselor-based change scores have not been fully explained. Only potential users who regard counselors' ratings as an absolute criterion for the validity of client reports, however, should be put off by the observed client-counselor discrepancies.

Although tailored for FSA agencies, the questionnaire consists primarily of generic questions which are certainly applicable to many child welfare agencies as well. Some minor modifications in wording would be needed (for example, changing references from "counselor" to "social worker"), and individual child welfare agencies might well find it desirable to delete certain existing questions or add special questions of their own. Though non-FSA agencies must obtain permission to modify the forms, FSA is apparently receptive to such requests (Beck and Jones 1980:88). With reasonable modification, the FSA Questionnaire appears to be appropriate for child welfare agencies that believe in the value of client follow-ups and are able to make the necessary investment.

SOURCE: *The manual (Beck and Jones 1980) and forms are available from: Family Service America, 11700 West Lake Park Drive, Park Place, Milwaukee, WI 53224*

TITLE   *Client Outcome Questionnaire*
AUTHOR   *Margo Koss, Harry Hatry, Annie Millar, and Therese Van Houten*
CONTENT: *Comprehensive assessment of client functioning, well-being, and satisfaction with social services.*
SUBJECT: *The "primary client" and other family members.*

Description

The Client Outcome Questionnaire is designed to monitor changes in the status of clients receiving social services. Preservice and follow-up information is collected for the following areas, arranged in separate "modules":

1. Physical Health
2. Performance of Activities of Daily Living
3. Physical Abuse
4. Mental Distress
5. Alcohol and Drug Abuse
6. Family Strength
7. Quality of Substitute Care (if applicable)
8. Child Problem Behavior and Parenting
9. Economic Self-Support and Security
10. Client Satisfaction with Services (follow-up only)
11. Background Information
12. Services Received (follow-up only)

There are a total of 125 questions, almost all having structured response formats. The following example from the Child Behavior and Parenting section illustrates a typical wording and response:

78. In the past month, have adults in the household had problems with disciplining or training the children? Were there [READ RESPONSES]:

1. No problems	3. Medium problems
2. Minor problems	4. Major problems

At follow-up, clients are also asked for their perceptions of change in each problem area. For example, the change question for Child Problem Behavior and Parenting is:

> 94. Now think about whether there are any problems with the child(ren)'s behavior when we first interviewed you [PAUSE]. When you compare then and now, would you say things *now* are [READ RESPONSES]:
>
> | | |
> |---|---|
> | 1. Much better | 4. Somewhat worse |
> | 2. Somewhat better | 5. Much worse |
> | 3. About the same | 6. No problems then or now |

Because of difficulties in identifying presenting problems and determining which areas of functioning might be affected by which services, the authors decided on a "whole client" approach rather than designing separate instruments for different social services. Clients are asked about all problem areas regardless of their present problems and the services they receive. The focus is on "end" outcomes; that is, reduction of problems, rather than on "intermediate" outcomes, that is, provision of services.

Scoring

Koss et al. (1979) suggest several ways of tabulating and summarizing the outcome information. For individual clients, the authors suggest computing problem change scores by weighting responses ("no problem" = 0, "minor problems" = 1, and so on), summing the weights for each problem area, and subtracting the follow-up score from the preservice score (Koss et al. 1979:A1–4). For grouped data, the change question ratings may be summed over all problem areas, or average severities of preservice and follow-up problems may be compared.

Administration

Clients are interviewed on the questionnaire either in person or by telephone, both at a preservice and at a follow-up time. Interviewers may be trained agency clerical or paraprofessional employees or outside interviewers supplied by a contracting survey firm. The coordinator of the effort should be an agency professional.

Field tests were conducted with 245 clients at two country social services departments. The preservice interviews took an average of 24 minutes and the follow-up interviews 50 minutes. Sixty percent of the interviews were conducted by telephone, 36% in person at clients' homes, and 4% in person at the agency. The system worked best, in that in-person interviewing and refusals to participate were both lowest, when intake workers obtained written consents from clients for questionnaire interviews during the agency's intake interview.

The authors estimate that preservice and follow-up interviews could be completed for 700–800 clients annually by two to three full-time interviewers and by a one third to one-half time coordinator. This assumes interviewers would conduct three to four interviews a day.

An excellent manual is available covering in detail all aspects of designing, implementing, and interpreting the results of an outcome study using the questionnaire (Koss et al. 1979).

Reliability

Stability of client responses was tested by reinterviewing 25 clients after 3 or 4 days. The authors report that "clients' responses in the preservice interviews substantially agreed with their responses on reinterview" (Koss et al. 1979:A3-3).

Alternate forms reliability was examined by comparing client responses to several pairs of questions asking for similar information in different ways. Included were 41 clients interviewed both at intake and follow-up. For instance, answers to whether "health troubles stood in the way of doing things" were compared with ratings of physical health. Correlations for 11 such pairs of questions were fairly high, except for correlations between different measures of *change* in physical and mental health. For example, Kendall's tau = .27 between clients' overall perception of mental health change and the mental health change score based on clients' responses to 10 specific mental distress items. The 10 items themselves, drawn from the Denver Community Mental Health Questionnaire, displayed good internal consistency (alpha = .80 for preservice, .93 for follow-up). It was therefore suggested that "clients' self-report, which requires recall of health status changes over time (in this case, 9 months) is probably an unreliable indicator of actual change" (Koss et al. 1979:A4-4). (Similar analysis of change measures for the other client problem areas would have been useful.)

The authors note difficulties with question content in some modules: "There were a few questions that were difficult or sensitive for some clients—questions on family earnings, abuse, and drugs and alcohol—and we have some concern about the reliability [sic] of these data" (Koss et al. 1979:xi).

Validity

To determine content validity, material in 50 case records was compared with questionnaire items. Except for the area of family planning, "the problems and outcomes in these cases were quite well-covered in the questionnaire" (Koss et al. 1979:A3-3).

Convergent validity of the background information was examined by comparing case records of 42 clients with questionnaire responses. Clients' responses on items such as age, family composition, income, and employment "substantially agreed" with the case records.

Convergent validity of problem ratings was tested by asking workers of 85 interviewed clients to rate their clients' problem severity in six areas at both preservice and follow-up. (It was necessary to exclude Activities of Daily Living and Economic Security/Self-Support.) Workers' ratings were "similar" to clients' ratings for 78% of the ratings made overall; the low was 61% for Parenting and Child Behavior, the high was 99% for Physical Abuse. "Similar" meant that ratings differed by no more than one point on the following scale: 1 (no problem), 2 (minor problem), 3 (medium problem), 4 (major problem). The questionnaire's authors note that very high agreement rates were obtained for Physical Abuse and Alcohol/Drug Abuse because nearly all clients and workers reported "no problem" in those areas.

In 16% of the ratings overall, clients indicated more serious problems than did workers, and in 6%, clients indicated less serious problems ("more" and "less serious" meant a difference of at least two rating points). Dissimilarity was especially high for Parenting and Child Behavior, where clients indicated more serious problems in 38% of the cases. The questionnaire's authors are unsure whether this pattern reflects deficiencies in information available to workers, or whether the results are attributable to clients "overestimating their problems." The only way to disentangle this would have been to obtain some descriptive information from respondents about the nature of the problems being referenced (Koss et al. 1979:A3-3, passim).

It is unclear whether the authors' definition of "similarity" is the most useful way to judge agreement between workers and clients. Since the nature of the problem is not specifically described, it is unknown whether workers and clients are using the same definitions of "no," "minor," "medium," and "major" problems. Consequently, it may be that convergent validity for the problem ratings has not been demonstrated at all. Using pre-post differences of problem ratings as measures of change would appear to require additional justification at this stage of the questionnaire's development.

Wherever possible, the questionnaire incorporated previously developed instruments to measure client status. For instance, the Alcohol and Drug Abuse area includes the four questions of the "CAGE" instrument (Mayfield et al. 1974). Family Strength includes two questions from the FSA Follow-up Questionnaire (Beck and Jones 1980). Activities of Daily Living include typical questions from several existing physical functioning scales, and Mental Distress includes 10 modified items from the Denver Community Mental Health Questionnaire (Ciarlo and Reihman 1974). Available data on the validity and reliability of these instruments contributes to the credibility of their use on the Client Outcome Questionnaire.

Sensitivity to Change

The questionnaire is designed to determine change in two ways: by comparing clients' problem severity ratings at preservice and follow-up and by obtaining clients' retrospective assessments of change. In the pilot tests, the majority of clients appeared to change: either to improve significantly or to deteriorate, across all problem areas.

Norms

Distributions of client responses to questionnaire items, and of computed change scores, are available for 245 clients participating in pilot testing at two county social services departments in North Carolina and Virginia. The sample consisted primarily of adult and family service cases; only 22 child protective service or foster care cases were included. There are plans to extend the work into child welfare services (personal communication).

Completeness/Response Rates

In the field tests, 60–65% of the eligible clients completed both the preservice and follow-up interviews. About half the loss was due to refusals and the other half to inability to locate clients. Analysis indicated that there were only small differences in demographic characteristics and problem severity at preservice between those clients completing both interviews and those who did not. Completers, however, received greater amounts of service than noncompleters, indicating the advisability of presenting outcome data broken down by amount of service.

For 13 child protective service cases, the completion rate was lower than average—31%. The authors conclude that "it seems likely that interview data alone will be insufficient for assessing protective service outcomes" and suggest supplementation with information from social workers and state reporting systems.

Discussion and Recommendations

The Client Outcome Questionnaire was developed to meet the need for a single instrument that covered the range of client problem areas required for comprehensive social service outcome monitoring. It achieves this objective in many respects. For several reasons the questionnaire at this stage seems more useful for adult and family services than for child protective services: there are relatively few questions related specifically to parenting; the validity of the physical abuse module is in doubt; and there has been insufficient field work to demonstrate the questionnaire's feasibility with protective service cases. Potential users for child protective services may wish to revise or augment the modules on Physical Abuse and Parenting/Child Behavior.

SOURCE: *Koss et al. (1979). Available from: The Urban Institute, 2100 M Street, N.W., Washington, D.C. 20037*

TITLE: *Knowledge Scale*
AUTHOR: *Ann S. Epstein*
CONTENT: *Knowledge of age-appropriate behaviors in children's development, birth to 24 months old.*
SUBJECT: *Parent or other individual.*

Description

The Knowledge Scale consists of 73 questions designed to determine the respondent's expectations regarding child development in the first years of life. The items are grouped into three subscales:

1. Basic Care
   (9 items; e.g., "When do most babies begin to . . .
   • be ready to start toilet training?"
   • turn and suck on a nipple, either their mother's breast or a bottle?"
   • sleep through the night, that is, about 8 hours at a stretch?")
2. Physical and Motor-Perceptual Development
   (23 items; e.g., "When do most babies begin to . . .
   • use their fingers to explore their own faces?"
   • sit without any support?"
   • dress themselves?")
3. Cognitive, Language, and Social Development
   (41 items; e.g., "When do most babies begin to . . .

- say their first real word, that is, correctly name a person or things?"
- be aware they can fall off things?"
- understand when an adult says 'No'?")

Possible responses to each question are "Birth to 1 month; 1 to 4 months; 4 to 8 months; 8 to 12 months; 12 to 18 months; 18 to 24 months." The intervals used were derived from Piaget's substages of sensormotor development.

Scoring

The computation of three scores is recommended: the mean numbers of "appropriate," "early," and "late" answers to the items. "Early" answers indicate expectations for mastery earlier than typical for that skill or behavior, and "late" answers indicate expectations for behavior acquisition later than typical.

Interpretation of these scores must take into account that the chance occurrence of "late" responses is considerably larger than the chance of "early" responses. This result occurs because the three younger age ranges (birth to 8 months) contain about two-thirds of the "appropriate" answers to items. Random answering on the scale would lead to an average of 17% "appropriate," 33% "early," and 50% "late" responses. To draw conclusions about respondents' degree of knowledge and types of errors, it is necessary to compare this distribution of answers expected by chance to the distribution actually observed (Miller 1983).

Degrees of inaccuracy in "early" or "late" responses may be indicated by the number of age categories the actual response is from the correct response. In attempting this, however, it must be recognized that the age ranges themselves are not equal intervals in terms of months.

The age ranges as defined overlap (see Description). Apparently the intended categories are: Under 1 month; 1 to 3 months; 4 to 7 months, and so on, where age in months here corresponds to the lay definition of age.

Administration

The scale is completed through a card sorting routine, with questions read to the respondent by an interviewer. Each question is typed on a card and read to the respondent, who is then asked to place the card on one of six piles corresponding to the six given age ranges between birth and 24+ months.

The scale might also lend itself to self-administration by respondents with adequate reading ability. The procedure for this would have to be developed by the user, however. Thus far, the scale has been used only in the context of a longer research interview with parents.

Administration of the scale has averaged 20 minutes.

One page of Administration Instructions and a copy of the scale marked with recommended "appropriate" answers are available from the author. Cards for sorting must be constructed by the user.

Reliability

Internal consistency estimates for the three subscales are available from Miller's (1983) study of 184 teenage mothers. The alphas were: Total Scale (.86), Cognitive (.73), Physical

(.74), and Basic Care (.51). The relatively small number of items (nine) on the Basic Care subscale may contribute to its low reliability.

The items for the subscale were grouped by Epstein solely on a conceptual basis. Factor analysis of Knowledge Scale items did not identify a clear factor structure (S. H. Miller, personal communication).

Validity

To assess convergent validity, teenagers were asked to "observe, describe, and react to videotapes of infant behavior and of mothers interacting with their infants." The number of "appropriate" answers on the scale correlated positively with higher observance and awareness of child development on a videotape measure ($r = .49$ to $.57$). The number of "late" responses correlated negatively with the videotape measure ($r = -.53$ to $-.62$) (Epstein 1980).

Construct validity was assessed using a mother-infant interaction observational measure Knowledge Scale. Scores displayed low but statistically significant correlations with how teenaged mothers behaved with their infants. "Late" expectations were positively correlated with a "nontalking" interaction style ($r = .31$), and "early" expectations were negatively correlated with a "sharing" interaction style, one characterized by "verbal and physical mutuality" between mother and infant ($r = -.23$) (Epstein 1980).

Miller (1983) examined the predictive validity of the scale, finding unexpectedly that mothers' child development knowledge several months after delivery was not related to their children's performance at 18 months, as measured by the Developmental Profile (Alpern and Boll 1972). Miller suggests that the mothers' learning deficits might have been too small to result in substantial cognitive deficits in their children at this early age and also notes that the children's development was influenced by other adult caretakers.

Sensitivity to Change

No information is available.

Norms

The Knowledge Scale has not been formally normed. The score distribution for a sample of teenage mothers, however, is given by Miller (1983).

The "appropriate" answers to the items were determined by the author from various sources in the child development literature, though no specific sources have been cited. It must be noted that available age norms for specific skills and behaviors are still often based on studies of white children conducted in the 1930s and 1940s.

Completeness/Response Rates

Since the scale has been completed thus far only in the context of a broader interview, the interview response rates have been the determining factor. Respondents have apparently been able to understand and answer the questions.

Discussion and Recommendations

The Knowledge Scale is potentially useful for evaluating formal parent education programs and any other activities intended to increase knowledge of child development. The scale has good face validity but other validity data are sparse as yet. The scale is new and requires more experience before final judgments can be made.

To regard the scale as a proxy measure for adequate child care would be a potential misuse. Theoretical knowledge of child development may have no obvious relationship to tolerance and sensitivity in parent-child interaction. The scale should not be used in isolation from other types of measures in service outcome studies.

SOURCE: *Single copies may be obtained from: Ann S. Epstein, High/Scope Educational Research Foundation, 600 North River Street, Ypsilanti, Michigan 48197*

The report [Epstein (1980)] is available from: High/Scope Press, 600 North River Street, Ypsilanti, Michigan 48197

TITLE: *Preschool Behavior Rating Scale*
AUTHORS: *William F. Barker and Annick M. Doeff*
CONTENT: *Behavioral skills in three areas: psychomotor, cognitive, and social.*
SUBJECT: *Children aged 3–6 years.*

Description

The Preschool Behavior Rating Scale (PBRS) was developed to meet the need for a simple but accurate instrument to measure the developmental status of children in settings such as day care and Head Start. It is intended as an alternative to valid, but costly and time-consuming, direct testing of children. An explicit developmental perspective is used, where skills increase from lower to higher levels. The PBRS's objectives are to identify children who show incipient or manifest development problems and to enable the monitoring of progress in specific behavioral skills over time.

The PBRS has five conceptual dimensions, incorporating a total of 20 scales, as follows. The dimensions, and examples of rating scales on each, are:

    I. Coordination (2 scales; e.g., Gross Motor; Fine Motor)

    II. Expressive Language (3 scales; e.g., Vocabulary; Grammar)

    III. Receptive Language (6 scales; e.g., Story Listening; Memory)

    IV. Environmental Adaptation (5 scales; e.g., Organization; Initiative)

    V. Social Relations (4 scales; e.g., Cooperation; Consideration of Others)

Each rating scale consists of four or five descriptions ordered from lower to higher levels of skill. An example is:

15. Initiative
>   (1) Almost never initiates any activity. Almost always at a loss for what
>   to do.
>   (2) May verbalize a wish to do something but can't seem to decide or
>   needs adult support to follow through.
>   (3) Can organize or suggest activities for self but tends to choose the
>   same activities again and again.
>   (4) Can usually find a variety of acceptable activities to do either by self
>   or with others.

Scoring

There are two alternative procedures for scoring, the first based on the five conceptual dimensions (above) derived through factor analysis (discussed below). In both procedures, scale ratings are summed to obtain scores for each dimension. A total PBRS score can also be computed. Comparison to distributions from a normative study show whether a child is "typical, questionable, or atypical" on any dimension (discussed below).

It may also be useful to calculate a discriminant function score (discussed below).

Administration

The PBRS was designed to be completed by a child care worker able to observe directly the behavior of children. The scales are intended to be completed through observations made over a period of time, to avoid inaccuracies due to possible day-to-day fluctuations of behavior.

Average time for completion and scoring "after the first few" is 10 minutes (personal communication).

There is a short, well-written manual explaining the administration and scoring of the PBRS (Barker and Doeff 1980a). Answers are given for questions that might arise in completing the instrument. Scoring sheets are available for individual children and for recording group profiles.

Reliability

The PBRS focuses on concrete behaviors in an effort to minimize observer subjectivity or distortion.

Inter-rater reliability was determined by having nine pairs of preschool teachers rate a total of 85 children; Pearson r's averaged .85 on the conceptual dimensions.

Internal consistency of the dimensions computed for the normative sample averaged .85.

Alternate forms reliability was determined by presenting teachers with two item formats. The first format was the usual one with each scale having four or five rank-ordered choices. The second format consisted of taking each scale choice, putting it into a true-false format, and then randomly sequencing these true-false items. The correlation between the two PBRS forms averaged .90 for the conceptual dimensions, measured for seven teachers rating a total of 56 children. (Reliabilities for the 20 individual scales are not reported separately.) Overall, reliabilities were somewhat higher for dimensions with more scales and for comparisons using the same rater (Barker and Doeff 1980b). All additional data are from this reference.

Validity

Content validity was determined through consultation during scale development with professional and paraprofessional mental health workers and educators.

The authors conducted a factor analysis of PBRS data for 1367 children supplied by 124 teachers in a variety of urban, suburban, and rural preschool settings. The children were 51% male and 59% black. The authors regard this as a confirmatory factor analysis; that is, it supported their hypothesis that three distinct factors would emerge from a factor analysis of the scales. These are: a Language factor consisting of the language scales in dimensions II and III; a Social factor consisting of the relational scales in dimensions IV and V; and a Psychomotor factor consisting of the sensory scales in each dimension. Two scales, Organization and Initiative, loaded heavily on both the Social and Psychomotor factors.

Since the factor structure does not parallel the conceptual dimensions, the issue of the latter's trait validity has not been satisfactorily resolved.

An analysis of variance of PBRS scores for this same sample showed statistically significant differences by age and sex, but none by race, socioeconomic status (SES), or race-SES interaction. This result is unexpected, since developmentally delayed children are usually found more frequently in disadvantaged families. This finding may be attributable to the crude measure of SES used in the study, rather than a problem with the validity of the scale. Children were designated as "low" SES if the program restricted entrance to families with low income levels and were designated as "middle high" SES if the problem had no such restriction. Perhaps most children in the latter category came from low-income families also, thus making the child sample more socioeconomically homogeneous than the scale's authors have assumed.

The concurrent validity of the PBRS was examined by attempting to differentiate between "typical" and "atypical" children, the latter being those "previously diagnosed as having a problem." The analysis was limited to 579 low SES children, of whom 55 were diagnosed "atypical" on the basis of psychiatric evaluation and psychological testing (personal communication). A discriminant function analysis using child's age, sex, and the 20 PBRS rating scales resulted in correctly classifying 93% of the "typical" and 85% of the "atypical children." Other discriminant functions, using age, sex, and either the five conceptual dimension scores, the three factor-based dimension scores, or the total PBRS score, did not result in accurate classification. Such findings are unusual. Among other possibilities, it could suggest that certain individual rating scales are responsible for the discriminatory power of the PBRS, but that their effect is attenuated when combined with the nondiscriminatory scales into summed indices. This issue requires more investigation, and users of the PBRS must be alert to it.

The authors also report that a previous version of the PBRS was compared with scores on the Denver Developmental Screening Test, concluding that "the two approaches to screening provided about the same reasonably good results" (p. 9).

Sensitivity to Change

No data are reported on this issue.

Norms

The sample of 1367 children was used to establish norms for the PBRS. Means and standard deviations are published for 12 age-sex categories, with age broken down by 6-month intervals from 36 to 71 months.

Also provided are norms for each age-sex category in terms of ranges of individual scale scores labeled "atypical," "questionable," and "typical." The ranges are not derived from the discriminant function analysis but are judgments based on the percentile score distributions.

The authors did not recommend computing the scores for the discriminant function that differentiated well in their concurrent validity analysis because "it is unreasonable to expect teachers to calculate a discriminant function score for each child, which requires using age, sex, and the 20 scale scores" (p. 14). However, simply computing scores that weight the scales equally, but whose validity has not been demonstrated, may not be the most useful approach. Actually, a little multiplication can yield the desired discriminant function score in several minutes. The authors have offered to provide the function weights to interested users (personal communication).

Completeness/Response Rates

The scales measure behaviors that would ordinarily be observable in, and pertinent to, preschool settings. The authors note, however, that difficulties in completion can arise when a setting does not provide opportunities for certain activities. There may also be instances when certain scales are not applicable, such as with a handicapped child. Addition of "unknown" or "not applicable" choices could be helpful. No information is given about specific scales' frequency of noncompletion in the normative study.

Discussion and Recommendations

The PBRS shows promise as an alternative to direct testing of children in program evaluation. Its intended use is in preschool settings, but it could be useful as well to social workers and clinicians in other service contexts for assessing the developmental status of children aged 3–6 years. No applied work with the PBRS other than that conducted by its authors has come to attention as of this writing, however.

The most appropriate scoring procedures remain to be determined, as there are now several alternatives (conceptual dimension scores, factor-based dimension scores, discriminant function scores). This will depend on further experience with the PBRS, taking into account the objectives of specific users. Reliability of scoring seems excellent, however. Overall, this is a potentially superior instrument for use in program evaluations of services to preschool children.

SOURCE: *Barker and Doeff (1980a; 1980b).*
Available from: Child Welfare League of America, c/o CSSC, 300 Raritan Center Parkway, Edison, NJ 08818.
For additional information: Annick M. Doeff, 425 Homestead Road, Wayne, Pennsylvania 19087

TITLE: *Developmental Profile II*
AUTHORS: *Gerald D. Alpern, Thomas J. Boll, and Marsha S. Shearer*
CONTENT: *Child's level of functioning in five areas: physical, self-help, social, academic, and communication.*
SUBJECT: *Children, birth to age 9.*

Description

The Developmental Profile was developed to permit a multidimensional description of children's development intended to be "relatively quick, inexpensive, (and) accurate" and usable by persons "not specifically trained" in psychological and developmental testing.

The profile consists of 186 age-graded "pass-fail" items arranged into five scales. The age levels proceed in 6-month intervals from birth to age 4 and by one-year intervals thereafter. The ages are those at which children are typically expected to pass the items (see Norms). Most of the age levels within each scale contain three items.

The five scales, and examples of items on each, are:

I. Physical Developmental Age Scale
(39 items; e.g., 4-year-old level: "Does the child catch a ball (any size) thrown by an adult who is standing five feet away? The child must catch the ball 50% of the time.")

II. Self-Help Developmental Age Scale
(39 items; e.g., 9-year-old level: "Does the child shop for several items? This means the child can go to more than one store, if all items are not available in one store, account for the money spent and the change received.")

III. Social Developmental Age Scale
(36 items; e.g., 4-year-old level: "Is the child allowed to play in her/his own neighborhood without being watched by an adult? This does not mean the child is allowed to cross the street alone.")

IV. Academic Development Age Scale
(34 items; e.g., 9-year-old level: "Can the child multiply through the sixth table with only a few errors? For example, the child will know the answers to six times nine, five times eight, four times three, etc.")

V. Communication Developmental Age Scale
(38 items; e.g, 4-year-old level: "Can the child tell people (by speaking or holding up fingers) how old s/he is now, how old s/he was last year, and how old s/he will be next year?")

Scoring

The profile yields a Developmental Age for each of the five scales, computed from the numbers of items passed. In addition, an I.Q. Equivalency Score (I.Q.E.) may be computed from Academic Developmental Age. Guidelines based on clinical judgment are provided for comparing the five Developmental Ages (based on normative data) with chronological age to determine whether the child can be considered "significantly retarded" in any area.

Administration

The profile is intended to be completed by the following: "Professionals and semi-professionals—[e.g.,] teachers, teachers' aides, physicians, nurses, social workers, psychologists." It is to be completed on the basis of a service provider's knowledge or observation of the child's skills, or, more likely, on the basis of an interview with the parent.

Not all 186 items have to be covered. As a shortcut, the instrument's authors recommend that a "double basal" be established (two consecutive age levels wherein all items are passed), and then items be administered until a "double ceiling" is reached (two consecutive age levels wherein all items are failed).

The most feasible mode of completing the profile appears to be interviewing the child's parent. The authors report the interview takes about 20 to 40 minutes to administer and score.

An attractive, color-coded manual with complete instructions, scoring sheets, and background information on the profile, is available (Alpern et al. 1980). Various issues involved in administering and interpreting the profile are discussed lucidly and in detail.

Reliability

Inter-rater reliability was examined by having 36 Head Start preschool teachers rate a demonstration interview with a mother of a 4½-year-old boy. The interview covered 30 items of a preliminary 71-item Academic Scale. Twenty-five teachers scored the boy identically on academic age, five were within one month of the modal age, and the remaining five were within two months; one teacher's scores were disallowed.

A second reliability test was made by having a rater interview 11 mothers and then having a second rater interview the same mothers two to three days later. (This reliability design combines aspects both of stability—test-retest for identical subjects—and of equivalence—different interviewers rating identical subjects.) The children, five boys and girls, ranged in age from 1 to 10 years. Scores (that is, Developmental Ages) on all five scales were calculated for each child at each of the two times. The mean differences in scores were as follows: Physical (1.5 months), Self-Help (2.4), Social (2.1), Academic (1.9), Communication (.8). The average difference for all five scales was 1.7 months, reported as not statistically significant.

Validity

Convergent validity was examined by comparing mothers' reports of their children's abilities on the profile with actual task performances by the children. Of 318 items in the prestandardized profile, which included items for children up to age 12, 197 were considered amenable to direct individual testing. The subjects consisted of 100 children who were tested while their mothers were interviewed in a separate room (55% male, 88% white, 3 months to 12 years of age). There were 8,709 total observations (that is, items with both a mother's report and a child's performance), resulting in 7,301 agreements (items where the mother's report and the child's performance coincided)—an agreement rate of 84%. Agreement rates for the five scales ranged from 81% to 87%. There were no significant or systematic differences associated with the race or sex of subjects.

It must be noted, however, that only 54% of the items on the final version of the profile were validated in this way. The results might not hold for the remainder, which were not amenable to direct testing.

The authors point out that distortions of mothers' reporting might take place if the test results are to be used for important decisions, such as placement in a certain grade or admission to a special school program. Of course, these also might be typical reasons for administering the profile in the first place. The mothers in the validity study were also volunteers who knew their children were being tested during the interview. The authors conclude that mothers *can* accurately report their children's developmental skills, but there is no guarantee that they will do so accurately in all real-life situations.

Convergent validity of the I.Q.E., derived from the Academic Scale, was determined by comparing the Stanford-Binet I.Q. with the I.Q.E. for a non-normally distributed sample of 70 children ranging in I.Q. from 20 to 148. The average difference between the I.Q. and the I.Q.E. was 1.6 I.Q. points. There was a tendency, however, to underestimate the I.Q. of above-average children and vice versa.

The profile items are intended to measure actual developmental attainment; they are not intended as "test" items that sample more general skills. The authors observe that practice on specific "test" (that is, knowledge) items, for example, $3 \times 8 = ?$, would artificially inflate an achievement test score, while practice on a developmental item, for instance, stairwalking, would result in actual developmental gain and thus would be legitimate. Unfortunately, some of the items on the profile can indeed be construed as "test" items in the authors' sense, primarily in the academic and communications areas; for example, "Does the child know by memory at least three telephone numbers or mailing addresses which s/he is able to use?"

The content validity of the profile as a pure developmental measure is reduced to the extent that it is susceptible to undesired practice effects, though perhaps the total elimination of practice effects is an unrealistic goal.

Different scales often appear to include similar items as indicants. For example, the following items for the self-help and communication scales, respectively, measure the same type of performance: "Does the child answer the telephone and tell the person called the right message?" "Can the child dial a number or ask the operator for a number correctly on a telephone when wanting to call someone?" The source of this problem is that competence on one of the five scale dimensions as defined often presupposes competence on one or more of the others; consequently the conceptual distinctions between dimensions may have proven difficult to put into operation. No correlations between scale scores are reported, but they may be expected to be high; overlap of item content would contribute to this.

Sensitivity to Change

Alpern (n.d.) reports before-and-after profile scores for 201 retarded children placed for the first time in a remedial education program; the developmental gains reported on the basis of services were recorded by the profile.

Norms

The Developmental Age scores on the scales are based on normative data obtained in a major standardization study involving 3008 parent interviews in 1970–72[2].

The purpose of the study was (1) to place a preliminary pool of development items at appropriate age levels for a "normal" child population and (2) to develop scales that are unbiased in terms of sex, race, or social class. Though mothers were apparently drawn from the general population by convenience sampling, only children who had no prenatal or postnatal complications and had never had a serious physical or mental illness or handicap were eligible subjects for the profile.

The preliminary profile, consisting of 318 items, was reduced to 217, as follows. First, items that did not satisfactorily differentiate among age levels were eliminated. In the final profile, an item is placed at the age level where about 75% of the normative population passed, where most subjects at the next younger level failed, and where most subjects at the next older level passed. Second, items showing large differences by sex or race were eliminated. Items showing small race or sex differences were retained but "balanced" so that the overall scales do not differentiate by sex or race. Third, items showing discrepancies between what mothers reported about the child's abilities and what abilities the child demonstrated were eliminated on the basis of the validity study described previously. Finally, some items were eliminated to reduce social class differences, though small differences "reflective of genuine differences between social classes" remain.

In 1980 the profile was reduced to the present 186 items by eliminating items for children aged 10–12. An undesirable ceiling effect had been demonstrated for children of this age. Tables are published showing the percentage of children passing each item by sex, race, and social class. The authors indicate that the norms permit comparisons only for white and black children from large urban areas. Hispanic, Oriental, mixed race, and rural children were insufficiently represented in the standardization sample.

Unfortunately, means and standard deviations of scores on the five scales for the normative sample were not published.

Completeness/Response Rates

Scoring of the profile requires that all items (or all items needed for the shortcut method) be answered. When there is uncertainty, the authors recommend either testing the child or "guessing." No information is given about how often actual testing or guessing has proven necessary in using the profile. Since some guessing apparently was involved in the validity test described previously, the implication is that guessing on the profile tends to be accurate. Guessing on the profile might well be a matter of degree, since judgments regarding many of these specific tasks, on which the child may never have been observed, probably derive from making analogies to similar but not identical tasks on which the child has been observed.

Discussion and Recommendations

The profile appears useful as a multidimensional assessment of children's development, subject to the limitations previously noted. Although the profile was originally designed as a screening device, the authors report it has been used to assess change in handicapped or developmentally delayed children in clinical settings. Since developmental delay is often an issue in child abuse and neglect situations, the profile has a potential application as an evaluation device to a wide range of child welfare programs.

SOURCE: *Psychological Development Publications, P.O. Box 3198, Aspen, Colorado 81611*

TITLE: *Child Behavior Checklist*
AUTHOR: *Thomas M. Achenbach*
CONTENT: *Problem behavior and social competency.*
SUBJECT: *Children aged 4 to 16 years.*

Description

The Child Behavior Checklist (CBCL) was developed to allow standardized and detailed behavior discriminations among disturbed children. Its purpose is to aid in choosing appropriate services, facilitate determination of prognoses, and measure behavioral change that may occur in response to interventions. Achenbach (1978:480) states that "the items are intended to provide a broad but non-redundant coverage of behavioral problems that can be rated with a minimum of inference."

The CBCL consists of 118 behavior-problem items and seven social competency items. The behavior-problem items are organized into separate and different Child Behavior Profiles for six sex-age groups: males and females each in the age ranges 4 to 5 years, 5 to 11 years, and 12 to 16 years. The eight behavior-problem scales for girls aged 12–16, and examples of items on each, are:

    I. Internalizing Scales

        1. Anxious Obsessive (e.g., "Too fearful or anxious")

        2. Somatic Complaints (e.g., "Nausea, feels sick . . . without known medical cause")

        3. Schizoid (e.g., "Hears things that aren't there (describe:)")

        4. Depressed Withdrawal (e.g., "Withdrawn, doesn't get involved with others")

    II. Externalizing Scales

        5. Cruel (e.g, "Cruelty, bullying, or meanness to others")

        6. Aggressive (e.g., "Temper tantrums or hot temper")

        7. Delinquent (e.g., "Hangs around children who get into trouble")

    III. Mixed Scale

        8. Immature Hyperactive (e.g., "Can't concentrate, can't pay attention for long")

Each behavior-problem item has three alternative responses: "not true"; "somewhat or sometimes true"; or "very true or often true." The time period considered is to be "now or within the past six months." The scale labels are intended to be descriptive only, not clinical diagnostic categories.

There are three social competency scales, each composed of several multipart items.

These scales—Social, Activities, and School—are the same for all sex-age groups, except for the last, which is scored only for school-age children. A typical multipart item, this from the Social scale, is:

- Please list any organizations, clubs, teams, or groups your child belongs to. (*Space to list*)
- Compared to other children of the same age, how active is he/she in each? (*Responses:* Less active; average; more active; don't know).

Scoring

For the behavior problem items, "somewhat or sometimes true" is scored "1" and "now or within the past six months" is scored "2." The items for each scale are then summed, and scale totals may also be summed to yield separate Internalizing and Externalizing Scores. Similarly, responses to items on each social competence scale are assigned numbers, and these are summed to yield a total scale score.

Scoring can be done by hand, using templates on the CBCL that show where to enter responses to each item on the score sheets. The score sheets contain a graphic display of percentiles and T-scores for the raw scale scores. A computerized program for raw data entry and scoring can also be used. These scoring aids are available from the CBCL's author.

Administration

The CBCL is a four-page instrument composed almost entirely of precoded items. It was specifically designed for ease of completion by parents but could also be completed by parent surrogates, child care workers, and clinicians. Instructions are short and printed on the form. Items are written in what seems to be standard English, not laced with technical terms or outright jargon.

The author reports average completion time of 15–17 minutes (personal communication).

There is a comprehensive user's manual, as well as a computer program for automated scoring of the CBCL.

Reliability

The CBCL scales for each sex-age group were derived through separate factor analysis. In addition, second-order factor analysis showed that the scales could also be dichotomized into broader Internalizing and Externalizing factors, as illustrated previously for girls aged 12–16.

To examine test-retest reliability, interviewers obtained two CBCLs at a 1-week interval from mothers of normal (that is, nonclinic) children. Mean Pearson r's computed over all the scales were .89 (boys aged 6–11, $N = 12$), .82 (boys 12–16, $N = 13$), .88 (girls 6–11, $N = 16$), and .90 (girls 12–16, $N = 8$). There was a slight tendency for behavior problem scores to decrease between administrations.

Inter-rater reliability of CBCL scores was determined by having mothers and fathers of mental health clinic children independently complete the instrument. Mean Pearson r's for the paired scores were .74 (boys aged 6–11, $N = 37$), .79 (boys 12–16, $N = 16$), .63 (girls 6–11, $N = 20$), and .54(girls 12–16, $N = 24$) (Achenbach 1979:35).

Cluster analysis was used to develop a classification system for children (Child Behavior Profile), based on behavior-problem scales derived through factor analysis. Inter-rater reliability for these Child Behavior Profile types was determined for mothers and mental health practitioners. For 67 boys and girls aged 6–16, mean percentage agreement on the computed types was 74% and the mean kappa coefficient was .64 (Edelbrock and Achenbach 1980:465).

Supplementary reliability information may be found in Achenbach and Edelbrock (1981).

Validity

The behavior-problem items on the CBCL were originally compiled from a survey of the existing literature, analysis of case histories of 1000 child psychiatric patients (Achenbach 1966), and consultation with clinicians. Factor analysis of the items was performed on 450 6- to 11- and 12- to 16-year-olds of each sex, and 250 4- to 5-year-olds of each sex. The children had been referred for mental health services in 42 settings on the East Coast, including publicly funded guidance clinics, health maintenance organizations, and private practices. The sampling was designed to ensure that the CBCL would be applicable to a wide range of children in diverse settings. Factors were retained as scales only if they consistently appeared across both orthogonal and oblique rotations of the data (Achenbach and Edelbrock 1979:224). This method improves the chances of replicating the factor structure in cross-validations of the CBCL.

Selection of the social competence items was based primarily on substantive, rather than statistical, considerations. Following a survey of the literature, descriptions of positive behavioral characteristics were piloted in various formats with parents. The items finally chosen seemed less susceptible to social desirability bias (that is, near universal endorsement) than items typically found on social competence indices.

The generalizability of the CBCL's factor structure is supported by the author's review of the literature (Achenbach and Edelbrock 1978). Behavior syndromes similar to the CBCL Aggressive, Delinquent, Hyperactive, and Schizoid factors were identified in eight to 12 previous studies, while syndromes similar to the Depressed, Immature, Sex Problems, Withdrawal, and Somatic Complaint factors were found in two to four studies each.

It has been pointed out that the names assigned to the CBCL's factor-based scales should not be taken literally, as there is considerable overlap of "anxious" and "depressed"thought and behavior items on the scales (Eisen et al. 1980:46). That is, a conceptual classification of anxiety vs. depression items would yield indices different from those obtained through factor analysis.

Sensitivity to Change

Boys aged 12 to 16 ($N = 35$) were followed up after child guidance clinic care was terminated, approximately 1½ years after the CBCL had been originally completed by parents. The average number of clinical interviews was 15. This follow-up sample could be classified into two Child Behavior Profile types: Hostile-Withdrawal-Immature and Hyperactive-Delinquent. The former showed a slight increase and the latter a sharp decrease in total problem behaviors between intake and follow-up. Evidently the CBCL is sensitive to changes in problem behaviors of different Child Behavior Profile types. Demographic characteristics, length of follow-up, and number of interviews were unrelated to outcomes (Achenbach 1979).

Norms

Norms for the CBCL scales were obtained through interviews with parents in randomly selected homes in the Washington, D.C. area. Data were aggregated for 250–300 subjects for each age-sex category. The sample excluded children who had received mental health services in the previous year: it was 80% white and averaged 3.8 on Hollingshead's seven-step scale for head of household's occupation (Achenbach and Edelbrock 1979:224). These norms in the form of normalized T-score and percentile distributions for each age-sex category are available from the scale's author.

Completeness/Response Rates

No specific information is available regarding this issue. Some items apparently ask respondents to make inferences about the subjects' feelings, attitudes, or preferences (for example, "feels too guilty," "fears he/she might think or do something bad," "wishes to be of opposite sex"). It is possible that such items may cause difficulty for respondents, since the observational referents (for instance, child's statements?) are left ambiguous.

The author has not reported any problems in completion by lower socioeconomic status parents, assuming their ability to read (personal communication).

Discussion and Recommendations

The CBCL has been carefully developed, using appropriate research techniques and large impaired and general population samples. Both the equal representation of girls and boys in the samples and the large age range are unique and clearly advantageous. It would be helpful to have ethnic and socioeconomic status breakdowns in the norms. Users should examine the item content of the factor-based scales carefully in interpreting results, as the scale names may not provide the best guide. The inclusion of both behavior-problem and social competency scales is a strength, though relatively little empirical work with the latter has yet been done.

The CBCL is now beginning to be used for program evaluations (personal communication). It would seem particularly useful when a single, easy-to-administer instrument is desired for both parents and service providers. Child welfare agencies serving emotionally and behaviorally disturbed children should give it careful consideration for routine outcome measurement.

SOURCE: *The manual and instrument are available from: Thomas M. Achenbach, Child, Adolescent, Family and Community Psychiatry, University of Vermont, 1 South Prospect Street, Burlington, Vermont 05401*

TITLE: *Behavior Problem Checklist*
AUTHORS: *Herbert C. Quay and Donald R. Peterson*
CONTENT: *Assessment of aggression, withdrawal, immaturity, and socialized delinquency.*
SUBJECT: *School-age children (grades K–12).*

Description

The Behavior Problem Checklist (BPC) was developed to measure the types and degrees of behavior problems in children. It has been used in educational, mental health, medical, and correctional settings for research and program evaluation purposes.

The BPC consists of 55 items, most of which are grouped into four scales. The scales, and examples of items on each, are:

> I. Conduct Problem (CP)
> (17 items; e.g. "Disruptiveness, tendency to annoy others"; "profane language, swearing, cursing")
> II. Personality Problem (PP)
> (14 items; e.g. "Self-consciousness, easily embarrassed"; "anxiety, chronic general fearfulness")
> III. Inadequacy-Immaturity (II)
> (7 items; e.g. "Short attention span"; "preoccupation, 'in a world of his own'")
> IV. Socialized Delinquency (SD)
> (6 items; e.g. "Belongs to a gang"; "stays out late at night")

The BPC also contains four "flag items for psychotic behavior" and six items not part of any scale.

Scoring

An item is marked when the problem is believed to be present for a child; otherwise it is left blank. The score for a scale is the total number of items checked for it. Computing a total score has not been recommended by the authors.

Administration

The BPC is a one-page form with brief instructions directly on it. Both parents and professionals of various types have served satisfactorily as raters.

"Ratings, in most instances, can be completed in ten minutes by anyone well acquainted with the child" (Quay and Peterson 1979:2).

A manual with administration and scoring instructions, also detailing the development and usage of the BPC, has been published (Quay and Peterson 1979). A scoring template is also available.

Reliability

Evans (1975) examined test-retest reliability by comparing ratings over a two-week interval for 97 inner-city fourth graders. Test-retest correlations on the four scales averaged .81 for boys and .88 for girls.

Inter-rater reliability has also been investigated. Correlations between ratings of two different teachers for kindergarten children were .77 for CP and .75 for PP (Peterson 1961). For seventh and eighth grade pupils, respectively, correlations between teachers were .71 and .58 for CP, and .31 and .22 for PP (Quay and Quay 1965). The authors suggest that the lower reliabilities in the latter study were attributable to teachers averaging only one hour per day of contact with the adolescents they rated. It is also possible that the BPC is less reliable for older children than for younger ones.

Quay et al. (1966) obtained mother-teacher correlations of .33 for CP and .41 for PP, and father-teacher correlations of .23 for CP and .32 for PP. This may indicate that children's behaviors vary considerably between the school and home situations, or that parents and teachers are applying quite different standards for their ratings. It would be important to explore the source of this disagreement, since the results of follow-up studies of intervention that depend on parent ratings could be adversely affected.

Internal consistency of the BPC scales has been examined for samples of delinquents. Quay and Parsons (1971) report KR-20 reliabilities of .89 for CP, .83 for PP, and .68 for II. Mack (1969) found split-half reliabilities of .92 for CP, .81 for PP, and .26 for II.

Validity

To achieve content validity, items for the BPC were selected by reviewing over 400 representative case records of children in a child guidance clinic. The BPC was then used to rate 831 kindergarten through sixth-grade students; factor analysis yielded the Conduct Problem and Personality Problem behavior factors (Peterson 1961). The Inadequacy-Immaturity factor was found in a subsequent study involving older children (Quay and Quay 1965). These three factors have since been cross-validated by many studies (Quay and Peterson 1979; Achenbach and Edelbrock 1978).

The fourth scale, Socialized Delinquency, did not arise from research leading to the scales above but was constructed from items appearing as factors in case record studies of juvenile delinquency.

Quay and Peterson (1979) give a thorough review of studies supporting the instrument's convergent and construct validity. Generally, the BPC has been effective in differentiating between children with and without independently diagnosed behavioral or emotional problems. The BPC has also correlated moderately well with other instruments designed to measure similar variables, such as the Devereux Elementary School Behavior Rating Scale and the Conners Parent and Teacher Questionnaires. Evidence for construct validity appears in studies relating BPC scores to such variables as academic achievement, delinquency recidivism, activity level, perceptual preferences, and chronic illness/disability.

It should be noted that the BPC focuses exclusively on the presence of unacceptable or disturbed behaviors. Interventions whose purpose is to increase appropriate behaviors instead of, or in addition to, decreasing inappropriate ones, could not be evaluated using this instrument.

Sensitivity to Change

The BPC has been used in several studies to measure behavior change in response to drugs, to psychological therapy, and to educational programs. In what is perhaps the most methodologically sophisticated study, the BPC was found both to differentiate between guidance clinic and nonclinic children and to reflect improvement after treatment, based on parent ratings (Zold and Speer 1971).

Quay and Peterson (1979:10) have suggested that the BPC can be used to "select extreme scorers from a larger pool of potential subjects" for research purposes. This practice is not recommended, as even reliabilities as high as the ones reported above do not protect against possible regression artifacts in panel designs (Campbell and Boruch 1975).

Norms

Quay and Peterson (1979) have published scale means and standard deviations for numerous samples of both "normal" and "deviant" children. Users can make comparisons with the sample(s) most pertinent to their studies. The authors recommend that local norms be established by large-scale users.

Also given are statistics from two studies showing the percentage of children for whom each of the 55 BPC items was endorsed. These latter statistics, though useful, must be approached with care, because the scale reliabilities found probably do not extend to the individual items comprising any scale. It has been reported for behavior rating scales that reliabilities can be as high as .95 for total scores, but can drop to .10 for individual items (Cimenero and Drabman 1977:55).

Completeness/Response Rates

Mentions of difficulty in completing the BPC are rare, probably because raters have generally been persons in extensive contact with the children (teachers, parents, child care workers). The confidence with which the instrument is completed, however, may depend on a rater's access to sufficient or representative information on a child. The authors suggest at least one instance where lack of adequate information on the part of teachers may have resulted in low reliability coefficients (see Reliability). Addition of an "unknown" response category might be helpful.

Discussion and Recommendations

The BPC has been used in many studies over a 20-year period, accumulating extensive reliability and validity data. It is perhaps the best documented of the available child behavior checklists and rating scales. Some questions about it remain to be answered, as indicated earlier. Overall, the BPC seems very useful in evaluating services to behaviorally or emotionally disturbed children.

SOURCE: *Donald R. Peterson, School of Professional Psychology, Busch Campus, Rutgers University, New Brunswick, New Jersey 08903*

NAME: *Children's Pathology Index*
AUTHORS: *R. R. Alderton and B. A. Hoddinott*
CONTENT: *Disturbed functioning, behavior, attitude, relationships, and emotional response.*
SUBJECT: *Children aged 6 and over.*

Description

The Children's Pathology Index (CPI) was developed to meet a need for quantifying the subjective assessments of child care staff in clinical settings. The descriptions are generally behaviorally oriented and address the typical concerns of treatment staff.

The CPI has four dimensions, incorporating a total of 25 rating scales. The dimensions, based on factor analysis, and examples of scales on each, are:

 I. Disturbed Behavior Toward Adults (10 scales; e.g., Guilt; Adult-seeking Behavior)

 II. Neurotic Constriction (5 scales; e.g., Over-control; Spontaneous Play Behavior)

 III. Destructive Behavior (5 scales; e.g., Impulsivity; Hostility-General).

 IV. Disturbed Self-Perception (5 scales; e.g., Relationship with Children of Opposite Sex; Attitude of Other Children Toward the Child)

Each rating scale contains five descriptive statements ordered from worst to best adjustment. An example is:

 3. Attitude of Other Children Toward the Child

  (1) Disliked by almost all the other children

  (2) Liked by a few children, but disliked by most

  (3) Neither particularly liked nor disliked by the other children

  (4) Disliked by a few children, but liked by most

  (5) Generally popular, liked by almost all the children

Scoring

Scores for each of the four dimensions (or factors) are obtained by summing the ratings (1 to 5) for the scales comprising the given dimension.

Administration

The CPI is intended to be completed by a service provider in a clinical setting. According to the authors, "little training is required" (Alderton and Hoddinott 1968:360).

The CPI reportedly takes 20 to 30 minutes to complete.

There is no manual available as yet.

Reliability

Various tests for reliability of CPI scores were conducted for boys and girls aged 6 to 12 years who were admitted to a psychiatric hospital because of severe, acting-out behavior disorders (Alderton and Hoddinott 1968).

Inter-rater reliability among four raters on the CPI factors was calculated for 42 children; coefficients of concordance ranged from .62 to .70. Though these reliabilities are moderately high, the authors suggest that in using the CPI the results of several raters should be pooled whenever possible.

Analyses were conducted examining stability of the factor-based dimension scores under repeated administration over short time intervals. Two ratings about one month apart on 41 children produced test-retest correlations averaging .75. Also, 23 children were rated six consecutive times at approximately 42-day intervals; the average test-retest correlations between pairs of ratings for Factors I to IV were .71, .64, .74, and .71, respectively. Correlations between ratings decreased as the time interval between them increased, which may well be the result of treatment effects rather than unreliability. (Reliability data are reported from four different treatment settings.)

Validity

Validity data on the CPI are available for 40 children in five different treatment settings (Alderton and Hoddinott 1968). Scores on Factor I, Disturbed Behavior Toward Adults, were correlated at .59 with time sample observations of observed aggression to adults as the criterion and were correlated at .82 with psychiatric prognosis at discharge. Discharge scores on Factor I were significantly associated with children's status at follow-up in the community (rated as "good adjustment" vs. "definite problems" requiring treatment vs. "currently institutionalized"). Follow-up status was independently rated by three professionals, at least two of whom had to agree for a child to be included in the analysis. Factors III and IV were less successful predictors, although they did differentiate the "good adjustment" group from the others.

Predictive validity was also examined in another follow-up study of 16 boys discharged an average of 21 months from a psychiatric hospital (Alderton 1970). The home visitor who made follow-up ratings on the boys' home, school, and community adjustment nearly 2 years after discharge had no knowledge of CPI scores at discharge. Scores on Factor I were dichotomized and found to be related to adjustment at follow-up. Scores on the other three factors did not aid in predicting status at follow-up. Unfortunately, no correlations between subjects' ungrouped factor scores and follow-up adjustment were computed. The cutting point chosen for Factor I scores in this study might not be effective in predictive studies with larger samples or with different client populations.

Sensitivity to Change

Alderton (1972a) determined that satisfactory outcomes of residential treatment were best predicted by total absolute change in Factor I scores (negative or positive) during the first 6 months of treatment ($N = 20$). Apparently the CPI is picking up "the extent to which the program modified the child's customary defenses and behavior within that period, irrespective of whether this resulted in an increase or reduction in disturbance." Children showing little or no early change on Factor I made no progress during the latter half of their stay.

Norms

Mean scores at admission and discharge on CPI Factor I, Disturbed Behavior Toward Adults, are published for 56 children in psychiatric hospitals (Alderton 1972b).

Completeness/Response Rates

No information is given on the extent of missing information that might be expected or how that should be handled in scoring.

Discussion

The CPI has considerable face validity, is short and easy to administer, and has demonstrated acceptable reliability in residential treatment settings. Validity and normative data, however, are sparse for factors other than Factor I, Disturbed Behavior Toward Adults. Thus far it appears to have been used only by the authors themselves with small samples of younger (age 6–12) children. Experience with it is needed in a greater variety of service settings and with older children. The CPI has been specifically designed as an outcome measurement instrument and deserves consideration for use in residential program evaluations.

SOURCE: *Harvey R. Alderton, Sandringham Professional Building, Suite 205, 3995 Bathurst Street, Downsview, Ontario M3H 5V3, Canada*

NAME: *Health Insurance Study (HIS)—Child Health Status Measures*
AUTHORS: *Marvin Eisen, Cathy A. Donald, John E. Ware, Jr., and Robert H. Brook*
CONTENT: *Physical, mental, social health; general health ratings; satisfaction with development; behavior problems.*
SUBJECTS: *Children birth to age 13, for most content areas.*

Description

The Child Health Status measures were developed as part of a national field experiment to investigate the effects of different health care financing arrangements on medical services and health status. The measures are designed to be applicable to a general (rather than clinical or chronically ill) child population and to serve as meaningful outcome indicators of differential health care (rather than as a screening or diagnostic device). Emphasis was placed on measuring separable health constructs and on minimizing any overlap in operational definitions of each construct (Eisen et al. 1980:5)

The operational definitions of physical health focused on functional limitations (rather than disease descriptions); those of mental health focused on psychological states (rather than somatic states); and those of social health on quality of interpersonal interactions.

The health dimensions, their subcategories, and some examples of items are:

I. Physical Health
   1. Physical activity (5 items for age 5 to 13, 1 item for birth to 4; e.g., for ages 5 to 13, "Does this child's health limit the kind or amount of vigorous activities he or she can do, such as running, lifting heavy objects, or taking part in strenuous sports?")
   2. Role activity (3 items for each age group; e.g., "Does health limit this child in any way from doing anything he or she wants to do?")
   3. Self-care activity (1 item for each age group; for 5 to 13; e.g., "Because of health does this child need help with eating, dressing, bathing, or using the toilet?")
   4. Mobility (4 items for 5 to 13, none for birth to 4; e.g., "Does this child's health limit him or her in any way in using public transportation or a bicycle?")

All items are answered "yes" or "no" and followed up with a question on duration of this limitation: "Less than 1 month; 1–3 months; more than 3 months."

II. Mental Health (only for ages 5 to 13)
   1. Anxiety (5 items; e.g., "How much of the time during the past month did this child seem to feel relaxed and free of tension?")
   2. Depression (3 items; e.g., "How much of the time did this child seem to feel lonely during the past month?")
   3. Positive Well-Being (4 items; e.g., "How much of the time during the past month did this child seem to be cheerful and lighthearted?")

Item response categories are: "All; most; a good bit; some; a little; none of the time."

III. Social Health (3 items, only for ages 5 to 13; e.g., "During the past three months, how well has this child gotten along with other children?")
IV. General Health Ratings
   1. Current health (3 times, all ages; e.g., "In general, would you say this child's health is excellent, good, fair, or poor?")
   2. Resistance/susceptibility (2 items; e.g., "This child seems to resist illness very well")
   3. Prior health (2 items)
V. Satisfaction with Development (4 items, only for birth to 4; e.g., "How do you feel about this child's eating habits?")
VI. Behavior Problems (15 items only for ages two to 13; e.g., "Argues a lot?")
   This is an adaptation of Achenbach's (1978) Child Behavior Checklist.

Scoring

A dichotomous score is recommended for the Physical Health items—no limitations vs. one or more limitations of any kind (e.g., physical activity, role activity, self-care). For the other dimensions, each response on an item is assigned an equal-interval numerical value (e.g., "All of the time" = 6; "most of the time" = 5). Responses on items comprising each construct are then summed to yield the child's score. Items within the Mental Health and General Health areas may also be summed to form total scores for each area.

Administration

The information is obtained from parents by self-administered questionnaire. "Appropriate assistance and follow-up when needed [yielded] data of acceptably high quality, even among the least educated groups enrolled in the HIS" (Eisen et al. 1980:6). Respondents were compensated $2 for each child on whom a questionnaire was completed.

Complete documentation on the health status measures, as well as copies of the medical enrollment questionnaires where they appeared, is given in Eisen et al. (1980).

Reliability

The items for each physical health construct (physical activity, mobility, and so forth) for each age group were examined to see whether a cumulative (Guttman) scale could be formed. An examination proved impossible because of the small proportion of children with reported limitations on any item (1 to 2%). Where a test was possible, cumulativeness was not often found. For example, "it appeared that children who were reported as unable to go to school because of health were not necessarily limited in the kinds or amounts of schoolwork they were able to do" (Eisen et al. 1980: 104). A cumulative scale was found only for age 5 to 13 physical activity (coefficient of scalability = .73; Eisen et al. 1980:107–109) by grouping items to form a four-level scale.

The physical health constructs are very highly correlated (gamma = .80 to .99), indicating that children with limitations in one area (for example, physical activities) also have limitations in any other area (such as role activities) (Eisen et al. 1980: 126). The suggested scoring is based on this finding.

Reliability for the other health constructs, except Behavior Problems, was determined through multitrait analysis on the a priori summated scales. Two criteria were applied: a Likert-type criterion requiring that item-scale correlation (corrected for overlap) be greater than 0.3, and a discriminant criterion, requiring that an item correlate more highly with its hypothesized scale than with any other scale. Whenever an item failed to meet a criterion, an "error" was counted. The Likert-type criterion was satisfied for all seven construct-specific scales and the discriminant criterion was met in 145 out of 165 total comparisons (one "definite" error and 19 "probable" errors, the latter perhaps attributable to sampling fluctuation).

An overall summated Mental Health Index had far fewer discriminant errors than the construct-specific scales on Anxiety, Depression, and Positive Well-Being. Respondents either had some difficulty differentiating these constructs, or these symptoms may tend to occur together. Results of the multitrait analysis of nonphysical health items were generally confirmed by a factor analysis.

Internal consistency reliability of the health scales for the two age groups is as follows (Eisen et al. 1980: 124):

	Alpha Coefficients	
	Age birth to 4 (N = 678)	Age 5–13 (N = 1468)
Mental Health Index (Total)	—	.87
Anxiety	—	.72
Depression	—	.69
Positive Well-Being	—	.77
Social Relations	—	.80
General Health Ratings (Total)	.77	.76
Current Health	.75	.70
Prior Health	.53	.57
Resistance/Susceptibility	.59	.60
Satisfaction with Development	.54	—

Validity

To achieve content validity, the authors critiqued the literature in detail and drew on the best available materials in developing their health measures. Most of the scales are similar to those used in previous investigations in the various health areas.

The decision to exclude explicit behavioral content from the mental health measures, and rely on affective content, was based on the assumption that behavior and conduct problems were not malleable by medically oriented therapy, e.g., psychotherapy. As work on the HIS progressed, the field produced evidence that behavior modification techniques were having some success with hyperactivity and acting-out problems (Eisen et al. 1980: 143). Consequently, the authors constructed an adaptation of Achenbach's Child Behavior Checklist, consisting of 15 of the highest loading items across his age and sex groups in the following categories: aggression, delinquency, hyperactivity, and social withdrawal. These behavior items are now recommended for use with the measures on anxiety, depression, and positive well-being, to represent all major mental health dimensions described in the literature.

Construct validity was determined by correlating the health measures with other variables on the HIS enrollment questionnaire to which they should be theoretically related. These variables were presence of chronic/serious conditions (e.g., heart disease, asthma, lead poisoning); presence of acute illness/symptoms (e.g., colds, earaches, diarrhea); pain/distress caused by child's health; adults' worry caused by child's health; adults' worry about child's social relations; adults' health status ratings. Correlations were in the expected direction and low to moderate in strength. Although the results were encouraging, an important limitation is that the ratings for all variables come from the parent, so that systematic response bias may exist through item carryover effects. More useful would have been correlations with independent measures of child health status, if only for a subsample of the population.

The 13 health status and validity variables were jointly factor analyzed to summarize information relevant to construct validity. Two factors accounting for 47% of the total (common?) variance emerged; the first defined a "general/physical component of health status, and the second, a mental health component." The General Health Rating constructs appeared to reflect the physical rather than the mental component of health status (Eisen et al. 1980:134).

The adequacy of using parents as sole informants about child health is not entirely clear. Results from the National Health Examination Survey compared parents' and children's ratings of health for children aged 12 to 17. Parents seemed to exaggerate somewhat their children's general health status and underestimate their mental health status.

Supplementary findings on validity are reported in Eisen et al. (1980). Generally, the results support the adequacy of defining child health as a multidimensional concept.

Sensitivity to Change

The health status measures were developed for periodic outcome assessment, but no data are published as yet. An important concern is the low variability of the measures, especially the functional limitations index for physical health. For children aged birth to 4, about 4% had limitations of any duration; for those aged 5 to 13, about 6%. When unreliability in measurement is also taken into account, precision of measurement becomes a major problem; relatively large samples would be required to detect intervention differences between generally healthy groups of children. The problem may be less for a child welfare population, which has higher rates of child illness than the general population (Swire and Kavaler 1977).

Norms

Frequency distributions are published for individual health status items and summated scales (Eisen et al. 1980), based on 678 children aged birth to 4 and 1468 children aged 5 to 13 (Eisen et al. 1980: 112–113, 122–123). These are children in a "general" population participating in the HIS at six sites throughout the country. Low-income families were reportedly oversampled and Medicaid recipients were eligible (Eisen et al. 1980: 2). Demographic summary was 52% male; 77% white; mean educational level of family head = 12.3 years; and mean family income = $11,848 (1974).

Completeness/Response Rates

The frequency of missing data on individual health status items was essentially negligible: about 2% on the physical health items; 0.5% average on other items.

The low rate of missing data is attributable to automatic call-backs that were made when more than six items were missing on the enrollment questionnaire. Clients were also able to call for an interviewer to be sent to administer the instrument.

Discussion and Recommendations

The multidimensional conceptualization of health and the succinctness of the measures are important strengths. These measures appear to represent the state of the art in health status measurement for children, using survey techniques. Although reliabilities are not high enough to warrant comparison of individual scores, group comparisons are feasible. Validity remains a concern, so that evaluation studies should probably also incorporate potentially less subjective measures of health status (e.g., health visits, use of medical care, examination results), and sources of information other than the parent (e.g., children over 8, service providers). The measures deserve consideration as a relatively simple method of measuring child health for agencies where medically related services, provided or purchased, are an important component of the service program. Client populations with high proportions of children with developmental disabilities (physical, cognitive, or emotional) would be especially relevant.

SOURCE: *Eisen et al. (1980) is available from: Rand Corporation, 1700 Main Street, P.O. Box 2130, Santa Monica, California 90406-2138*

3

The
Child Well-Being Scales

Description

The Child Well-Being Scales are a set of standardized client outcome measures specifically designed to meet the needs of a program evaluation in child welfare services. The instrument measures a family's (or child's) position on 43 separate dimensions using fully anchored rating scales completed by social workers. The dimensions cover the four areas of parenting role performance, familial capacities, child role performance, and child capacities, as discussed in chapter 1. The scales focus on issues common to a broad range of child- and family-oriented services, with particular emphasis on problems encountered in child protection.

Each scale measures a concept that is related to one or more physical, psychological, or social needs that all children have: *the degree to which this set of needs is met defines a child's state of overall well-being.* There is no recourse to the ambiguous term "neglect" in constructing the scales. A failure in parenting may have many causes other than willful or careless negligence on the part of the parent(s). They may be powerless, in not having the financial or other resources to prevent or remedy a harmful situation; they may be mentally disturbed or incompetent; they may lack knowledge or appropriate education; or they may be unable to cope with a difficult child. Most of the scales focus on actual or potential unmet needs of children rather than on the ascribed causes of the unmet needs. Additional scales deal with parental capacities, motivation, or resources.

Each scale has between three and six levels ranging from "adequate" to increasing degrees of inadequacy on a given dimension. Each level of a scale is explicitly defined. The narrative "descriptors" at each level are phrased as much as possible in observable terms; that is, actual functioning and behavior of parents and children. Reliance on inferences and predictions is minimized. The descriptors for a given scale are intended to be mutually exclusive; a family or child is best described by only one of them. The text of the scales is given at the end of this chapter. A description of the purpose and interpretation of each scale follows.

1. Physical Health Care

This scale measures the adequacy of physical health care (not physical health itself) for the children in the family. It is intended to be applicable to any physical health problems, including injuries, illness, and disabilities, whether acute or chronic. The level of adequacy is indicated by the probable health consequences resulting from lack of treatment. The more serious these consequences, the more serious the lack of treatment is defined to be. Accurate completion requires some understanding by the rater of the implications and prognoses of common health problems. The major distinctions between levels 3, 4, and 5 are conditions that would or would not correct themselves in time, and among the latter, those that are or are not life-threatening in the absence of medical attention. Level 2, "marginal," is defined by lack of normal preventive health care.

The focus on children's physical health care, rather than on their actual health, was chosen because the connection between health care and health status is often unclear or tenuous. Health status is a logical outcome indicator for medical services, but for child welfare services it seems more reasonable to measure only whether children receive proper medical care.

2. Nutrition/Diet

This scale focuses on the quality and quantity of food available to the children in the family and on the health consequences of inadequate feeding. Quality of food takes into account both nutritional balance, usually a less serious problem, and wholesomeness (i.e., spoilage), usually more serious. Quantity of food is defined in terms of meal preparation and the accessibility of foodstuffs to children. The worst situations are those resulting in actual physical symptoms of malnutrition, dehydration, food poisoning, lack of growth (failure to thrive), related conditions ("seriously inadequate"), or required hospitalization ("severely inadequate"). In cases where children are ill, it may require a medical diagnosis to link such illness with inadequate feeding. Social workers should be sensitive to the possibility of illness in situations where poor nutrition is suspected.

The scale is not intended to imply that parents are deliberately or neglectfully failing to provide adequate food to their children. The intent is to measure the degree of adequacy of nutrition and diet, without necessarily attributing blame. Causes of the problem may be indicated by the appropriate completion of other scales. For instance, deliberate withholding of food may be rated on Scale 30, irresponsibility in child care on Scale 19 and 20, and mismanagement of finances on Scale 15.

3. Clothing

This scale measures the adequacy of children's clothing. Factors taken into account include amount, condition, and appropriateness. The more serious situations are when engagement in normal and necessary activities is hindered, or when clothing is insufficient for protection from the elements. Actual physical injury or illness attributable to exposure is expected to be very rare; therefore this situation is not explicitly described, though "seriously inadequate" would be the correct categorization.

Cleanliness of the clothes worn by the children should not enter directly into the rating of this scale. It may be that children often wear dirty clothes because they do not have enough changes of clothes. It is also possible, however, that there is enough clothing, but that it is not washed regularly. In that case the problem is not one of clothing as defined by this scale, but one of hygiene, and should be so rated on Scale 4, Personal Hygiene.

4. Personal Hygiene

The scale involves bodily cleanliness (skin, hair, teeth) and cleanliness of clothing, on the assumption that the two usually are related. The more serious descriptors involve grossly soiled clothes, bodily odor, complaints by others, and, in the most extreme case, actual illness attributable to poor personal hygiene. Again, rating the latter may have to rely on a medical diagnosis.

5. Household Furnishings

This scale focuses on the existence and condition of essential furnishings, including appliances and on the amount and balance of furnishings in relation to family needs. The more serious descriptors involve lack (or inoperability) of what are usually considered essential items, such as a refrigerator.

6. Overcrowding

This scale takes into consideration the amount of available living space in relation to family size and composition, privacy needs of adults and older children of opposite sex, and the ability of family members to pursue normal and necessary activities at home. The more serious situations involve lack of appropriate segregating in sleeping, constant competition for and arguments about space, and the breakdown of essential household functions such as meal taking and cleaning.

Inadequate furnishings and overcrowding will probably be related in many cases, insofar as small living quarters may lack physical space for all the furnishings a family commonly needs. In such instances both scales should be rated as applicable. In other cases, however, there will be few furnishings though sufficient physical space exists, or furnishings will be adequate but packed so closely that there is no room to "move around." Consequently, the ratings on the two scales may be quite different.

Children might also have an inappropriate sleeping arrangement not because of over-crowding but because of parental ignorance of or insensitivity to sexual development. In an extreme case this situation could constitute a form of sexual abuse, but the scale is not intended to address this eventuality. Such a situation would most likely be associated with sexual molestation and should be rated on Scale 33, Sexual Abuse.

7. Household Sanitation

This scale evaluates the cleanliness of the home, including such items as general orderliness, amount of dust and debris, disposal of garbage, proper storage and consumption of perishable foodstuffs, cleanliness of kitchen and bathroom, and presence of vermin. The more serious situations involve threats to the health of children because of filth or actual illness attributable to grossly inadequate sanitation.

8. Security of Residence

This scale measures the availability of housing for a family. Factors that may threaten or cause forced housing loss include overdue rent, uninhabitability of residence, and sale of residence. The most serious situation is when a family has no adequate, permanent quarters, or when their loss is imminent.

9. Availability of Utilities

This scale deals with common threats to the habitability of a residence. Included are problems with heat, water, lighting, cooking appliances, and plumbing facilities. The most serious situation exists when essential utilities are off for days at a time, and the landlord habitually fails to accept his responsibilities. Both this and the preceding scale are phrased mainly in tenants' terms, but the scales may also be completed for homeowners. In that case some references to "landlord" may not be relevant, or "landlord" should be understood as "owner."

10. Physical Safety in Home

The scale assesses physically dangerous conditions in the household or building in which the family is living. Taken into account are both the number of dangerous conditions and whether a child has sustained any injury as a result. No attempt is made to distinguish between relative degrees of danger posed by specific types of conditions. Most conditions could result in either mild or severe injury, depending on particular circumstances. The scale simply assumes that the more dangerous the conditions, the higher the risk of eventual injury to children. The most serious situation is defined as the actual occurrence of injury, accompanied by the continuing existence of several hazardous conditions that pose risk of additional injury. The examples given are typical but should not be considered all-inclusive.

The scale does not address the issue of dangerous environmental conditions, such as high neighborhood crime rates or vacant or condemned buildings. Many families receiving child protective services live in neighborhoods dangerous in this sense. These are the sorts of social conditions that cannot be affected by personal social services. Thus, although it might be possible to relocate families to a better building, or alert parents and children to hazardous neighborhood conditions, there is little likelihood that families can be insulated from the larger urban context of crime, economic deprivation, and often inadequate municipal services. This aspect is the arena of political action.

11. Mental Health Care

This scale is analogous to that for Scale 1, Physical Health Care. The severity of lack of mental health treatment is indicated by the degree to which the mental problem disrupts the child's everyday life. Taken into account are both the child's performance in various life roles and the reactions of others to the child. The most serious situation is when the child is excluded from normal activities or otherwise harshly sanctioned by others.

To measure severity, the scale focuses on the social interactional consequences of mental illness, not on specific psychiatric diagnoses. The rater must clearly make an inference about the existence of mental illness, however, in order to judge whether mental health care is required. In some cases a child may have been treated for a mental health problem previously, and the current problem may be a continuation or recurrence of that. In other cases a clinical diagnosis may have been made, but adequate treatment has not been provided or accepted. The cases with greatest ambiguity are those where a child's behavior seems to indicate a mental problem, but there is no formal diagnosis of mental illness. If the worker plans to recommend mental health evaluation for such a child, then a tentative rating of need for mental health care should be made—but such a rating is not intended to "label" a child before a proper evaluation is available.

12. Supervision of Younger Children (Under Age 13)

This scale measures the amount and quality of attention given to children when they are engaged in play or free activities. Factors included are children's location (inside vs. outside the home), parental concern or awareness of children's activities, dangerous circumstances in which children may have been found, and actual injury to children attributable to inadequate supervision. The scale implies parental responsibility (though not necessarily "blame") for inadequate supervision; possible mitigating circumstances are not considered in rating the scale. The focus is on danger or harm to the child, which remains the same no matter what the cause of inadequate supervision may be.

The scale assumes that problems in supervision constitute a pattern in the family. A single, isolated observation of less than perfect supervision would not warrant rating a family as "marginal" or "inadequate" in this area.

13. Supervision of Teenage Children

A separate scale for supervision of teenagers was constructed because the problems posed here are primarily supervision of social activities rather than of physical play activities. Factors included are rule and limit setting, concern about children's activities, use of appropriate sanctions when warranted, ability to command children's respect, and sensitivity to community norms for child behavior. Again, the scale assumes that a pattern of inadequate supervision exists that has been reported or that can be observed over a period of time.

While the scale is phrased in terms of parental responsibility, it is of course true that some children cannot be controlled by their parents despite their best efforts. Even if that is the case, supervision should still be rated at some level of "inadequacy." The intent of the scale is to document how well parents are supervising their children, independent of their inherent supervisory abilities or how difficult their children might be to control.

14. Arrangements for Substitute Child Care

This scale measures the adequacy with which parents arrange for the care of their children when they are temporarily absent—ranging from going out for an evening to being away for several days for any reason. The scale considers several factors relating to increasing risk of harm to the child(ren): the competency of the substitute caretaker; the age and competency of the child(ren) for self-care; and the timing of the parents' return. The most severe situation is leaving alone a young child incompetent to handle his or her basic needs who becomes physically harmed and/or emotionally distressed.

15. Money Management

This scale measures the adequacy with which the parents manage their "disposable income," that is, the income they have some control over spending. The issues include both budgeting and borrowing. Income production is not considered. The scale is suitable for describing a family irrespective of their level of income or their source of income. For example, for families on welfare the scale will describe how well they handle the small amount of income they have. Of course, they may be using their funds wisely and appropriately, yet not be able to meet all the necessities of life. In this case, Money Management would be rated "adequate"; the consequences of inadequate family income are indicated by other scales.

In defining the seriousness of the problem, the scale considers the following factors: spending priorities (necessities vs. luxuries), planning and timing of expenditures, attention to value in purchasing, and frequency and amount of borrowing. The greater the resulting deprivation of necessities, and the higher the debts, the more serious the defects in money management are considered to be for the family.

16. Parental Capacity for Child Care

This scale considers the degree to which a parent's child-caring capacity may be limited; the source of the limitation may be physical, mental, emotional, or behavioral. No distinction is made as to whether the parent has voluntary control over the problem. The scale defines the severity of the problem partially in terms of the type of treatment needed by the parent. Thus, the scale does not provide an "independent" measure of parental limitations, defined for example in terms of what the parent cannot or will not do for the children. Such measures are provided by the other scales, however. Severity of parental limitations is defined in terms of the duration of the problem, the ability of the parent to reside and function at home, and the need for substitute care for the children.

17. Parental Relations

This scale measures the quality of interaction between the parents or parent figures in the household. Poor relations between the parents may be detrimental to children indirectly through effects on child care, or, more directly, through involvement of the children in parental disputes. The emotional effect on children cognizant of or exposed to high levels of tension between their parents is an important reason for including such a scale. The following factors are considered in assessing the adequacy of parental relations: amount of argumentation and conflict; methods of dispute resolution, including resort to threats or violence; degree to which children are drawn in or are the focus of disputes; amount of positive interaction between parents despite conflicts; and the degree and permanency of parental separations.

18. Continuity of Parenting

The rationale for this scale is children's need for the stable presence of parent figures to whom they are attached (Goldstein et al. 1973) The scale takes into account the frequency of disruptions in regular parenting; the length of time the parent is away; the preparation given children for any break; the familiarity to the child of substitute caretakers; and the permanency of any current disruption in regular parenting.

The scale does not explicitly take into account the emotional impact of parenting discontinuity on the child. Clearly, children are not all equally vulnerable to adverse effects from a given situation. It is difficult, however, to attribute any emotional problems a child may have to a particular cause such as unstable parenting. It was considered preferable, therefore, to document observable instability independent of any disturbance that might be exhibited by the child. (Functioning disturbance is measured by Scale 42, Coping Behavior of Children.)

19. Parental Recognition of Problems

This is one of several scales that explicitly consider parental attitudes toward and understanding of their family's problems. This scale considers the degree to which parents understand the nature and severity of the problem situation, understand their own contributions to the problems, and accept appropriate responsibility. Clearly, these attributions are made from the perspective of the service provider. Recognition of problems may often be a prerequisite to problem resolution; thus, improvement on this scale may signal an increased potential for case progress. Changing parental orientation does not in itself alleviate harm to children, however. In an extreme case, parents might accept responsibility, yet lack the inner strength or other resources to alter their behavior.

20. Parental Motivation to Solve Problems

This scale measures the concern parents demonstrate about the problems that have been identified, irrespective of whether they believe themselves "responsible," and their willingness to work to resolve the problems. The scale may be considered to measure acceptance vs. rejection of the parental role. Some aspects of this are willingness to make sacrifices, avoidance of carelessness or mistakes, development of confidence in oneself and avoidance of apathy, and ability to empathize with their children.

21. Parental Cooperation with Case Planning/Services

Part of parents' capacity to deal with family problems involves their willingness to cooperate with the agency. Such cooperation is facilitative although it does not guarantee problem improvement if, for example, the services are of the wrong kind or not sufficiently intense. The scale measures the degree of cooperation by considering following through on referrals, keeping appointments, actively participating in case planning and in proposing alternatives, making maximum use of services offered, maintaining contact with the agency, accepting service for oneself as well as for the children, displaying some autonomous action, and adhering to plans except when extenuating circumstances arise.

22. Support for Principal Caretaker

This scale is concerned with parents' informal social networks that may assist in relieving personal stress and domestic burdens. Social isolation has been noted as a factor associated with maltreatment of children (Garbarino et al. 1980). The scale is an adaptation of the Family Support Index (Polansky et al. 1981:87), which is a grounded typology developed from actual parent interview responses. In the Polansky study, construct validity of the scale was indicated by the large differences in social support found between parents who were and were not referred for child neglect.

The scale measures the level of informal supports by the closeness of the relation (immediate family vs. other relatives or friends) and by the number of persons who can be called on to help when needed. Obviously, this does not measure the quality or exact intensity of the help available, but it is assumed that these factors are correlated with the given indicators.

23. Availability/Accessibility of Services

The scale is the only one focusing explicitly on the adequacy of service resources for a family in the community. It is possible that this area is entirely out of the control of both the client and the worker. The scale relates to parental capacity for parenting in that it measures limitations on resources needed by parents. In this sense it also constitutes a measure of limitation on successful casework.

It may be possible, however, to increase availability of resources through changes in agency programs, advocacy in the community, or skilled mediation with other agencies on behalf of particular clients. Clients may sometimes be able to help themselves by changing their residence or establishing eligibility. Improvement on this scale, then, is clearly an outcome that facilitates resolving a family's problems.

24. Parental Acceptance of/Affection for Children

This is the first of five scales that measure components of what is known as "emotional care" of children. The scales are defined so as to cut across the concepts of "emotional neglect" and "emotional abuse." The scales are based on current understanding of what constitutes effective methods of child socialization; that is, methods that result in adequate internalization of normative behavior without incurring undesirable emotional consequences (Toby 1974).

The acceptance scale measures behavior reflecting unconditional positive regard of children. Such behavior includes verbal expressions of affection, encouraging physical contact, sharing affection with all children, and accepting children's requests for affection. Without this kind of acceptance, children may be unable to undertake the tasks leading to emotional maturity, involving risk taking in their relationships with others (Patterson and Thompson 1980: 62–63).

25. Parental Approval of Children

This scale focuses on whether sanctions are exercised primarily through rewarding appropriate child behavior or punishing inappropriate behavior. Effective and permanent learning has been shown to take place under the first condition of positive reinforcement, but not under the second of aversive conditioning (Bandura 1971). The scale also takes into account the linkage between sanctions, whether positive or negative, and actual child behavior; the "proportionality" of sanctions; and sanctioning inconsistencies due to parental overreactions.

26. Parental Expectations of Children

The scale focuses on the appropriateness of the behavioral demands made on the children. The difference between levels 2 and 3 is that, in the former, parents are open to adjusting their unrealistic demands, while in the latter they seem committed to them. Level 4 is defined by the extreme nature of the lack of realism in parent-child interaction. This scale includes the concept of "role reversal" between parent and child that has been identified as a cause (or at least as a concomitant) of child abuse (Helfer et al. 1976). Note that both inappropriate parental expectations for less or more mature behavior are compatible with the scale definitions. In role reversal, both types of situations may occur.

27. Parental Consistency of Discipline

This scale concerns the degree to which parents maintain a uniform and understandable pattern of discipline for the children.

28. Parental Teaching/Stimulating of Children

This scale concerns the extent to which parents provide opportunities for learning and encourage competence in task behaviors. Adequacy on this scale contributes both to intellectual development and to confidence and self-esteem, a "sense of mastery," on the part of children. Thus the scale has emotional as well as cognitive implications for adequate child development.

29. Abusive Physical Discipline

This is the first of the scales concerned with various types of abusive behavior.

Abusive Physical Discipline focuses on the use and severity of physical force with children, which is most frequently interpreted by parents as disciplinary behavior. The scale applies as well, however, when the use of force has a less "rational" basis—for example, parents' emotional disturbance. The scale assumes that any "culturally acceptable" physical punishment will not result in physical injury or the infliction of great pain. The severity of unacceptable punishment, examples of which are given, is defined in terms of the degree of injury to the child.

The risk of injury, when no actual injury occurred, is not considered in measuring severity. Nevertheless, it is possible that life-threatening behaviors may occur, even if no injury was sustained. Instead of attempting to equate actual and potential injuries, this type of situation is taken into account by Scale 34, Threat of Abuse. In general, it is difficult to scale "risk" because the actual extent of risk, which essentially involves a prediction, cannot often be readily determined.

30. Deliberate Deprivation of Food/Water

This scale measures the type and degree of deprivation of nourishment when practiced as a disciplinary technique.

31. Physical Confinement or Restriction

This scale measures the use of confinement or restriction as a disciplinary technique.

32. Deliberate Locking-Out

This scale is concerned with deprivation of shelter for the child by the parent. It is particularly applicable to those children who have been termed "push-outs" or "throwaways."

33. Sexual Abuse

This scale indicates the level of sexual abuse experienced by children. The type of abuse and the person committing it are rated separately. Empirical work with the scale, to be described later, showed that abuse committed by a parent or guardian is usually considered more serious than abuse committed by another adult. The scoring of the scale takes this into account.

34. Threat of Abuse

This scale defines the risk of physical abuse where none has yet occurred. The chosen indicators of risk are the actual verbalizations and behaviors of the parent, ranging from general or vague threats, to direct threats, to physical actions that could have resulted in injury. Such physical actions can also be interpreted as symbolic threats against the child.

35. Economic Exploitation

This scale concerns children's participation in inappropriate work roles, whether or not the child voluntarily performs such roles. The most serious situation is engagement in illegal activity.

36. Protection from Abuse

Part of a parent's responsibility is to protect children from harm by others. It is not uncommon in abuse and neglect cases for someone other than the parent to abuse the child. In defining the severity of the situation, the scale considers the adequacy of the parent's judgment, the parent's knowledge of maltreatment, and the parent's willingness to take corrective action.

Active collaboration in the abuse is always considered "seriusly inadequate" protection. The parent's actions and their consequences for the child would then also be rated on one or more of the previous abuse scales.

37. Adequacy of Education

This scale focuses on the degree to which the child's educational needs are being met. The scale does not assume that any deficiency is necessarily the parent's responsibility, although this situation may be at least partly true.

38. Academic Performance

This scale concerns the child's actual grades or other performance indicators in school. The scale measures performance in relation to the child's intellectual potential; that is, a child of below-average intelligence (as measured by I.Q.) who receives below-average grades may reasonably be considered performing "acceptably." Clearly this scale requires the rater to have some knowledge of the child's potential. Parents and teachers are usually aware of a child's potential, so that the social worker may draw on this information. If a child is educationally appropriately placed, however, the scale assumes the child should not be failing the grade, or be in danger of failing.

39. School Attendance

School attendance is often viewed as a particularly good indicator of a child's overall adjustment to school, so it is separately scaled here. Poor attendance may be the responsibility of the child, the parent, the school, or all three. The detrimental impact on the child is in all cases quite similar; that is, falling behind educationally.

40. Children's Family Relations

This scale focuses on the type and degree of conflict in the home between a child and other family members. It is applicable to children of at least school age. The scale considers such factors as problem-solving efforts, tolerance among family members, amount of contacts, and requests for separation.

41. Children's Misconduct

This scale involves the type and seriousness of children's behavior in the home, school, and community. Seriousness is defined both in terms of the harm done to others and the consequences to the child.

42. Coping Behavior of Children

This scale involves the adequacy of a child's relations with others, as defined by the following concepts: delay of gratification, assertiveness, resistance to authority, independence, withdrawal, impulse control, and so forth. It is potentially applicable to children of any age, but particularly to younger children. This scale is an adaptation of Barker's (n.d.) Emotional Development Scale for Children.

43. Children's Disabling Conditions—Degree of Impairment

This scale focuses on limitations in role functioning of children attributable to specific physical or emotional conditions. Factors taken into account in defining the severity of limitations are effects on "major" roles vs. "secondary" role activity, amount of disruption of others' activities, extensiveness of symptoms, reactions of others to the child, amount of stress or difficulty in performing roles at a given level, and prognosis for the future. The type of impairment is also coded.

Scoring

A rating form (see Figure 3-1) has been designed to facilitate completing the scales on a case. Scales 1 through 28 receive a single rating for the entire family; Scales 29 through 43 receive a rating for each child in the family (or, alternatively, for each child receiving services). These scale ratings are then used to compute individual and summary scale scores, as described below.

Seriousness Scores

The scoring of the scales was refined by empirically deriving seriousness scores for each level of each scale. These scores make it possible to compare the seriousness of situations harmful to children described on different scales. Additionally, the scores may be used to form composite or summary scores from the individual scale ratings.

The desirability of using seriousness scores may be seen by considering the limitations of the individual scale ratings for evaluative research purposes. The situations described for each scale are intended to increase in seriousness when going from one level to another. Precise differences of seriousness between levels are not specified, however. All that can be said is that one level is more or less serious than another level. Some levels may be conceptually close together in seriousness, while others may be far apart. This makes it difficult to interpret changes on the scales. For example, does a change from level 3 to level 2 on Physical Health Care represent improvement that is greater than, less than, or equal to a change from level 2 to level 1?

Similarly, with only the scale ratings it is not possible to compare the seriousness of descriptors on different scales. For example, what is the seriousness of level 3 for Nutrition/Diet as compared with level 3 for Clothing? And how much improvement is represented by a change from level 3 to level 2 on Nutrition/Diet compared with the same change in levels on Clothing?

By the method to be discussed in chapter 4, seriousness scores were assigned to each level of each scale (refer to table 3-1). These scores are, in effect, a set of seriousness "weights" that make it possible to compare as well as to combine ratings on different scales. The scores may be interpreted as the *relative seriousness of each described situation for the welfare of the child.* The range of the scores is from 0 (most serious) to 100 (adequate). Equal numerical differences in scores represent equal differences in seriousness. For instance, the difference in seriousness between 50 and 60 is the same as that between 80 and 90. The seriousness scores assigned to the levels of each scale may now be used to form composite or summary scores for the scales.

Total Score

The seriousness scores enable all individual scale information to be combined into a total score for the family, here termed the "Child Well-Being Score" (CWBS). It would be impermissible to add individual scale ratings (e.g., "1," "2," "3") to obtain a summary score, because these ratings are not true numbers, but rather only labels for the level of each scale. In contrast, the seriousness scores as derived are numbers that may be justifiably added and averaged.

There is no single "best" way to construct a total score, but the following procedure may be the simplest and suitable for most applications. The CWBS is defined as the mean of the seriousness scores of the individual scale ratings:

$CWBS = SUM/N$, where
SUM = sum of the seriousness scores for the scales rated (from table 3-1)
N = Number of scales rated

For any scale rated on individual children, the seriousness scores for the children are averaged to obtain a single family seriousness score on that scale. This average score is then

Rating Form for Child Well-Being Scales

FAMILY IDENTIFIER: EVALUATION PHASE:

                                          INTAKE _____

DATE COMPLETED: FIRST FOLLOW-UP _____

                                          SECOND FOLLOW-UP _____

PERSON COMPLETING: CASE CLOSING _____

INSTRUCTIONS: *Write in numerical rating for each scale using the manual as reference.*

		Family's Rating
1	Physical Health Care	
2	Nutrition/Diet	
3	Clothing	
4	Personal Hygiene	
5	Household Furnishings	
6	Overcrowding	
7	Household Sanitation	
8	Security of Residence	
9	Availability of Utilities	
10	Physical Safety in Home	
11	Mental Health Care	
12	Supervision of Younger Children	
13	Supervision of Teenage Children	
14	Arrangements for Substitute Child Care	
15	Money Management	
16	Parental Capacity for Child Care	
17	Parental Relations	
18	Continuity of Parenting	
19	Parental Recognition of Problems	
20	Parental Motivation to Solve Problems	
21	Parental Cooperation with Case Planning/Services	
22	Support for Principal Caretaker	
23	Availability/Accessibility of Services	
24	Parental Acceptance of/Affection for Children	
25	Parental Approval of Children	

Rating Form for Child Well-Being Scales (cont)

FAMILY IDENTIFIER: EVALUATION PHASE:

                                      INTAKE _____

DATE COMPLETED: FIRST FOLLOW-UP _____

                                      SECOND FOLLOW-UP _____

PERSON COMPLETING: CASE CLOSING _____

INSTRUCTIONS: *Write in numerical rating for each scale using the manual as reference.*

26	Parental Expectations of Children	
27	Parental Consistency of Discipline	
28	Parental Teaching/Stimulating of Children	

		Child's Number					
		First	Second	Third	Fourth	Fifth	Sixth
29	Abusive Physical Discipline						
30	Deliberate Deprivation of Food/Water						
31	Physical Confinement or Restriction						
32	Deliberate Locking-Out						
33A	Sexual Abuse—Type						
33B	Person Committing Sexual Abuse						
34	Threat of Abuse						
35	Economic Exploitation						
36	Protection from Abuse						
37	Adequacy of Education						
38	Academic Performance						
39	School Attendance						
40	Children's Family Relations						
41	Children's Misconduct						
42	Coping Behavior of Children						
43A	Children's Disabling Condition—Type						
43B	Degree of Impairment						

Figure 3-1   Rating Form for Child Well-Being Scales

Table 3-1 Seriousness Scores for Child Well-Being Scales

Scale Name	Scale Level (Descriptors)					
	1	2	3	4	5	6
Physical Health Care	100	81	56	34	9	
Nutrition/Diet	100	71	50	32	22	9
Clothing	100	83	74	46		
Personal Hygiene	100	82	53	39	31	
Household Furnishings	100	88	64	54		
Overcrowding	100	82	62	51		
Household Sanitation	100	71	38	21	18	
Security of Residence	100	94	71	64		
Availability of Utilities	100	86	78	53		
Physical Safety in Home	100	44	31	25	20	
Mental Health Care	100	69	50	15		
Supervision of Younger Children (Under Age 13)	100	74	71	41	23	
Supervision of Teenage Children	100	93	62	39		
Arrangments for Substitute Child Care	100	79	70	50	33	14
Money Management	100	90	66	52		
Parental Capacity for Child Care	100	63	48	13		
Parental Relations	100	61	53	33		
Continuity of Parenting	100	79	68	44	13	
Parental Recognition of Problems	100	55	43			
Parental Motivation to Solve Problems	100	70	62	50	31	
Parental Cooperation with Case Planning/Services	100	59	54	46		
Support for Principal Caretaker	100	96	85	73	67	56
Availability/Accessibility of Services	100	77	68	57	29	
Parental Acceptance of/Affection for Children	100	70	45	35		
Parental Approval of Children	100	78	72	63		
Parental Expectations of Children	100	80	65	47		
Parental Consistency of Discipline	100	85	70	53		
Parental Teaching/Stimulating of Children	100	84	70	41		
Abusive Physical Discipline	100	93	22	18	13	1
Deliberate Deprivation of Food/Water	100	75	42	15	4	
Physical Confinement or Restriction	100	94	24	13		
Deliberate "Locking-Out"	100	53	30	30	8	
Sexual Abuse—Parent or Guardian	100	48	18	18	18	6
—Other Adult[a]	100	38	30	25	25	12
Threat of Abuse	100	54	46	17		
Economic Exploitation	100	50	46	13		
Protection from Abuse—Intake	100	50	23			
—Follow-up	100	30	12			
Adequacy of Education	100	73	61	41		
Academic Performance	100	76	64	45		
School Attendance	100	80	45	42	35	
Children's Family Relations	100	72	52	31		
Children's Misconduct	100	56	50	42	33	23
Coping Behavior of Children[b]	47	68	100	65	30	
Children's Disabling Conditions—Degree of Impairment	100	92	71	51	31	26

Note: High scores indicate high well-being (and low seriousness).

[a] Parent vs. other adult determined from Part B of the scale.

[b] Level 3 is defined as "adequate" for this scale.

entered into the formula above. A maximum of 43 seriousness scores, one for each rating scale, may enter into the CWBS computation.

CWBS scores for a family may range from 1 to 100. A score of 100 would be obtained if a family was ranked at level 1 (= 100) on all scales that were rated. Clearly, extremely low numerical scores are unlikely if only because few scales have any level with seriousness scores close to 1.

In evaluative research the scales would be completed on a family at two points in time, at least. Change (or lack of change) on the CWBS could then be a measure of service outcome, if a research design is used that properly allows observed client change to be linked to services received. A linear change score can be constructed by subtracting a family's initial score from a follow-up score.

Factor-Based Scores

Composite scores may also be computed based on the results of a factor analysis conducted on our field test data (see chapter 4). Three factors were found, accounting for 43% of the common variance of the individual scale scores. The three factors, and the number of scales belonging to each, are as follows:

Factor Name	No. of Scales
Household Adequacy (HA)	10
Parental Disposition (PD)	14
Child Performance (CP)	4

Three factor-based scores may be computed, using the same formula as for the CWBS; that is, the mean of the seriousness scores for the rated scales belonging to that factor. For HA, a maximum of 10 scales could enter into the computation. The maximum score possible for the factor-based scales is 100; the minimum possible score depends on the individual scales involved in each computation.

Other Composite Scoring

The total and factor-based scores described above are not the only plausible ways of forming composite scores. Because the seriousness scores are numbers measured on an interval-level continuum, any subset of individual scale scores may permissibly be added or subtracted (though not multiplied or divided). Different subscores may be constructed for different evaluative purposes. For instance, a subset of scales with some common conceptual element, for example, related to physical abuse or emotional care, may be combined into a summary score.

Administration

The scales are designed to be completed by a service provider, usually a social worker, based on all credible information available on a family. Accurate completion requires some direct contact with and home observation of a family, but the scales are not a structured observation device. The person completing them must obtain and synthesize information on a family from many sources. Completion should be on the basis of intake studies or other comprehensive assessments by service providers.

The scales are designed to be completed several times during the term of a case, so that change (or lack of change) in problems over time can be determined for families. Suitable time periods for administration would be every 3 or 6 months. The scales are intended to track relatively long-term changes, rather than changes from day to day or week to week (if indeed such short-term client changes are even plausible for child welfare services).

Time estimates for training and completion were obtained from field tests of the instrument. The average length of time required to complete the scales, once a social worker is familiar with their content, is 25 minutes. Completion is facilitated by the fact that client families were found to have problems (ratings below "adequate") on an average of only 11 scales at any given time. On most scales, then, workers need only read and mark the descriptor for "adequate," thus saving considerable time.

Staff members who were to complete the scales for the field tests participated in a 1-hour training session conducted by the authors. This seemed to be sufficient for familiarizing the staff with the concept of the scales and the rating format. The scales are written so as to be self-explanatory, but some self-study is required to become familiar with their content. This process usually takes place in completing the scales on the first few cases. The authors now recommend that staff members complete the scales on one of their cases as part of the training session; 90 minutes may then be required for training.

No special qualifications are needed by the person leading the training, other than familiarity with the documentation on the scales in this book and, if possible, some personal experience in completing them. A potential individual or agency user of the scales should have access to the documentation in this book.

Reliability and Validity

These are thoroughly discussed in chapters 4 and 5.

Sensitivity to Change

This issue was addressed by examining the reliabilities and standard errors of the change scores for the composite scales. These statistics and the associated 95% confidence intervals for observed change scores of zero are presented in table 5-9. For example, reliable positive changes on the CWBS was identified for 44.6% of the families in the normative sample, and reliable negative change for 20.7%.

Change scores on the individual rating scales are not reliable enough to assess change for individual families. Changes for groups on individual scales may be assessed and compared, however, as discussed in chapter 5.

The scales are being used in several evaluation studies where their sensitivity to measuring service and program effects will be tested (see Discussion).

Norms

The normative sample consists of 240 families drawn from the population of families who had completed the intake process and had been newly accepted for service during 1981 at three public agencies in Texas, Minnesota, and Florida. Two of the agencies are child protective service agencies, the third serves multiproblem families at risk of involvement with the child protective or juvenile justice systems. Only families with at least one child at home were eligible for the study. At one site, sexual abuse cases were deliberately oversampled. Demographic characteristics of this intake sample are given in appendix 1; more details on sample selection are given in chapter 4.

The individual Child Well-Being Scale ratings at the time of intake are presented in table 3-2. The set of scales rated is the version before the final revisions of the instrument, as described in chapter 4. Thus table 3-2 does not include Continuity of Parenting, nor is Supervision of Children divided between teenage and younger children. Also the number of levels has changed for some scales.

The scale distributions are highly skewed toward "adequate" (= 1), which indicates that most families are free of problems in most areas. Any comprehensive family assessment might show similar results. Also note that the percentage of cases rated at a given scale level decreases as the seriousness of the level increases. This suggests that nontrivial problems are being registered at the higher scale levels, as intended.

The means and standard deviations for the composite scales (CWBS, HA, PD, and CP) are given in table 5-5. The means and standard deviations of the change scores for these composites are given in table 5-9. To compute those change scores, the intake cases were followed up 5 to 6 months from the date of referral.

Completeness/Response Rates

Information on completeness of responses is available for the normative sample (refer to table 3-2). Social workers were able to rate the family (or at least one child in the family) on a given scale an average of 85% of the time. There was insufficient information ("unknown") to rate a scale an average of 11% of the time, and a scale was coded "not applicable" an average of 6% of the time. Percentages in table 3-2 do not add to 100% because they are category averages.

There is some pattern to the "unknown" responses. Four of the five scales involving emotional care of children have above-average rates of missing data, which may indicate the relative difficulty of a practitioner observing such interaction. The above-average rates of "unknown" for some of the scales involving living conditions are more difficult to understand. Several scales were expected to show, and did show, frequent "not applicable" responses because of the absence of a spouse in the household (Parental Relations), because there was no

Table 3-2   Child Well-Being Scale Distributions (Intake Data, N = 240)

	% of Families			Level of Scale (% of Cases)					
Scale Name	With Information	NA	UNK	1	2	3	4	5	6
Physical Health Care	96	*	4	82	7	8	3		
Nutrition/Diet	92	*	8	82	13	2	1	2	*
Clothing	96	*	4	81	14	4	1		
Personal Hygiene	93	*	7	80	13	5	1	1	
Household Furnishings	81	2	17	79	10	9	2		
Overcrowding	89	2	9	80	12	4	4		
Household Sanitation	75	3	22	76	18	4	2		
Security of Residence	89	1	10	86	8	2	4		
Availability of Utilities	85	2	13	94	2	2	2		
Physical Safety in Home	74	2	24	87	8	4	1	1	
Mental Health Care	88	4	8	71	18	7	4		
Supervision of Children	93	1	6	66	11	15	7	1	
Arrangements for Substitute Child Care	92	3	5	79	11	7	1	2	
Money Management	86	*	14	78	9	8	5		
Parental Capacity for Child Care	95	0	5	61	27	8	4		
Parental Relations	65	28	7	46	19	14	21		
Parental Recognition of Problems	97	0	3	47	30	15	8		
Parental Motivation to Solve Problems	95	0	5	54	14	17	11	4	
Parental Cooperation with Case Planning/ Services	88	3	9	60	23	11	6		
Support for Principal Caretaker	91	*	9	61	12	6	9	5	7
Availability/Accessibility of Services	96	*	4	79	16	5	*		
Parental Acceptance of/ Affection for Children	90	0	10	59	25	12	4		
Parental Approval of Children	74	3	23	41	35	17	7		
Parental Expectations of Children	85	1	14	44	37	11	8		
Parental Consistency of Discipline	75	2	23	43	34	7	16		
Parental Teaching/ Stimulating of Children	78	2	20	49	26	19	6		
Abusive Physical Discipline[a]	84	7	9	42	43	5	8	1	1
Deliberate Deprivation of Food/Water[a]	88	5	7	91	6	3			
Physical Confinement or Restriction[a]	86	4	10	79	20	*	1		
Deliberate Locking-out[a]	89	7	4	96	2	2	*		
Sexual Abuse—Parent[a,b]	88	5	7	89	1	1	*	3	6
Threat of Abuse[a]	84	4	12	88	5	6	1		

Table 3-2   (Continued)

Scale Name	% of Families			Level of Scale (% of Cases)					
	With Information	NA	UNK	1	2	3	4	5	6
Economic Exploitation[a]	87	10	3	98	1	1			
Protection from Abuse[a]	16	59	25	41	37	21			
Adequacy of Education[a]	78	19	3	83	7	5	5		
Academic Performance[a]	66	24	10	72	14	7	7		
School Attendance[a]	71	5	24	83	6	8	3		
Children's Family Relations[a]	86	4	10	70	18	8	2	2	
Children's Misconduct[a]	86	5	9	71	14	7	3	3	2
Coping Behavior of Children[a,c]	76	7	17	16	16	58	8	2	
Children's Disabling Conditions—Degree of Impairment	87	5	8	80	7	5	7	1	*

*Less than 1%

[a] For the child-specific scales, "level of problem" distributions were computed by summing all children in the family rated at each level. The "% of cases" is the % of all children for whom there is information who were rated at each level.

[b] Includes Dallas, where oversampling occurred. Excluding Dallas: 1, 96%; 2, 1%; 3, 1%; 4, *; 5, 1%; 6, 1%.

[c] Level "3" defined as "adequate"

Note: There are certain differences between some of the Child Well-Being Scales described in this chapter and the corresponding scales in table 3-2. See the section on Norms, in this chapter.

current or past child abuse by a third party (Protection from Abuse), or because there were no school-age children in the family (Adequacy of Education, Academic Performance).

Discussion and Recommendations

The Child Well-Being Scales are a multidimensional measure of child welfare problem situations specifically designed for use in outcome evaluation research. Extensive reliability and validity testing have been done with large samples under realistic agency field conditions. The results indicate that the scales compare favorably with the best alternative measures currently available. The scales are one of the few measures tailored for child welfare service evaluation, which should make them particularly attractive to agencies.

The Child Well-Being Scales are being used in two major applications as of this writing. The scales have been selected as the outcome measurement procedure for the Colorado Department of Social Services' new statewide computerized management information system for child welfare. The Virginia Department of Social Services is using the scales to evaluate the impact of a statewide group of preventive services demonstration projects.

Source

The Child Well-Being Scales, the rating form, and complete instructions and documentation are published in this volume. Permission is granted to reproduce the scales and rating forms directly from the book for non-profit research or evaluation purposes only. Alternatively, multiple copies of the scales and rating forms may be obtained from: *Publications Department, Child Welfare League of America, 440 First Street, N.W., Suite 310, Washington, DC 20001*

The Child Well-Being Scales

Rating Instructions for Social Workers

The purpose of the Child Well-Being Scales is to document possible changes in the well-being and caretaking environment of children. The scales should be completed based on all information available concerning the family.

When completing the instrument at the end of the intake process, each scale should describe the family situation and behavior at the time of referral to the agency. The intake process should be considered a period of discovery. Incidents or conditions that were discovered to be reasons for the family's referral must be included (unless such reasons were shown to have been false). If some change in the family's situation occurred during the intake assessment, only the initial situation at referral should be described. When completing the instrument at follow-up (that is, after some period of service, or when the case is closed), the scales should describe the family's then-current situation and behavior. This does not necessarily mean on the day the scales are completed, but rather should reflect the latest information available on the family.

Before completing the scales, review the description of each one for content. (Some training and practice on the schedule should already have been provided.) After making a judgment on the scale level that *best* describes the family or child, write in the numerical rating on the scoring sheet. Do not force an answer. When information in a particular area is not available (or cannot be easily obtained), a "don't know" response is preferred. In some cases a "not applicable" response may be appropriate, such as academic information when a child is not of school age.

If you believe an explanation of any rating is needed, please make a comment on the rating sheet.

Scales 1 to 28

On these scales the family should be rated as a unit. Write in one rating on each scale for the family.

At Intake

Choose the rating that *best describes* the situation at the time the family came to the agency (at referral).

At Follow-Up

Choose the rating that *best describes* the situation *now*, based on the most recent information.

If the situation is not the same for all children in the family, indicate the most serious problem experienced by any child.

If there are two caretakers (for example, mother and father) who do not provide the same quality of care, indicate the lowest quality of care that constitutes an adverse influence on the children. For example, if one of the children in the family is emotionally rejected while others are not, the rating on scale 24, Acceptance of/Affection for Children, should reflect the harsh behavior toward that one child.

Scales 29 to 43

These scales are child-specific and a rating is made for *each child* in the family or under the agency's supervision. (The agency should decide which.) On the rating sheet, write in one code for each child for each scale.

At Intake

Choose the *most serious* abuse or problem identified for each child at referral to the agency.

At First Follow-Up

Choose the *most serious* abuse or problem experienced by each child during supervision by the agency (since referral).

At Subsequent Follow-Ups.

Choose the *most serious* abuse or problem experienced by each child since the last follow-up.

If more than one incident has occurred, or if a single situation contains different elements, you should indicate the most serious condition. For example, a child has been molested and sexual intercourse occurred. On the Sexual Abuse scale Sexual Intercourse would therefore be coded for that child.

Remember that the examples given are just that. The situation, condition, or behavior in your case may be different in its particulars but may still be comparable to the examples given. You will need to decide what scale level most closely resembles your own case. Not every example under a given level need hold true for you to decide that the level constitutes the best description. Experience has shown that social workers' ratings on these scales are reasonably reliable, so you should have confidence in your ability to complete the instrument satisfactorily.

The
Child Well-Being
Scales

Stephen Magura
and
Beth Silverman Moses

Complete documentation on the Child Well-Being Scales is given in Stephen Magura and Beth Silverman Moses, *Outcome Measures for Child Welfare Services*, Washington, D.C.: Child Welfare League of America, 1986.

Development of the Child Well-Being Scales was funded by Grant No. 90-CW-2041 from the Administration for Children, Youth and Families, Office of Human Development, Department of Health and Human Services, Washington, D.C.

Child Welfare League of America, Inc.
Washington, D.C.

1. *Adequate*

There are no children with untreated injuries, illnesses, or disabilities that could benefit from medical treatment

Children are taken for checkups promptly when symptoms of illness appear.

All children receive normal preventive health care for their age.

2. *Marginal*

There are no children with untreated medical conditions that could benefit from medical treatment.

But preventive medical or dental care (e.g., immunizations, dental checkups) should be improved.

3. *Moderately inadequate*

At least one child is not receiving medical care for an injury or illness that usually should receive treatment. The child's condition will probably correct itself even without medical treatment. However, medical treatment now would reduce risk of complications, relieve pain, speed healing, or reduce risk of contagion.

4. *Seriously inadequate*

At least one child has an illness or disability that interferes with normal functioning. Neither medical care nor a diagnostic assessment has been sought. With treatment it could be corrected or at least controlled. However, without treatment the illnesss or disability will worsen (though it is not life-threatening).

Include situations where a child has had some physical symptoms (e.g., pain or signs of contagious disease) for some time, but has not been taken for a medical exam.

5. *Severely inadequate*

At least one child is not receiving medical treatment for an injury, illness, or disability. If left untreated, the condition is life-threatening, or will result in permanent impairment, or is a serious threat to public health.

U *Unknown*—insufficient information

Z *Not applicable*

1. *Adequate*

   Children provided with regular and ample meals that usually meet basic nutritional requirements.

2. *Marginally adequate*

   Prepared meals often nutritionally unbalanced and occasionally skipped.
   Children get food themselves at home or supplement diet outside home.

3. *Mildly inadequate*

   Meals irregular and often not prepared at all, but usually one meal a day is provided.
   Children often take food on their own, but sometimes only nutritionally inadequate food in insufficient amounts is available.

4. *Moderately inadequate*

   Periods where meals have not been provided at all for several days.
   Almost no food in home and/or children unable to feed themselves.
   May eat nonfood items or spoiled food.
   Children may be quite hungry, but there is no actual illness.

5. *Seriously inadequate*

   Children suffer from some clinical symptoms of malnutrition, dehydration, or food poisoning.
   Medical attention and/or rehabilitative diet required.
   Hospitalization not ordinarily required for medical reasons (although children may be temporarily hospitalized for their protection).

6. *Severely inadequate*

   Children so severely malnourished or dehydrated (severe weight loss, anemia, etc.), or food poisoned (fever, vomiting, etc.), that hospitalization is required for this reason.

U *Unknown*—insufficient information

Z *Not applicable*

Scale 3   Clothing

1. *Adequate*

Children have all essential clothing items and enough changes of clothes to be neat and clean.

Clothes need not be new, but are in good condition and fit adequately.

Clothes are consistent with time, place, and weather. For example, children have seasonally appropriate clothes (rainwear, gloves, lightweight items).

2. *Mildly inadequate*

Children have all essential clothes, but may have limited changes of clothes, or may lack some seasonally appropriate items.

Clothes are worn and often obviously mended, but not ripped, torn, or dirty.

Some clothes may not fit properly (sleeve length wrong, unable to button).

3. *Moderately inadequate*

Children are missing one or two essential clothing items, or some essential items are in such bad condition that they shouldn't be worn.

They manage by adapting what clothes they have (e.g., wearing extra sweater instead of coat) or by wearing clothes that are not designed for the setting or weather in which they're being worn.

Children may be improperly dressed for some of their normal and necessary activities, e.g., school, but they are able to participate or attend.

Clothing is sufficient to protect children from the elements.

4. *Seriously inadequate*

Children are lacking many basic and essential items of clothing.

There are so few clothes, or so few of the right kinds of clothes, that children are sometimes unable to perform normal and necessary activities (going outdoors, to school, etc.).

Clothes are sometimes insufficient to protect children from the elements.

U *Unknown*—insufficient information

Z *Not applicable*

1. *Adequate*

 Children wash or bathe daily.
 Hair is combed and clean.
 Clothes are changed regularly, even if not outwardly dirty.
 Clean underwear is worn daily.
 Soiled diapers promptly changed.

2. *Mildly inadequate*

 Children wash or bathe when they are outwardly dirty rather than on a regular basis.
 Hair may be uncombed but tends to be clean.
 Clothes are changed only when soiled.
 Soiled diapers changed fairly regularly.

3. *Moderately inadequate*

 Children do not regularly wash or bathe even when they are dirty.
 Hair is visibly dirty.
 Children may emit body or mouth odor.
 Clothes are noticeably soiled and children may wear the same soiled clothes for days.
 Soiled diapers may not be changed for several hours.

4. *Seriously inadequate*

 Children have not bathed for at least several weeks.
 Children emit strong body odor and/or mouth odor.
 Teeth encrusted with green or brown matter.
 Clothes are soiled and stained and probably beyond cleaning.
 Complaints about children's hygiene have been made by others (school, etc.). Peers will not play with children.
 But children are not suffering from any illnesses due to poor personal hygiene.

5. *Severely inadequate*

 Children are suffering from several of the conditions described under (4), "seriously inadequate."
 Due to this poor hygiene, at least one child is physically ill (e.g., with intestinal disorder) requiring medical treatment.

U *Unknown*—insufficient information

Z *Not applicable*

1. *Adequate*

Has basic, essential furnishings, kitchen (stove, refrigerator) and bathroom facilities, that are in fair to good condition and in working order.

Needed repairs or replacements made quickly.

Has specialized infant/child care items (e.g., crib, high chair, carriage), if needed.

No more than one or two minor problems (e.g., needs more glassware; repairman on call; desire for nicer furniture).

2. *Mildly inadequate*

Has all essential appliances and facilities in working order.

Has most basic furnishings, but some are very worn though usable.

Needs one or two furniture items (e.g., another bed, table, more chairs) or infant care items.

Quantity of several items insufficient in relation to family size (linens, towels, blankets, glassware, utensils).

3. *Moderately inadequate*

Has all essential appliances and facilities, but most are old and in need of frequent repairs, resulting in non-operable periods (e.g., a hot plate might substitute for a stove, frequent inability to refrigerate perishable foods, etc.)

Needs several additional furnishings (e.g., some mattresses on floor, or family members must crowd on beds, or no large table for family meals).

Many items are insufficient in quantity in relation to family size.

Available utensils or furnishings often used for other than intended use (e.g., pots as bowls, sofa as bed).

May lack space heater or fans when needed seasonally.

4. *Seriously inadequate*

Essential household and sanitary functions cannot be pursued due to lack of (or inoperability of) essential kitchen appliances or bathroom facilities.

Few furnishings, most beyond repair or functional use.

There are no (or almost no) linens, towels, blankets, utensils, pots, pans. Makeshift items used (e.g., crates for tables or seating).

Household has a "bare" look."

U *Unknown*—insufficient information

Z *Not applicable*

Scale 6   Overcrowding

1. *No overcrowding*

Space for family completely adequate.

There are designated, separate areas for various household functions and personal activities (eating, sleeping, cooking, recreation).

There is sufficient space for normally private activities for all family members.

2. *Mild overcrowding*

Adults and children have separate sleeping areas, but children 6–8 years of opposite sex may be sharing same bed.

Up to four children may be sleeping in an average size bedroom.

Some but not all household functions may share same space (living room may double as bedroom, no separate kitchen, etc.).

Space can be made available for personal activities (homework, reading, play, etc.).

3. *Moderate overcrowding*

Parents and children age 5 or older may be sharing same bedroom.

Other adults of same sex may be sharing room with children.

Children ages 9–12 of opposite sex may be sharing same bed.

All rooms serve multiple functions.

There is competition for space among family members for personal activities (people "get in each other's way"), but essential household functions can be pursued with difficulty.

Sometimes normal in-home activities must be shifted to outside home (taking meals, doing homework).

4. *Serious overcrowding*

There is no segregation of sleeping areas; children and adults of any ages may be found sharing same bed.

Space is inadequate to pursue essential household functions in timely manner (cooking or cleaning often can't be done; proper sleep often impossible). There is almost no space to "move around."

Severe competition for space among family members.

Family members spend as much time as possible outside home; fights and arguments about space may be common.

Kitchen and/or bathroom facilities may be shared with other household(s).

U *Unknown*—insufficient information

Z *Not applicable*

1. *Adequate*

Generally clean and orderly.

Carpet and tile swept often and washed as needed (but some lint, threads, paper scraps may be seen).

Regular dusting (no more than thin layer of dust on tables).

Pleasant to neutral odors.

Home is orderly (but articles for daily living may be around: newspapers, books, coats not hung up).

Dishes washed or at least put in sink after each meal.

Groceries properly stored.

Linens clean; no vermin.

2. *Mildly inadequate*

Untidy, dusty, minor dirt buildup.

Carpet and tile have many particles of debris and are spotted; swept sometimes but rarely washed.

Tables, shelves, objects are very dusty; cobwebs in corners.

Stale, stuffy odors. Garbage not kept in proper receptacle.

Home is not picked up; things are all over (but no "piles" of trash)

Dirty dishes lay around home; washed at night or next day.

Groceries lay all around (but perishable foods generally refrigerated).

Some creeping vermin, but few in number, appearing mainly at night (no rats).

Walls, windows, doors, bathroom fixtures are spotted, stained, streaked with dirt.

3. *Moderately inadequate*

Carpet and tile have dirt buildup; carpet smells.

Dust and dirt are layered all over and accumulated in corners.

Home smells of mildew, rot, spoilage; bathroom has strong smells of urine/feces (but little visible).

Trash is around, and some corners or rooms are used to pile up junk or trash, which is rarely moved; garbage not kept in any receptacle.

Dishes only washed when no clean ones are left.

Perishable food found unrefrigerated and sometimes spoiled.

Creeping vermin frequent during daylight; home may have mice (no rats).

Walls, doors, bathroom fixtures are discolored from and smeared with dirt and grease.

Linens used after becoming dirty.

4. *Seriously inadequate*

Carpet, tile, walls, doors, bathroom fixtures are layered with encrusted dirt, debris, food wastes; human or animal waste prominent.

Thick dust and grease coat everything.

Home smells overwhelmingly of urine/feces/spoilage throughout.

Trash and junk piled up and layered on the floor so that it is difficult to get around.

Dishes are not washed; family eats off dirty dishes, or doesn't use them.

Perishable foods found spoiled; spoiled foods not promptly discarded.

Heavy rodent infestation; creeping vermin have "taken over."

Family sleeps on dirty mattresses, or on linens black with dirt and soil.

But no children are ill as a result.

5. *Severely inadequate*

   Household exhibits many of the conditions described under (4), "seriously inadequate."

   As a result of this poor sanitation, at least one child is physically ill (e.g., intestinal disorder, food poisoning) requiring medical treatment.

U *Unknown*—insufficient information

Z *Not applicable*

1. *Residence is secure*

Rent or mortgage payments up-to-date and family able to meet future payments.

If family is moving (by choice, by eviction, or by inability to meet rent) specific permanent living arrangement at affordable cost has been made (not a shelter or "doubling up" with another family).

2. *Some problem(s) with security of residence*

Rent/mortgage payments overdue by a month, but as yet no threat of eviction. Or, rent is being paid, but family needs less expensive rental.

There is no imminent threat of loss or forced relocation.

3. *Serious problems with security of residence*

Landlord has begun eviction proceedings, or has indicated family must vacate for some reason (continued overdue rent, damaging property, sale of residence, condemnation of building, etc.).

Must find alternate living arrangements but can remain in current residence for at least a while, e.g., earliest eviction or vacate date several months in future.

4. *Loss of residence*

Family currently does not have any permanent living quarters (may be on street, in a shelter, or "doubling up" temporarily). Includes loss of residence, (e.g., eviction, condemnation, burned out, etc.).

Family has received notice from court or landlord that they must vacate in one month or less. Have no specific alternative living arrangements.

U *Unknown*—insufficient information

Z *Not applicable*

Scale 9 Availability of Utilities

1. *Available and dependable*

No regular or long-standing problems with availability of heat, water, lights, electricity, or fuel for cooking.

2. *Available but threatened loss*

This family currently has all utilities (heat, water, electricity, fuel for cooking) available, but there is a threat of turnoff or reduction of service (e.g., tenant or landlord has not paid bills for several months).

There has not been a previous pattern of service loss.

3. *Erratic availability*

The essential utilities are on in this family's home, but service is inadequate or inconsistent. For example, though the heat is working it does not provide sufficient warmth or is turned off part of the day. Or, the water pipes burst frequently.

But complaints are usually responded to and repairs made in reasonable time.

4. *Seriously undependable or unavailable*

This family has been without at least one essential utility for several days or more (e.g., heat, water, lights, electricity, fuel for cooking). Or, there have been many such breakdowns of service recently.

It always takes a long time for service to be restored. The landlord often can't be found or doesn't respond to complaints. Sometimes the family has to move out temporarily.

U *Unknown*—insufficient information

Z *Not applicable*

Scale 10   Physical Safety in Home

1. *Safe*

There are no obviously hazardous conditions in the home *(see examples below)*.

2. *Somewhat unsafe*

There are one or two hazardous conditions in the home (but child has not sustained injury as a result).

3. *Moderately unsafe*

There are many hazardous conditions in the home (but child has not sustained injury as a result).

4. *Seriously unsafe*

There are one or two hazardous conditions in the home. Child has sustained a physical injury requiring medical treatment as a result.

5. *Severely unsafe*

There are many obviously hazardous conditions in the home. Child has sustained a physical injury requiring medical treatment as a result.

U *Unknown*—insufficient information

Z *Not applicable*

Examples of hazardous conditions:

> Leaking gas from stove or heating unit.
> Peeling lead-based paint.
> Recent fire in living quarters or building.
> Hot water/steam leaks from radiators.
> Dangerous substances or objects stored in unlocked lower shelves or cabinets, under sink,
or in the open.
> No guards on open windows.
> Broken or missing windows.

---

1. *Entirely adequate*

All children who could benefit from professional treatment for a mental, emotional, or psychological problem are receiving such service(s).

Includes children with behavior problems (e.g., delinquency) who are known to service providers, but for whom mental health services are not now planned.

2. *Marginal* (performs with difficulty, no significant impairment in performance of major roles)

At least one child who could benefit from mental health treatment is not receiving such service.

Child has an emotional condition that causes him/her some stress and discomfort and may require others to make minor adjustments in their relationship with the child, i.e., give special help, make allowances. However, the child remains able to maintain his/her normal levels of role performance, though with difficulty. Child's condition will probably not deteriorate, despite the absence of treatment.

Includes situations where the child has early symptoms of emotional disturbance ordinarily requiring professional evaluation.

3. *Moderately inadequate* (definitely impaired performance in one or more major roles)

At least one child who could benefit from mental health treatment is not receiving such service.

Child has an emotional condition that impairs his/her performance in major roles (e.g., as family member, as student, as friend, or as citizen). However, child does continue to perform all roles at a minimal level.

Child has considerable problems in relating to others. May disrupt others' activities to the point where some sanctions are used against the child, e.g., others limit their interactions with child, or are forced to punish child. The child's role performance will probably continue to deteriorate without treatment.

4. *Severely inadequate* (inability to function in one or more major roles)

At least one child who could benefit from mental health treatment is not receiving such service.

Child has an emotional condition that makes him/her unable to function at all in one or more major roles (e.g., in school, with friends, or as family member).

Child is completely unable to function in one or more major roles, and/or makes it impossible for persons involved with him/her to function in theirs. The child is experiencing isolation from others and/or considerable physical punishment.

Child may present a danger to the safety of others and/or of self.

U *Unknown*—insufficient information

Z *Not applicable*

1. Adequate

Parent provides proper and timely supervision of children's activities inside and outside of the home.

Parent knows children's whereabouts and activities, whom they are with, and when they return.

Definite limits are set on children's activities.

2. Marginal

Parent has difficulty supervising younger children while they are in the house. Tends to leave younger children unobserved and doesn't always know what they're doing. Children are often "getting into" things that they shouldn't. Sometimes children are found engaging in rough play. However, no child has ever been injured as a result of this. Parent is known to be careful about supervising children's activities outside the house.

3. Moderately inadequate

Younger children play in off-street areas adjacent to home. Parent knows children's location but does not check on them often enough. May depend largely on others to "keep an eye on" the children. Parent may be unable to access children's play area quickly if necessary. However, no child has ever been injured as a result of this.

4. Seriously inadequate

Parent exercises little supervision over the younger children, either inside or outside the home. Children may have been found playing at home with objects that could hurt them. Children may have been found playing in unsafe circumstances outside (e.g., in street, in a dump, or with older strangers). Parent often does not know where one of the younger children is. Child wanders to unfamiliar areas and sometimes needs stranger's help to return home. In general, family's younger children are given far too much responsibility for their own safety.

However, no child has been physically injured as a result of such a situation.

5. Severely inadequate

The younger children in this family have been improperly supervised by the parent(s). As a result, one or more of the children has been injured, requiring medical treatment, or has been victimized (molested, etc.).

U   *Unknown*—insufficient information

Z   *Not applicable*

1. *Adequate*

Parent provides proper and timely supervision of teenage children's activities inside and outside of home.

Parent knows children's whereabouts and activities, whom they are with, and when they return.

Definite and reasonable limits are set on children's activities.

2. *Marginal*

Parent makes rules for the older children and generally enforces them. But children sometimes persuade parent to allow or to tolerate certain activities that are against the parent's better judgment (e.g., staying out too late; attending an unchaperoned party).

Parent does try keeping track of children's activities and uses discipline when things get "out of hand." Children respect parent for the most part.

3. *Moderately inadequate*

Parent makes rules for older children, but has difficulty enforcing them. Children often engage in inappropriate activities without parent's knowledge.

Parent sometimes does not make enough effort to find out what children are up to, or does not react with necessary sanctions when rules are broken.

Parent has difficulty getting children's respect, but has not lost it entirely.

4. *Seriously inadequate*

Parent has few, if any, rules for the older children, and rarely enforces any. Children often stay out all night without parent knowing where they are or when they may return.

Parent usually has no idea what children are doing and makes no attempt to find out. Children are known to be "wild."

Parent shows little or no interest in children's activities, as long as parent is not inconvenienced by them. Parent(s) may say they are helpless to control children, or may defend children's independence ("They have to find out what the world is like for themselves").

U *Unknown*—insufficient information

Z *Not applicable*

1. *Adequate*

Parent makes safe and appropriate substitute child care arrangements when needed (including babysitting and overnight arrangements).

Or,

Children are old enough so that they do not normally require arrangements for substitute child care.

2. *Marginal*

The parent usually leaves the children in the care of a responsible babysitter or adult, but there is a problem with this. For example: Parent returns home much later than substitute caretaker expected; substitute caretaker unwilling to provide child care services under present conditions (e.g., without financial compensation).

3. *Mildly inadequate*

Very young children are never left alone when the parent goes out. But older children able to fend for themselves sometimes do not know where their parent is at night or when he or she will return. The children would be able to get help in an emergency if necessary.

4. *Moderately inadequate*

A child is left in the care of an incapable person (i.e., another young child, adult invalid) when the parent goes out. But the parent comes back before any problem develops.

5. *Seriously inadequate*

A child left alone at home is unable to handle his/her basic needs, such as getting something to eat or calling for help in an emergency. However, the parent does return before the child's needs become acute, or before a problem develops.

6. *Severely inadequate*

A child who is unable to handle basic needs (e.g., eating, toilet, avoiding accidents) is left alone at home. The parent does not return before the child's needs become acute. The child is at least emotionally distraught or hungry, and may have had an accident requiring medical treatment.

U *Unknown*—insufficient information

Z *Not applicable*

1. *Adequate*

Parent/guardian spends available money wisely, putting needs of the children first. Food, rent, essential clothing have priority.

Is able to budget funds over a period of time; when necessary, manages to "stretch" money to avoid "running short." Rarely has to borrow money.

May buy things other than necessities, but rarely at the expense of necessities.

Tries to maintain some reserve money for unexpected but important needs.

If family is economically deprived, or if no reserve can be kept, that is because of insufficient income, not poor money management.

2. *Mildly inadequate*

Parent/guardian spends money appropriately, putting needs of children first. Food, rent, essential clothing have priority.

Has a problem budgeting funds over a period of time; tends to "run short." This is not due to insufficient income.

Has to borrow often from friends and relations, but usually manages eventually to pay it back.

Never has reserve funds; spends all that comes in, even if income would allow a small reserve.

Sometimes wastes money buying poor quality items, or overspends for items that are available cheaper at same quality, or buys too many perishable goods at one time.

3. *Moderately inadequate*

Parent/guardian sometimes displays poor judgment regarding spending priorities, e.g., dips into rent money to buy nonessentials, or buys toys for children instead of food.

Sometimes spends money on nonessentials for self, while children lack an essential; but these things do not happen regularly.

Budgeting poor; sometimes has to put off important expenditures because of lack of planning and impulse buying.

Borrows regularly from friends and relatives; finds it difficult to get out of debt, or sees no necessity for doing so.

4. *Seriously inadequate*

Family has constant or frequently recurring monetary crises. This is not primarily due to insufficient income.

Constant exercise of poor judgment in expenditures leads to children being regularly and seriously deprived of necessities. There may be threatened loss of housing due to nonpayment of rent.

Parent may be unable to hold on to money (e.g., "drinks the money up," spends it on others, loans it to others with no hope of recovery, "gambles it away," etc.). This is a chronic situation.

Buys nonessentials on credit, usually without prospect of being able to pay the money back. Bill collectors are in constant contact.

Heavily in debt. May borrow money from disreputable sources at high interest.

U *Unknown*—insufficient information

Z *Not applicable*

1. *Adequate*

No personal limitations on capacity for child care.

Parent has no significant physical, mental-emotional, or behavioral limitations that interfere with his/her ability to care for the children.

2. *Marginally adequate*

Parent has a physical, mental-emotional, or behavioral problem that threatens to interfere with his/her child caring ability (or that has already caused some erratic child care quality).

Examples are chronic physical illnesses, physical disabilities, mental or emotional illnesses, substance abuse, criminal activity.

Parent requires, and may be receiving, help or treatment for this problem, but there is no current necessity or plan for hospitalization, institutionalization, or incarceration of the parent.

Problem is not of long duration, or if it is of long duration, has recently improved. Supportive services (counseling, medical care, etc.) seem sufficient to stabilize the situation or to further improve it.

3. *Moderately inadequate*

Parent has a physical, mental-emotional, or behavioral problem that is of long duration, or if it is of short duration, has recently deteriorated. Problem may be recurring and not be completely curable.

Parent will be, is now, or recently was, hospitalized, institutionalized, or incarcerated.

Parent will resume (or is resuming) at least partial child care responsibilities, but longer term provisions for supplementary child care (day care, homemaker, etc.) may be required.

Temporary substitute care for the children will be, is now, or was, used during parent's absence, or used as a respite service, but long-term substitute care not necessary.

4. *Severely inadequate*

Owing to a physical, mental-emotional, or behavioral problem, parent has no current capacity to care for the children, even with supplementary child care services, and no change is expected in the near future.

If parent is, or is due to be, hospitalized, institutionalized, or incarcerated; this is expected to be long-term.

If parent is at home, he/she is not capable of more than personal self-care tasks, perhaps requiring assistance.

In either case, long-term arrangements for substitute care of the children are required.

U *Unknown*—insufficient information

Z *Not applicable*

For this scale, "parental relations" should be defined as including relations between unmarried, regularly cohabiting adults.

1. *No significant discord*

Parental relations are good; only infrequent, normal arguments occur.

There is mutual tolerance and conflicts are resolved quickly; channels of communication kept open.

Parents have close, positive emotional ties. Child(ren) are never drawn into arguments between parents.

There is never any physical violence between parents, and never any talk of separation.

2. *Moderate discord*

Parents have more than usual amount of arguments.

There are attempts at problem solving, but these are not always successful; channels of communication may temporarily close.

Threats of separation or divorce are sometimes made, but not carried out.

Children are sometimes drawn into arguments between parents.

Nevertheless, there seems to be a close emotional tie between parents and they support each other in serious matters (e.g., involving their children).

Rare instances of fighting (hitting, slapping) may occur. *(If there is a pattern of violence, or if a serious injury occurred, always code 3 or 4 instead.)*

3. *Serious discord*

Parents seem to have more periods of arguments than of peace and harmony.

Since contacts between parents tend to result in conflict, contacts on all except essential matters tend to be avoided.

There is little tolerance and "grudges" are harbored for long periods of time.

Parents may have a diminished emotional tie and may seek satisfaction outside the marital relationship.

Children may not only be drawn into arguments, but may be the focus of arguments.

Parents have talked about separation and one may have stayed away from home for several days on several occasions. But no legal separations or long periods of separation have occurred, and no legal action is pending.

There may also be some hitting or slapping but no injuries have occurred.

4. *Severe discord*

There is a pattern of serious discord as described in (3) above.

In addition, physical violence resulting in injury has occurred and there are threats of more violence.

Family income may be disrupted.

Separations are occurring and divorce proceedings may be imminent or may have begun.

U *Unknown*—insufficient information

Z *Not applicable*

1. *Continuous parenting*

No breaks in parenting for the children for at least one year (at intake) or since referral (at follow-up). If there are two parents or guardians, they have remained together without separations. If one parent or guardian, he or she has maintained primary responsibility for the children. If parenting is shared with relatives, this is part of an extended family network, and children are well-acquainted with and completely comfortable with these relatives. No permanent or extended absence of a parenting figure has occurred.

2. *Marginal stability*

One of the parents has provided continuous, stable care for the children in the past year (at intake) or since referral (at follow-up).

The other parent has not been in the household consistently or was away an extended period of time (due to marital difficulties, institutionalization, etc.). Or, the parents may have separated and the other parent now only makes visits.

This has required adjustments in the lives of family members.

3. *Moderate instability*

One or two unexpected (but temporary) breaks in parenting have occurred in the last year (at intake) or since referral (at follow-up).

Children had to receive care for an extended period of time by a person who does not normally care for them. But parent(s) did not leave abruptly. Parent(s) maintained some contact during the absence.

Parent has returned to resume caretaking (or is expected to return shortly).

4. *Serious instability*

Children have experienced a series of breaks in parenting during the last year (at intake) or since referral (at follow-up). Parent(s) left children for extended periods of time on short notice with persons who are unfamiliar to the children and do not normally care for them.

Parent(s) has (have) left abruptly without preparing the children for this. Children have been shifted from one home to another. However, the parent(s) has (have) always returned to resume caretaking responsibility; children have not been deserted.

5. *Desertion/abandonment*

Children have been deserted or abandoned by their parent(s) or guardian(s). This was abrupt and there is no indication that parent(s) intend to return.

Children have been shifted from one home to another. Future plans for them are uncertain at this time.

U *Unknown*—insufficient information

Z *Not applicable*

1. *Adequate: good understanding and recognizes responsibility*

Parent/guardian understands the types of problems the family has and generally agrees with others about the severity of those problems.

Is aware of the degree to which children's physical, social and/or emotional needs are not being met.

Parent understands own part in or contribution to the problems (to the extent that he or she is responsible for their existence at all). Accepts full responsibility (if warranted).

2. *Moderately inadequate: partial understanding, recognizes only limited responsibility*

Parent/guardian understands the types of problems existing, but does not agree with others about their severity (believes problems less severe).

May lack adequate knowledge about child development and parenting.

Consequently, accepts only limited responsibility for existence of the problems (to the extent that he or she is responsible for their existence at all).

Fuller understanding of the problems might lead to greater acceptance of responsibility (if warranted).

3. *Seriously inadequate: recognizes no personal responsibility*

Parent/guardian may have some understanding of family's problems, but entirely fails to recognize own part in, or contribution to, these problems.

Accepts no responsibility for children's unmet needs, even though some responsibility should be taken.

May bring up question of cultural bias, even though most members of client's cultural group would not agree.

Is adamant that other family members, society, etc., are solely to blame, when this is not so.

U *Unknown*—insufficient information

Z *Not applicable*

Scale 20   Parental Motivation to Solve Problems

1. *Adequate: shows concern and has realistic confidence*

Parent/guardian is concerned about children's welfare; wants to meet their physical, social, and emotional needs to the extent he or she understands them.

Has realistic confidence that he or she can overcome problems and is willing to ask for help when needed (e.g., to negotiate the "system" or to acquire knowledge).

2. *Marginally adequate: shows concern, lacks confidence*

Parent/guardian is concerned about children's welfare and wants to meet their needs.

Lacks confidence that he or she can overcome problems (feeling of futility), making failure a self-fulfilling prophecy. May be unwilling for some reason to ask for help when needed.

But uses good judgment whenever he or she takes some action to solve problems.

3. *Moderately inadequate: seems concerned, but careless*

Parent seems concerned about children's welfare and claims he or she wants to meet their needs.

But has problems with carelessness, mistakes, and accidents in trying to meet those needs.

May be disorganized, not take enough time, or pay insufficient attention; may misread "signals" from children; may exercise poor judgment.

But does not seem to intentionally violate proper parental role. Shows remorse.

4. *Seriously inadequate: indifferent, apathetic*

Parent is not concerned enough about children's needs to resist "temptations," e.g., competing demands on time and money. This leads to one or more important physical, social, or emotional needs of the children not being met.

Parent does not have the right "priorities" when it comes to child care; may take a "cavalier" or indifferent attitude. There may be a lack of interest in the children and in their welfare and development.

But parent does not actively reject the parental role.

5. *Severely inadequate: rejection of parental role*

Parent actively rejects parental role, taking a hostile attitude toward child care responsibilities. Believes that child care is an "imposition," and may ask to be relieved of that responsibility. May take the attitude that it isn't his or her "job."

U *Unknown*—insufficient information

Z *Not applicable*

Scale 21 Parental Cooperation with Case Planning/Services

1. *Adequate*

Parent is fully and actively involved in case planning, services, and/or treatment. This holds both for services directed toward the children and toward self.

Accepts and actively uses suitable services, including following through on referrals to other agencies or providers.

Keeps appointments, makes self available as needed, and follows directions to best of his or her ability.

Shows concern about impact of services or treatment; complains about inadequate service when warranted.

May not agree with everything suggested, but tries to be constructive in proposing alternatives.

When problems in cooperation develop, there tend to be extenuating circumstances.

2. *Mildly inadequate*

Parent is not as fully or actively involved in case planning and/or services as he or she could be. This may be because parent is rather disorganized and/or somewhat ambivalent about services.

Accepts and uses suitable services, but doesn't always make best use of them, or drops them too early; follows through on referrals, but sometimes not in a timely manner.

Makes appointments, but often postpones them and sometimes doesn't keep them, with no extenuating circumstances.

May cooperate satisfactorily with services for children, but may cooperate less well with personal services believed to reflect poorly on self.

Tends to wait for worker to suggest and act; may complain without proposing alternative, but does accept advice.

3. *Moderately inadequate*

Parent is only minimally involved in case planning, services, and/or treatment. There is a pattern of passive resistance to service providers.

Accepts services verbally, but doesn't use them or follow through on referrals without constant prodding and direct assistance (e.g., has to be taken there every time, even though own transportation can be arranged).

Often has to be cajoled, coerced, and/or "chased after."

Makes appointments, but rarely keeps them; doesn't reschedule in advance, even if there are extenuating circumstances.

When services used, participates without much enthusiasm or at the minimal acceptable level.

Generally doesn't refuse to accept services, doesn't act consistently hostile, and doesn't actively sabotage services.

Agency able to remain in contact with family.

4. *Seriously inadequate*

Actively resists any agency contact or involvement.

Parent refuses to accept any service, or actively sabotages services when persuaded or coerced into using any.

May threaten service providers, or otherwise discourage them from attempting to engage client in service.

Family may be very difficult to contact or remain in contact with; may relocate mainly to avoid agency contact.

U *Unknown*—insufficient information

Z *Not applicable*

Scale 22   Support for Principal Caretaker*

The person taking the maternal role, usually the child(ren)'s mother, is defined as the principal caretaker.

1. Supported

One *or more* members of the immediate family and *two or more* friends or other relatives can be called on to help when needed.

Immediate family members are defined as: the other parent; a grandparent; a brother, sister, or adult child of the principal caretaker.

2. Family and friend related

One *or more* members of the immediate family and *one* friend or other relative can be called on to help when needed.

3. Family bound

Two or more members of the immediate family can be called on to help when needed.
There are no friends or other relatives that can be called on.

4. Friend dependent

Only one person can be called on to help when needed.
That person is a friend or relative outside the immediate family.
There are no members of the immediate family that can be counted on.

5. Family dyad

Only one person can be called on to help when needed.
That person is a member of the immediate family.
There are no friends or other relatives that can be called on.

6. Completely isolated

No one can be called or counted on to help when needed, or principal caretaker states that the only person that can be counted on is a social worker or other professional helper.

U *Unknown*—insufficient information

Z *Not applicable*

*Adapted from the Family Support Index, in Polansky et al. (1981).

130

Scale 23   Availability/Accessibility of Services

1. Adequate

All essential services that family needs are available in the amount and of the quality desired. The services are convenient and accessible.

Family is able to meet out-of-pocket expenses, if any, needed to take advantage of or gain access to the services. (Or, family will receive grant for such out-of-pocket costs.)

Services may be considered available and accessible despite being rejected by family.

2. Marginal

All essential services that this family needs are available at least in part, though they may be shorter in duration or less intensive than desired.

Some services are not easily accessible because of overutilization (e.g., long waiting times) or because of poor location.

The family manages to obtain services, though there are times when appointments are missed due to access problems.

Sometimes the most appropriate service may not be available, but a similar substitute can be found (e.g., group counseling instead of individual counseling).

3. Moderately inadequate

One essential service that is needed by this family is not available in the community or is not accessible, though other essential services are.

This means that a part of the case plan cannot be carried out, or that the most desirable case plan cannot be written.

The family is receiving other needed services, however.

4. Seriously inadequate

This family is unable to obtain several essential services that are needed, because the services either are not available or are not accessible. The case plan originally developed for this family cannot be carried out. Work with the family is restricted to social worker counseling or monitoring.

5. Severely inadequate

This family cannot get any of the essential services it needs. The services are not available in the community or are not accessible. The agency involved does not have the resources to provide even a minimum service, such as social worker counseling. Consequently, this case will be closed.

U *Unknown*—insufficient information

Z *Not applicable*

Scale 24   Parental Acceptance of/Affection for Children

1. *Very accepting and affectionate*

Parent/guardian is accepting and affectionate toward the children (e.g., frequently uses spontaneous expressions or gestures of affection for children).

Encourages and warmly responds to children's overtures for physical contact and emotional response.

Often speaks about children's accomplishments and good behavior.

2. *Fairly accepting and affectionate, but with reservations*

Few if any spontaneous expressions or gestures of affection, but will describe child positively if asked.

Rarely initiates physical contact, but will usually allow children to initiate contact and will respond. Places limits on type, time, or length of contacts.

May sometimes prefer some children over others, but doesn't exclude any.

3. *Not affectionate, but not openly rejecting or hostile*

Parent tends to describe and speak to children in matter-of-fact or objective terms.

Does not appear to like physical contact with children (e.g., will allow contact, doesn't push away, but rarely responds warmly).

Tries to restrict contacts to functional ones, (e.g., feeding, dressing).

Seems uncomfortable when children express affection; may complain that children demand too much, want to be kissed, etc.

May show persistent favoritism (e.g., affectionate to some children, cool or indifferent to others).

Seems confused about feelings toward children.

4. *Openly rejecting or hostile*

Consistently speaks to and about children in deprecating, resentful, or angry way.

Usually does not allow children physical contact, and tries to minimize or avoid even functional contacts (e.g., feeding, dressing).

May punish children's requests for affection. Declines to help and support children when they are in trouble.

May sometimes show affection to one child for sole purpose of making another envious, or to enhance effects of subsequent rejection.

U *Unknown*—insufficient information

Z *Not applicable*

Scale 25   Parental Approval of Children

1. *Approval is primary way of guiding children*

    Parent/guardian prefers to guide child by rewarding behavior rather than by punishing misbehavior.
    Praise may sometimes be spontaneous.
    Criticism is limited and constructive.
    Parent/guardian does not have retributive attitude.

2. *Approval and disapproval both used conditionally*

    Punishment and disapproval are used as readily as rewards and praise, depending on children's behavior.
    Approval given for specific acts, but not as general encouragement and not spontaneously.
    Parent values "eye for an eye" or "giving just dues."

3. *Disapproval is primary way of guiding children*

    Children rarely praised or rewarded for appropriate behavior, but often tend to be punished or criticized for misconduct.
    But tends to be "fair," in that punishment and disapproval are linked to behavior in consistent way.
    Parent/guardian is very retributive; may believe "goodness is its own reward" or that rewards are actually "bribes."

4. *Excessive and severe disapproval used*

    Children's faults and shortcomings are clearly overemphasized.
    Criticism/disapproval are disproportionate to actual behavior (children called "stupid," "worthless," etc.).
    Criticism/disapproval are not used in a fair and consistent way.
    Parent/guardian gives rewards only to compensate or "atone" for his or her own unfairness or overreaction.

U *Unknown*—insufficient information

Z *Not applicable*

Scale 26   Parental Expectations of Children

1. *Very realistic*

   Parent/guardian has good knowledge of (or good feelings for) age-appropriate behaviors.
   Gradually encourages increasingly mature behavior, but takes care not to frustrate children.
   Helps children on tasks as needed, but doesn't allow them to give up own efforts too soon.
   Displays flexibility in demands and offers options to children.
   May make some mistakes, but those are readily acknowledged and corrected.

2. *Somewhat unrealistic, but open to improvement*

   Parent/guardian has fair knowledge of age-appropriate behaviors, but children sometimes held to too high or too low a standard.

   Sometimes makes demands that frustrate both child and parent, or, alternatively, sometimes doesn't allow child to practice new behaviors.

   But only rarely punishes children for inability to comply with demands, or for trying new behavior; parent is more confused than angry.

   Is open to advice and guidance; wants to be realistic with children and understand their needs and capacities.

3. *Somewhat unrealistic, and not open to improvement*

   Same as description for (2) above, except that parent/guardian is indifferent or angry when children cannot comply with demands, or when they attempt exploratory behaviors.

   Parent/guardian is not very flexible and not open to advice.

4. *Very unrealistic*

   Parent/guardian either has very poor understanding of age-appropriate behaviors, or makes unrealistic demands of children despite some understanding.

   Often punishes children for inability to comply with demands, or for attempting more mature behavior; rarely tries to help children to comply.

   There may be daily conflicts about expectations regarding children's behavior; children have become reluctant to explore or innovate.

   Parent/guardian may refuse to acknowledge the concept of age-appropriate behavior, or may believe that his/her expectations are, in fact, appropriate; is hostile on this subject.

   Child may exhibit some developmental delays or emotional stress due to this situation.

U *Unknown*—insufficient information

Z *Not applicable*

1. *High consistency*

Parent/guardian always follows through on promised rewards and punishments with children; rarely will contradict herself or himself; children know what to expect; punishments fit behavior.

2. *Marginal consistency, but open to improvement*

Parent/guardian does not always follow through on sanctions. Sometimes will contradict herself or himself, but makes corrective efforts when inconsistencies are brought to attention.

Consistency is understood and valued, but parent/guardian sometimes forgets, acts impulsively, etc.

3. *Marginal consistency, but not open to improvement*

Same as description for (2) above, except that children do not always know what to expect and parent/guardian seems indifferent to this.

Parent/guardian does not seem to value consistency, or perhaps doesn't understand it.

4. *Low consistency*

Parent/guardian often reacts indiscriminately or inconsistently to children's behavior; punishments often do not fit behavior.

Parent/guardian may be hostile when problems are brought to attention.

May believe he or she is being consistent, according to own logic; may claim his or her behavior benefits children (e.g., helps them cope in the "real world").

U *Unknown*—insufficient information

Z *Not applicable*

Scale 28   Parental Teaching/Stimulating of Children

1. *High activity*

   Parent/guardian promotes and maintains conversation (or discussion). Encourages children to relate stories, give opinions, or demonstrate skills.

   Parent spends time most days with children engaged in a child-centered activity.

   Routinely makes an effort to teach younger children such things as colors, words, manners, etc.

   Asks often about progress in schoolwork and helps with homework if requested.

2. *Moderate activity*

   Parent/guardian doesn't usually encourage children to perform skills or give opinions, but will be attentive when initiated by children.

   Doesn't often initiate child-centered activities, but responds to children's requests to do so to extent possible.

   Will try to include children in activities that may not be child-centered, (e.g., visiting, shopping, cooking).

   Provides place to do homework and asks about it, but discourages requests for help.

   Seems open to guidance and advice on teaching and communicating with children.

3. *Passive approach, some deprivation*

   Parent/guardian tends to be inattentive or indifferent to children's attempts at conversation or at engaging parent in activities.

   Usually prefers children to teach or entertain themselves with toys, games, TV.

   May offer participation in activities that fit parent's interests, rather than child's interests.

   Little interest in children's homework, but allows them to do it without interruptions.

   Older children receive minimal interaction or guidance from parent, but allowed to participate in peer group activities.

   Seems to be "putting up" with children; shows little enthusiasm.

4. *Considerable deprivation*

   Parent/guardian tends to ignore or avoid children; attempts to gain attention may result in hostility.

   Children have few if any games, toys, or play materials of any kind.

   Older children participate little in peer group activities, due to parental discouragement.

   Children have no set place to do homework, or parent does nothing to prevent interruptions.

   Communication is monosyllabic (usually restricted to ordering children to quiet down) or is corrective in nature (pointing out errors), rather than constructive (showing the right way).

   Parent may think children are a "bother," or that they purposefully try to "get on my nerves."

U *Unknown*—insufficient information

Z *Not applicable*

Scale 29   Abusive Physical Discipline

1. *No physical discipline used with child*

Child never physically punished. Only non-physical, non-assaultive methods of discipline used (e.g., revoking privileges, verbal disapproval).

Caretaker does not allow others to physically punish child.

2. *Physical discipline used, but not excessive or inappropriate (not abusive)*

Only culturally acceptable mode(s) of physical punishment used, typically spanking on rear.

Punishment is not excessive and does not ordinarily leave physical marks or cause great pain.

Purpose of punishment is primarily to symbolize disapproval, not to hurt or inflict great pain on child.

3. *Excessive or inappropriate discipline used, but no resulting injury*

See definitions and examples of excessive or inappropriate force at end.

Child experiences considerable temporary pain, but is not physically injured, though potential for some injury was there. (*If actual injury did result, choose one of next codes.*)

4. *Excessive or inappropriate physical force used, resulting in superficial injury*

See definitions and examples of excessive or inappropriate force at end.

Typical superficial injuries are bruises, welts, cuts, abrasions, or first-degree (mild) burns. Injuries are localized in one or two areas and involve no more than broken skin.

Superficial injuries do not ordinarily require medical treatment; proper home remedies would suffice. (However, medical treatment may be received.)

5. *Excessive or inappropriate physical force used, resulting in moderately serious injury*

See definitions and examples of excessive or inappropriate force at end.

Moderate injuries should usually receive medical attention to reduce risk of complications, substantially speed healing, or reduce pain. But such injuries are not life-threatening and not likely to cause crippling, even in the absence of medical treatment.

Examples are sprains, mild concussions, broken teeth, bruises all over body, cuts needing suture, second-degree (moderately severe) burns, minor (small bone) fractures, etc.

Moderate injuries do not ordinarily require hospitalization for medical reasons. (However, child may be hospitalized for protection against repeat harm.)

6. *Excessive or inappropriate physical force used, resulting in severe injury*

See definitions and examples of excessive or inappropriate force at end.

Severe injuries always require prompt medical attention, often on an emergency basis; e.g., long bone fractures; internal injuries; third degree (most severe) burns; brain or spinal cord injury; eye injury; deep wounds or punctures that could result in systemic infection.

Injury may be life-threatening, or could result in physical or mental crippling, or could cause serious disfigurement, or could cause deep, chronic pain.

Hospitalization is usually required for medical reasons.

U *Unknown*—insufficient information

Z *Not applicable*

Definitions of excessive or inappropriate force:

  (a) Caretaker (or other) uses culturally acceptable mode(s) of physical punishment, but overdoes it, prolongs it unduly, or uses excessive force.

  Or,

  (b) Culturally unacceptable or inappropriate mode(s) of physical punishment used.

Examples: Continual or lengthy beating, slapping or whipping; hitting with fist; kicking, biting, twisting, shaking, dropping, bludgeoning, burning, scalding, poisoning, suffocating, using weapon, etc.

1. No deprivation

Food and water never deliberately or intentionally withheld from child when it is available. This is never used as a means of punishment.

But there may be restrictions on type of food (e.g., sweets, desserts) for nondisciplinary (e.g., health or economic) reasons.

2. Mild deprivation (but not abusive)

Some deliberate or intentional withholding of food within culturally acceptable bounds (e.g., child sent to bed without supper).

Water is never withheld.

3. Moderate deprivation

Child deliberately or intentionally not fed or given water for at least one day, or fed minimal and nutritionally inadequate food for several days.

No clinical symptoms of malnutrition or dehydration, although child may have become very hungry or thirsty.

4. Serious deprivation

Owing to deliberate deprivation of food or water, child suffers from some clinical symptoms of malnutrition or dehydration.

Condition requires medical attention and rehabilitative diet.

Hospitalization not ordinarily required for medical reasons (although child may be temporarily hospitalized for own protection).

5. Severe deprivation

Owing to deliberate deprivation of food or water, child so severely malnourished or dehydrated (e.g., severe weight loss, anemia) that hospitalization is required for medical reasons.

U Unknown—insufficient information

Z Not applicable

Scale 31 Physical Confinement or Restriction

1. *No physical confinement or restriction*

Child never deliberately confined, tied, or bound in any way as a means of punishment.

2. *Mild confinement (but not abusive)*

Confinement used occasionally in a culturally acceptable way to discipline child. For example, child may be confined to room for several hours; or not allowed to play outside (or speak to friends) all day.

But movements of child are never physically restricted by tying or binding.

Child is placed in no physical or emotional danger.

3. *Moderately excessive confinement or restriction*

Confinement and/or restriction used in culturally unacceptable way.

Examples:

Child confined to room all day and night; or not allowed to go outside for several days.

Child's movements are physically restricted by harnessing, tying, binding, etc., but for no more than several hours.

4. *Seriously excessive confinement or restriction*

There is potential for physical and/or emotional harm.

Examples:

Child confined to room for several days or more.

Confined in any cramped or dark enclosure (e.g., closet, bin, shed) for any period of time.

Child not allowed outside for a week or more.

Any sensory deprivation or placement in frightening situation.

Child is harnessed, tied, or bound for a day or more.

U *Unknown*—insufficient information

Z *Not applicable*

1. No problem with locking-out

Child never denied access to his or her home or expelled from home. This is never used as a deliberate means of punishment.

2. Some problem, low potential danger, no injury

Child was denied access to his or her home or expelled from home. He or she had somewhere to go (relative, friend, neighbor) *and* was old enough or capable enough to go there.

If out-of-home overnight, child was in safe location (another home or shelter).

Includes runaway child whose parent(s) refused to take him back and who came to police or social service agency for help.

Does not include any child who had to ask stranger for help.

3. Moderate to high potential danger, possible superficial injury

Child was denied access to or expelled from home.

Includes any child who had no safe place to go (relative/friend/neighbor) *or* who was not old enough or capable enough to go there.

Includes any child who would not be able to contact the police or social service agency without help from a stranger.

Includes any child who has been out several hours or more in very bad weather, or who is too young to cross streets safely.

As a result, child may have received some superficial injury (e.g., bruise) not requiring medical attention, or may have been scared or threatened. But there was no serious injury, accident, or crime victimization.

4. Serious consequences

As a result of being denied access to or expelled from his or her home, child sustains an injury or illness that usually requires medical attention, but *not* hospitalization.

Or, child is moderately victimized (e.g., robbed), but not physically or sexually assaulted or kidnapped.

Or, child commits a status offense during this time.

5. Severe consequences

As a result of being denied access to or expelled from his or her home, child sustains a severe injury or illness that usually requires hospitalization.

Or, child is seriously victimized (assaulted, kidnapped, etc.).

Or, child commits a delinquent offense during this time.

U *Unknown*—insufficient information

Z *Not applicable*

PART A: TYPE OF ABUSE

1. *No sexual abuse or impropriety*

   Caretaker does not sexually abuse or provoke child in any of the ways below, or allow anyone else to do so.

2. *Sexual suggestiveness*

   Sexually provocative comments are made to a child, or a child is shown pornographic photos.
   But there have been no sexual approaches to the child, and no molestation is suspected.

3. *Sexual harassment*

   Child is being harassed—encouraged, pressured, or propositioned—to perform sexually.
   But no sexual activity has actually occurred.

4. *Sexual exhibitionism*

   Person has exhibited himself or herself sexually in front of the child (e.g., exposure of genitals, masturbation). The child was pressured to participate, but did not do so.

5. *Sexual molestation*

   Person has sexually molested the child (e.g., fondled breasts or genitals; made child exhibit himself or herself). But there was no sexual intercourse between them.

6. *Sexual intercourse*

   Child was sexually abused—sexual intercourse occurred (oral, anal, genital).

U *Unknown*—insufficient information

Z *Not applicable*

PART B: PERSON COMMITTING SEXUAL ABUSE

1. Parent or legal guardian of child.

2. Other adult.

3. Other person *(Please explain).*

1. *No verbal or physical threat of abuse*

No verbal or physical threats of abuse or harm are made against child(ren).

Threat of culturally acceptable corporal punishment should not be considered a threat of abuse or harm.

2. *Indirect or implied verbal threat only*

No direct and specific threats of abuse or harm are made.

But parent/guardian says they "feel overwhelmed by the child(ren)" "might hurt child(ren)," "fear child(ren) might have an accident," "get so mad at child(ren) they don't know what might happen," etc.

3. *Direct verbal threat*

Direct, specific, verbal threats of abuse or harm are made against the child(ren); may also include indirect threats.

Threats are such that, if carried out, physical or emotional harm to the child(ren) could result.

Included would be threats of physical abuse, deprivation of food or water, sexual abuse, etc.

But there has been no attempt to carry out such threats.

4. *Direct physical threat, but no actual harm*

Child is placed in a dangerous situation (e.g., held out of window, held over scalding water, deliberately allowed to wander where potential for injury is high, etc.).

But no actual injury or harm occurs, though child may have been frightened.

If injury occurred, it should be indicated on Scale 29, Abusive Physical Discipline.

U *Unknown*—insufficient information

Z *Not applicable*

143

1. *No economic exploitation*

If any child works, he or she only engages in appropriate work (e.g., household chores, part-time job after school).

2. *Inappropriate work role at home*

Child forced to assume too much responsibility in household, given his or her age (e.g., babysitting long hours many days a week, cooking for the family regularly).

Responsibilities go beyond chores into normally adult responsibilities.

Work role at home interferes, or threatens to interfere, with child's health or with social and school activities.

3. *Inappropriate work role outside home*

Child forced (or allowed) to work in violation of child labor laws, or in socially disreputable activities (e.g., panhandling).

But not in criminal or illegal activities.

4. *Criminal work role*

Child forced (or allowed) to work in illegal or disreputable activities for financial gain (e.g., shoplifting, gambling, drug dealing).

Includes sexual exploitation for financial gain (e.g., prostitution, pornography).

U *Unknown*—insufficient information

Z *Not applicable*

This scale applies only if a "third party," i.e., someone other than the child(ren)'s parent or guardian has or had previously, abused or threatened to abuse any of the children. Otherwise code "Z" (not applicable).

1. *Adequate*

   At intake:

   Child was abused by third party despite the fact that parent/guardian used good judgment, i.e., did not give third party unlimited or unrestricted access to the child(ren).

   There did not seem to be any prior indications that abuse would occur and/or parent exercised reasonable precautions in attempting to protect children from any potential abuse.

   At follow-up:

   Third party who previously abused (or threatened to abuse) child(ren) no longer resides in household.

   > *And or,*

   Parent/guardian has severed his or her relationship with this person, or maintains only perfunctory relationship.

   Potential for further abuse seems virtually eliminated.

2. *Somewhat inadequate*

   At intake:

   Child was abused by third party and parent/guardian did not use good judgment in protecting child(ren) from potential abuse; i.e., third party was allowed unrestricted or unlimited access to children.

   Parent was too "trusting," or did not pick up on signals for potential abuse. But was not aware of abuse.

   Parent/guardian reacted rapidly and reasonably to the incident(s), e.g., reporting abuser or requesting help.

   At follow-up:

   Third party who previously abused (or threatened to abuse) children is still in household.

   > *And or,*

   Parent/guardian has not severed his or her relationship with this person.

   But parent has now restricted or limited third party's access to children; is aware of potential danger.

   This has reduced but not eliminated the danger of repeated abuse.

3. *Seriously inadequate*

   At intake:

   Child was abused by third party and parent took no steps to stop it, or to stop repeat incidents.

   May have passively stood by without protesting, or pretended he or she didn't know it was happening.

   Did not immediately report it or seek help.

   At follow-up:

   Third party who previously abused (or threatened to abuse) children is still in household.

   > *And or,*

   Parent/guardian has not severed his or her relationship with this person.

   Third party still has unlimited or unrestricted access to child(ren). Parent may say he or she is worried, but has taken no action to reduce danger of repeated abuse. Or, parent says there is no cause for worry.

   Parent shows little or no ability or inclination to stand up to third party and prevent repeated abuse.

U *Unknown*—insufficient information

Z *Not applicable*

1. *Educational needs adequately met*

Child enrolled (or scheduled to be enrolled) in class or program which is appropriate for child's abilities.

Specialized educational needs, if any, are being met (e.g., special class, tutoring, individualized instruction).

If child is performing poorly, it is not for lack of adequate support.

2. *Some problems with meeting educational needs*

Child enrolled in school but needs remedial tutoring or some specialized instruction in one or two subject areas.

Meeting this need would improve child's school performance.

3. *Serious problem with meeting educational needs*

Child enrolled in school, but has diagnosed educational, emotional, or physical disability that requires specialized curriculum, school, or environment.

Child's current school or educational program provides little benefit; child unable to keep up in all subject areas.

4. *Severe problem—not enrolled*

Child of school age not enrolled (and not scheduled to be enrolled) in any school or educational program.

Include child who "dropped out" prior to legal age or who was expelled.

U   *Unknown*—insufficient information

Z   *Not applicable*

1. *Acceptable*

Child receiving at least average grades in school,
> *Or,*

Child receiving below average grades, but it is believed child is performing up to his or her potential.

2. *Marginal*

This child's grades are below average but he or she is not failing any subjects. The child is believed to be performing below his or her potential.

3. *Moderately unacceptable*

The child is currently failing one or two major subjects in school. There is a risk that the child will not be promoted to the next grade. Remedial work and increased effort will be necessary to prevent this.

4. *Very unacceptable*

The child is failing so many subjects in school that he or she will not be promoted to the next grade, or will be transferred to an alternate school or remedial program. (If scheduled for a graduation, the child could not graduate.)

U   *Unknown*—insufficient information

Z   *Not applicable*—preschool child, not enrolled, etc.

1. *Average attendance*

> May have missed a number of days, but no more than most other students.
> Include child with above average attendance.

2. *Below average attendance*

The child tends to be absent from school more frequently than other students. But this does not seem to have affected the child's school performance. There has been one complaint to the parent from the school about this, but no other action is contemplated.

3. *Poor attendance, no strong school reaction*

The child attends school irregularly. The child is absent almost as often as he or she attends. This has adversely affected the child's school performance.

There have been several complaints to the parent from the school about this, but stronger action is not yet considered indicated.

4. *Poor attendance, strong school reaction*

The child does not attend school at all for weeks at a time, and is absent more often than present (but is enrolled). The child requires extensive remedial work to catch up in school.

There have been many complaints to the parent from the school, and more serious action has now been threatened (e.g., court action).

5. *No attendance—not enrolled*

> The child does not attend school at all because the parent has not enrolled the child.
> The child is being left far behind his or her peers academically.

U *Unknown*—insufficient information

Z *Not applicable*

1. *Child's family relations generally positive with few conflicts*

There is mutual tolerance and conflicts are resolved quickly.

Child participates adequately in family life. Include child whose family relations were good even though he or she may now be placed, for other reason (e.g., misbehavior)

2. *Child often in conflict with family members, but some contacts remain positive*

There are attempts at problem solving, though not always successful; some mutual tolerance exists. Child may be temporarily excluded from some family activities, or have some privileges revoked.

3. *Child's behavior very disruptive of family relations (but no requests for separation have been made)*

Other family members tend to avoid contact with child (or child tends to avoid contact with them). Some contacts attempted but usually result in conflict.

There are few attempts to solve problems.

4. *Child in danger of separation from family due to conflicts at home*

For example, parent has made status offender complaint; or has asked for out-of-home placement; or child desires placement; or refuses to go home.

U *Unknown*—insufficient information

Z *Not applicable* (e.g., child out of home)

For cases being rated at follow-up, consider only "serious consequences" that have followed (recent) misconduct, e.g., misconduct since referral to the agency or since the last follow-up.

1. *Recent conduct generally acceptable at home, in school or work, and in community*

    Child's recent conduct is comparable to that characterizing other children of same age.

2. *Some recent oppositional behavior at home or school, but no serious consequences for child*

    See examples of "oppositional behavior" and "serious consequences."
    Parent may be requesting help with child, but not placement. School may have complained to parents, but no threat of imminent suspension or expulsion. No police or court involvement.

3. *One or two recent incidents of moderately serious misconduct at home, in school, or in community, but no serious consequences for child*

    See examples of "moderately serious misconduct" and "serious consequences."
    Parent may be requesting help with child, but not placement. School may have complained to parents, but no threat of imminent suspension or expulsion. No police or court involvement.

3. *One or two recent incidents of moderately serious misconduct at home, in school, or in community, but no serious consequences for child*

    See examples of "moderately serious misconduct" and "serious consequences."
    Parent may be requesting help with child, but not placement. School may have complained to parent, but no threat of imminent suspension or expulsion. Child may have been "picked up" by police, but no arrest. No court involvement.

4. *Pattern of oppositional behavior at home or school that has resulted in some serious consequence(s) for child*

    See examples of "oppositional behavior" and "serious consequences."

5. *Pattern of moderately serious misconduct that has resulted in some serious consequences for child*

    See examples of "moderately serious misconduct" and "serious consequences."

6. *At least one recent incident of very serious misconduct (violent or felonious behavior)*

    Examples: Assault on parent or teacher; sexual assault; drug dealing; carrying weapon; burglary; hold-ups; arson; etc.
    Probably has (or will) result in serious consequences for child.

U *Unknown*—insufficient information

Z *Not applicable*

Examples of oppositional behavior:
At home: argumentative, rude; refuses to do chores, clean up after himself or herself; comes home late; refuses to say where going.
At school: refuses to follow directions, to complete work; or cheats.
Excludes property offenses, violent offenses, or behavior physically dangerous to the child.

Examples of moderately serious misconduct:
Steals from family members or peers; petty theft or shoplifting; breaks things or vandalizes; makes threats; runs away; unapproved sexual activity; using drugs or alcohol; bullies siblings or peers.
Excludes assaultive or felonious offenses.

Examples of serious consequences for child:
Out-of-home placement is requested or received; imminent or actual suspension/expulsion from school; police arrest; court petition or appearance; any serious injury to child.

Scale 42   Coping Behavior of Children*

Please note that code "3" defines the most desirable coping behavior for children. Codes "1" and "5" denote opposite extremes of undesirable coping behavior.

1. Relentlessly externalizing

Demands own way in virtually all situations.

Actively resists authority.

Insists that others gratify his or her needs. May whine and cajole incessantly.

Cannot tolerate any delay of gratification.

Has temper tantrums in reaction to stress, striking out indiscriminately at others or acting self-destructively; unable or unwilling to engage in other activities for some time after.

2. Overly externalizing

Tends to demand own way, but not in all situations.

Will respond to use of authority or persuasion.

Tries first to have others gratify his or her needs, but then may attempt some independent action.

Able to delay gratification sometimes in presence of adults, but only for short periods. With peers, exhibits little control. Stops whining or cajoling when it has no effect.

Strikes out at persons or objects who frustrate him or her, but not at others; able to engage in other activities afterward.

3. Balanced coping; adequate for age

Able to compromise with others and to share, as well as to stand up for own rights when necessary.

Generally able to function independently (as expected for age), but willing to ask for help when needed.

Seeks and accepts rewards, but delays gratification when necessary, with both adults and peers. Rarely whines or cajoles.

Doesn't strike out in frustrating situations, rather acknowledges feelings and acts to relieve the situation, but not by hurting others nor giving up prematurely.

4. Overly internalizing

Finds it difficult to stand up alone for own rights, but will try when supported by adult or peers.

Shows some ability to depend on others in realistic way, but under stress reverts to pseudo-independence (pushes others away, refuses to ask or accept help).

May try independent action, but gives up too quickly.

Fearful of asserting himself or herself or of satisfying own needs, but will do so if encouraged.

When confronted with problems, tends to withdraw from people or activities (or tends not to engage in worthwhile but potentially stressful activities). May seek out an adult or special friend for support.

5. Relentlessly internalizing

Unwilling to stand up for self in virtually all situations even when encouraged by adults or peers.

Refuses help, or doesn't know when or how to ask for help, even when that seems essential.

Almost no attempts to satisfy own feelings or needs (e.g., shows little emotion, seems to need nothing); extremely overcontrolled.

Withdraws totally under stress; may assume fetal-like position; or display "symptomatic" behavior (e.g., incessant rocking, thumb-sucking); or flees the situation.

U Unknown—insufficient information

Z Not applicable—e.g., infant

*Adapted from William F. Barker, Emotional Development Scale for Children (n.d.).

Scale 43 Children's Disabling Conditions—Degree of Impairment

PART A: TYPE OF CONDITION—(For each child, choose the most severe)

A Chronic Physical Illness/Handicap
B Developmental Disability/Retardation
C Diagnosed Emotional Illness

(Not misconduct or social maladjustment unless accompanied by diagnosed emotional illness)

D Specific Learning Disability
E Hearing, Speech, Sight Impairment
F Undiagnosed Disabling Symptoms Present
U Unknown—insufficient information
Z Not applicable

PART B: DEGREE OF IMPAIRMENT—(For each child, choose the most severe)

1. No symptoms observed or reported

2. Mild symptoms, no impairment, no difficulty

Symptoms exist, but there is no impairment in carrying out daily activities or in meeting role requirements.

This may be because the symptoms are very mild, or because the child is being provided with services which enable him or her to overcome more serious symptoms and function in the normal range (e.g., medicines, therapy, physical aid, etc.).

Child has no more difficulty in functioning than do other children.

3. Moderate symptoms, no significant impairment, performs with difficulty

Symptoms exist, and child maintains a normal level of functioning in daily activities and major roles only with difficulty and with increased effort. (Major social roles are family member, student, friend, and citizen.)

There may be definite impairment in ability to perform secondary roles (e.g., recreational activities).

This may be because the symptoms are moderate in strength, or because the services or therapy provided thus far have not fully compensated for the effects of more severe symptoms.

The condition may be causing some pain, discomfort, stress, or loss of time during child's activities. The condition may require others to make minor adjustments in relations with the child to accommodate him or her.

However, the end products of child's performances are in the normal range quantitatively and qualitatively (e.g., child in wheelchair who is "mainstreamed," some epileptic children with blackouts).

(If symptoms impair child's effectiveness in functioning, use one of codes below.)

4. Fairly severe symptoms, definite impairment, but can perform major roles at minimal level

Symptoms exist and there is definite impairment (loss of effectiveness) in carrying out daily activities or in performing major roles.

This may be because the symptoms are fairly severe, or because the services or therapy provided thus far haven't enabled the child to perform in the normal range, even with difficulty.

Child is able to function only at a minimal level in his or her normal environment, but would be able to perform (or does perform) some roles better in a specialized, supportive environment (e.g., special school).

Child's relations with others are outside the normal range (e.g., tends to be a disruptive influence on others, is often punished or sanctioned by others, may be isolated).

But symptoms are not severe enough to warrant institutionalization or to exclude child involuntarily from any major role activities. Child is not a danger to self or others.

5. *Symptoms very severe, unable to perform one or more major roles at any level, temporary placement*

Symptoms exist, and child is unable to perform one or more major roles.

This may be because the symptoms are very severe, or because the services or therapy provided thus far have not significantly improved those symptoms.

Child will not be (or is not) allowed to remain in one or more of his or her major roles (because remaining is of no benefit or even harmful to him or her; and/or because child makes it impossible for others to carry out their activities, even with difficulty; and/or because severe sanctions are threatened against child; and/or because child represents danger to self or others).

Child will be (or is) temporarily institutionalized, hospitalized, or placed in a residential setting. Long-term placement is not expected.

6. *Symptoms very severe, long-term or permanent placement anticipated*

Same as (5) above, except that symptoms are so chronic and pervasive, or have such a poor prognosis, that long-term or permanent institutionalization, hospitalization, or placement in a residential setting is anticipated.

U *Unknown*—insufficient information

Z *Not applicable*

4

Validity of the Child Well-Being Scales

Introduction

This chapter describes the methods used to validate the individual Child Well-Being Scales and to develop a valid composite scoring procedure. Generally, a measure may be termed valid to the extent that it does what it was designed to do. Specific tests for validity were built into the development of the instrument and guided its construction. Consequently the questions of how the scales were developed and whether they are valid are inseparable.

Understanding the process of development is also essential for correctly interpreting and using the information obtained. The methods chosen to construct and validate the scales, and their related statistical assumptions, could affect the conclusions of evaluation studies. The instrument's utility and credibility ultimately depend on the appropriateness of its development in relation to the objectives of potential users.

The following is an overview of the chapter. First are described the steps taken to ensure the content validity, defined as the relevance and comprehensiveness, of the Child Well-Being Scales. These steps included drawing on the child welfare literature, on the advice of professionals who reviewed preliminary drafts of the instrument, and on a pretest by social workers with families receiving child welfare services. The result of this initial developmental work was a series of itemized rating scales, each scale consisting of between four and six levels presumably ranked in order of importance or seriousness for a child's well-being.[1]

Second, a set of comparable "seriousness scores" was derived for the levels of all the Child Well-Being Scales, using successive intervals analysis, a psychometric scaling technique. The data were obtained through a nationwide survey of 765 child welfare professionals, who were asked to rate the descriptions of the scale levels according to their relative seriousness for children's well-being. The derived seriousness scores are used to assess the criterion-related validity of the Child Well-Being Scales and are also the means for constructing a statistically valid, composite Child Well-Being Score.

Third, the trait validity of the scales was examined using factor analysis conducted on data from 240 families accepted for child welfare services.[2]

Content Validity

The development of the Child Well-Being Scales began with a target concept, "child well-being," defined as a set of dimensions involving a child's caretaking environment and individual adjustment. The first basis on which dimensions were selected was their relevance; that is, that the subject matter addressed be related to the purposes of child welfare services. The second basis of selection was that the dimensions be comprehensive; that is, that all the most important subject matter be included. The instrument went through several drafts, each reviewed by members of the study's advisory committee, composed of consultants to the study and representatives from the participating agencies. Reviewers, of course, were essentially assessing the instrument's face validity. The work proceeded until the reviewers were generally satisfied with the instrument's content and format. The next step was the completion of the instrument by social workers on actual child welfare cases to test its relevance and comprehensiveness more formally.

Initial field work with a draft of the scales was conducted at two child protective agencies, the Baltimore County Department of Social Services and the Baltimore City Department of Social Services, during 1981. Case selection procedures were similar at the agencies. The instrument was completed both on cases at intake (to test its adequacy for describing presenting problems) and on continuing service cases open for various lengths of time (to test its adequacy for describing situations subsequent to intervention). To ensure coverage of a wide range of case situations, selection of continuing service cases was stratified in Baltimore City by type of abuse problem (sexual abuse vs. teenage abuse vs. all other abuse) and in Baltimore County by type of service (foster placement aftercare vs. protective services). Goals were established for the number of schedules to be completed, but the guiding principle was to collect only the data needed to revise the instrument and the administration procedures.

Several means were used in this pretest to help assess the adequacy of the instrument. In addition to the possible substantive ratings, each item allowed an additional choice of "not classifiable—categories above don't fit." An "explanation" box at the bottom of each scale asked workers to explain the reason for this choice, as well as the reason for any rating about which they were doubtful. A separate section at the end of the schedule labeled "Other Problem Areas" asked staff to "please describe any other problems that this family is having that have not been covered thus far." A total of 150 schedules were reviewed by the authors.

The major finding was that the items were insufficiently comprehensive. Certain areas of major concern to workers were being only peripherally addressed, or not addressed at all, in the scales as constructed. This could be seen both in the types of problems listed as "not classifiable" under particular scales and in the entries for "Other Problem Areas." The apparent need for additional dimensions was confirmed through meetings with the staff members involved in these pretests. As a result, 12 scales, involving mainly familial capacities for parenting, were added to the instrument.

The mean percentage of "not classifiable" responses in relation to all responses on the schedule was 5%. This result seemed to indicate that most scales were written so as to be interpretable by workers. Particularly high "not classifiable" rates were found, however, for Supervision of Children (39%), Arrangements for Substitute Child Care (17%), and Economic Exploitation (12%).[3] These scales were rewritten in an attempt to eliminate the ambiguities perceived by workers.

The physical abuse area, which had consisted of a checklist of abuse types in combination with a physical injury index, was reformulated to the simpler current Abusive Physical Discipline scale. In addition, a checklist of types of sexual abuse was changed to a scale of sexual abuse severity. Overall, the revisions of the instrument seemed to make it more comprehensive in content and more consistent in format.

After the scales were revised, seriousness scores for them were derived by means of a survey of child welfare professionals, as described in the following sections. Various additional studies of the scales' reliability and validity were conducted, using case samples from child welfare agencies. This latter work is reported in the trait validity section at the end of this chapter, and in chapter 5.

Derivation of Seriousness Scores

Purpose

The key assumption in constructing the Child Well-Being Scales is that the different categories (levels) of each scale represent different degrees of seriousness for the well-being of the child on each dimension. Rather than relying on the face validity of the scales in this respect, it was considered important to derive a suitable criterion of "seriousness" against which this assumption could be formally tested. The study method was to obtain systematic ratings of seriousness for all scale levels from a national sample of child welfare professionals, and then to derive seriousness scores for those levels, using successive intervals analysis, a psychometric scaling technique. These scores, based on the pooled judgments of child welfare professionals, then serve as the criterion of validity for the ordinality of the scales. For instance, level 5 on a scale should score higher in seriousness than level 4 (or any other level), if the assumption of ordinal measurement for the scale is correct.[4]

Deriving seriousness scores has a second important purpose, to enable the valid construction of composite child or family scores from the individual scale ratings—that is, to construct a composite score one needs to be able to compare the seriousness of scale levels across different dimensions. For example, what is the relative seriousness of level 3 for Nutrition/Diet as compared with level 3 for Clothing? The study method, as will be shown, yields interval measurement of the individual scale categories on a common, general attribute of "seriousness for the welfare of the child."[5] The derived seriousness scores may then validly be combined (with certain limitations) into composite indices of child well-being for the case.

Rating Format

The narrative descriptions ("descriptors") defining the levels of each scale were rewritten slightly into the form of "case vignettes." Survey respondents were thus instructed:

> This questionnaire is a series of vignettes describing various situations involving children. . . . Based on your professional experience . . . you should rank each vignette according to its overall *seriousness for the welfare of the child.* Use the following nine-point scale:
>
> 1   2   3   4   5   6   7   8   9
> Least   Most
> Serious   Serious

A complete example was then given. The instructions concluded: "Of course, you may not agree with this particular response. Remember, the questionnaire asks only for your *opinions.* There are no 'right' or 'wrong' answers."[6]

The rating task implicitly requires respondents to compare the seriousness of descriptors for different child well-being dimensions. We considered this possible, since all the dimensions focus on the degree to which children's needs are actually or potentially being met in various areas of concern. The less adequately any given need is being met, the more serious we may term the situation described.

Alternatively, we can say that asking respondents to perform this rating task is based on the premise that they are able to conceive of a general dimension of seriousness. This premise seems plausible, since child welfare practitioners are required daily to compare and weigh highly diverse family situations and individual behaviors. A cognitive mechanism therefore exists that renders commensurate this varied information, enabling the practitioner to reach conclusions, make decisions, and recommend actions. The survey essentially asks respondents to replicate their case assessment skills in rating the vignettes.

Construction of Vignettes

In constructing the vignettes, care was exercised to retain the original language of the descriptors, which were occasionally split into two vignettes for testing purposes when rather different situations had been combined a priori to form a single descriptor.

It is important to note that the descriptor "labels" appearing on the scales, for example, "mildly inadequate," "severely inadequate," were *not* part of the wording of the vignettes. Seeing such labels might easily have "cued" respondents as to the intended seriousness of the individual vignettes.

The descriptors for the levels defining the ceilings of the scales (usually labeled "adequate") were not included in the survey. These were considered reference points for scaling purposes. It did not make sense to include descriptors of "adequate" on the survey form because no "degree" of seriousness can be conceptualized for them.[7] Pragmatically, they can be considered located at either the ceiling or base of a derived seriousness continuum (depending on the choice of directionality).

Survey Format

The professional survey was conducted in two phases. The first, or primary, survey used the complete child well-being schedule as then constructed, and ultimately provided three-fourths of the data for the derivation of the seriousness scores. Results of the first survey led to the revision of several scales. A second, smaller, supplemental survey was then conducted to validate those revisions and provide the remaining data for the analysis.

A pool of 154 vignettes was developed for the primary survey, clearly too numerous to place on one form. A survey form that would take no more than one-half hour to complete was considered feasible, and we found that this limited the number of possible items on a form to about 40. A second important reason for developing multiple survey forms was to maximize the independence of responses to vignettes representing the same scale. A respondent presented with all the vignettes drawn from a given scale might well perceive their intended ordering on seriousness and respond to this perception alone. Ratings of different vignettes from the same scale obtained from different (that is, independent) samples of respondents would eliminate this possible source of bias favoring the hypothesized rank-ordering of descriptors.

Separating vignettes drawn from the same scale by distributing them among different forms has another advantage, namely, that respondents are "forced" to compare the seriousness of vignettes of diverse content. This coincides with the survey rationale in eliciting responses based on the cognitive process respondents use in their professional practice to assess diverse case situations, assessments presumably relying on some more general, integrative concept of "seriousness for the welfare of the child." Of course, there is no guarantee beforehand that respondents can perform this task satisfactorily, but separating vignettes from the same scale structures the task more validly for its intended purpose.

Four survey forms were constructed for the primary survey, each consisting of between 35 and 40 vignettes. Vignettes representing different levels of the same scale were almost always placed on different forms. Only in seven instances, where scales consisted of five levels below "adequate," was it necessary to place two vignettes from the same scale on the same form. (These were Nutrition/Diet, Support for Principal Caretaker, Abusive Physical Discipline, Sexual Abuse, Children's Misconduct, and Children's Disabling Conditions—Degree of Impairment.) In such instances the vignettes were widely separated on the form.

Vignettes were assigned at random to the four survey forms, subject to the condition that, where possible, only one vignette from a given scale should appear on a given form. This was intended to ensure similar distributions of seriousness for each of the four sets of vignettes.[8]

The best methodological procedure would have been to present the vignettes to each respondent in a unique random order. It was not possible, however, to construct and code nearly 900 individually unique forms. Consequently, the responses obtained are vulnerable to an item-sequencing effect.[9] In any event, respondents had the option of revising their previous answers to improve consistency with later answers, if they desired to do so.

On the supplemental survey, a less rigorous procedure had to be followed. Only those descriptors that had been revised were included, since it was not practical to repeat the survey in its entirety with all descriptors. The 43 revised descriptors came from only 13 scales. Since the supplemental survey was limited to one form, vignettes drawn from the same scale necessarily appeared together.

Sampling Procedures

The survey objective was to sample qualified and informed practitioner opinion in the child welfare field. This we defined as located among the more experienced and educated administrators, supervisors, and line workers employed in child welfare agencies. Formally enumerating this population for the purpose of national sampling would have been very difficult. The more practical, and we believe satisfactory, approach taken was to select individual staff members from CWLA-affiliated agencies. It is not known exactly how CWLA affiliates, estimated at 10% of child welfare agencies in the U.S., differ from the nonaffiliated. CWLA agencies, however, tend to be the more established agencies in the field and are expected to conform to relatively high standards for administration and practice.

Since the survey deals with child protection situations, broadly defined, two types of agencies were excluded from the sampling frame—those that were primarily residential treatment centers or maternity homes. All other CWLA affiliates, both public and voluntary, were included in the sampling frame, for a total of 275 agencies.

A two-stage, stratified sampling procedure was used in both the primary and supplemental surveys. In the first stage, eligible agencies were classified as public or voluntary, and random selections were made from both groups so that about two-thirds of the sample was voluntary and one-third, public. Voluntary agencies were oversampled because they usually have a more "professionalized" child welfare staff, defined as a higher proportion of M.S.W.s and higher average years of experience. To avoid placing too great a burden on the agencies, the number of respondents requested from each was geared to the agency's staff size.

In the primary survey, the smallest agencies (under 25 practitioners) received four forms to complete, the medium-sized (25 to 50), seven forms, and the largest (over 50), 10 forms. In the supplemental survey, small and medium agencies received nine forms and large agencies, 15. Since the public agencies (state and county) were disproportionately represented in the "largest" group, the number of individual survey forms requested from public agencies was 42% of the total requested.

An introductory letter to the executive director of each agency explained the purpose of the survey and requested that equal numbers of social workers, supervisors, and program administrators be asked to complete the enclosed survey forms. The director was asked to complete a form if he or she had the time, or to select an additional administrator instead. Other than that, the choice of respondents was left to the director on the basis of individual staff "interest and availability."

The sampling plan was based on a desire for at least 100, and ideally 150, respondents on each of the four survey forms in the primary survey. The plan was to send out about 200 of each form; a minimal 50% response rate would then yield 100 responses, while a 75% rate would yield 150. The results of a preliminary mailing of 214 forms in September 1981 indicated the response rate would be well over 50%, if follow-up telephone calls to agencies were conducted and data collection was allowed to continue for at least 2 months. On that basis the additional survey forms were mailed on November 1, 1981. Data collection for the primary survey continued until January 15, 1982.

The desirability of conducting a supplemental survey became apparent near the end of the project. The forms were mailed on September 1, 1982, and because of time limitations only those forms submitted within one month could be included in the data analysis (162 forms).

The authors had no firm reason to believe that either public or voluntary agency status or a respondent's agency position would be associated with differential responses on the survey. Nevertheless, there are probably enough differences between public and private agency environments to warrant explicit consideration of this contextual factor. Also, a respondent's position is associated both with different levels and types of professional responsibility, as well as with different individual demographic characteristics; any of these could conceivably influence survey responses. In any event, the sampling strategy seemed to promise a reasonably diverse, national sample of respondents weighted as intended toward the more experienced and educated professionals in the child welfare field.

Method of Successive Intervals

Survey respondents rated each vignette on a nine-point scale of seriousness. Deriving seriousness scores requires making some assumptions about the nature of the data. The simplest procedure would have been to compute the mean rating for each vignette and define that as its seriousness score. This assumes that the nine-point scale is an equal-interval scale; that is, that the perceived differences in seriousness between adjacent ratings ("1" and "2," "2" and "3," etc.) on the scale are equal.

It was believed unwise or unnecessary to use this common but often tenuous "method of equal-appearing intervals" for the survey. Essentially, this requires asking respondents to make highly refined discriminations in seriousness among a large set of diverse descriptors. This technique places the burden of placing the descriptors on an interval-level scale entirely on the respondents.

Research in other contexts has shown that respondents have difficulty in adhering to an equal-interval requirement. For instance, categorical sorting or rating yields response distributions that at the extremes tend to be truncated and skewed toward the center of the rating scale. In the present survey, this would result in placing descriptors of above- and below-average seriousness too close to the center of the seriousness scale (and thus too close to the descriptors located at the center).

The method of successive intervals avoids the equal-interval assumption in analyzing the rating data. Needed was only the less stringent assumption that the ratings are rank-ordered on the attribute of seriousness. In other words, the ratings on the nine-point scale are considered as ordinal; for example, a "2" rating is taken to denote greater seriousness than a "1," but the amount of the difference in seriousness between "1" and "2" is considered unknown. It is clearly more realistic to ask respondents simply to rank-order the descriptors on seriousness, as the present survey did, rather than to ask them to judge the precise differences in seriousness between descriptors.

The statistics used in the method of successive intervals allow the scaling task to be shared between respondent and investigator. The method allows respondents to make less exacting distinctions in seriousness among the descriptors, yet through appropriate analysis it yields the latent metric (that is, interval-level scale) most consistent with the set of responses given. The method may be thought of as a statistical technique that essentially transforms ordinal-level ratings into interval-level scores, coincidentally avoiding unrealistic demands on survey respondents. The final result is the desired seriousness scores (or "weights") for the descriptors comprising the Child Well-Being Scales.[10]

Data Analysis

Sample Characteristics

The five independent professional samples (four in the primary survey, one in the supplemental) were quite similar on respondent characteristics. Table 4-1 presents the frequencies for the pooled sample on agency affiliation, position at agency, education, social work experience, ethnicity, and age. The sample is composed predominantly of persons holding M.S.W.s with over 10 years of social work experience, most now serving as either supervisors or administrators.

Response Rates

Examining response rates is important because those not completing the forms might hold opinions systematically different from those who do complete them. High response rates help ensure that the seriousness scores derived adequately represent professional opinion.

Table 4-2 presents an analysis of response rates to the primary professional survey for each version of the form, type of agency, and respondent's position. There was an overall response rate of 70%; however, some variation appeared between different forms (60 to 80%), though we have no ready explanation for this. Voluntary and public agencies responded at similar rates, both in terms of percentage of agencies participating and percentage of forms returned. The administrators' response rate was slightly lower than those for supervisors and workers. Follow-up calls indicated that some agencies had very few administrators, and unless all or nearly all of them agreed to participate, these agencies could not meet our requested quota. On balance, the level of participation in all groups can be considered quite satisfactory.

Response rates were not calculated for the supplemental survey because the data collection period was unavoidably attenuated due to time limitations. Only the first 162 forms, submitted within one month, could be included in the final analysis.

Comparison of Sample Subgroups

If there were observed differences in rating patterns between subgroups in the pooled sample, the seriousness scores obtained would depend on the particular profile ("mix") of respondents surveyed. Consequently, these scores would not be generalizable to child welfare professionals as a whole. Different sets of seriousness scores for different subgroups might then be needed.

No differences in response patterns were found for any of the respondent characteristics examined, except for agency affiliation, where the results were ambiguous. The average rating of seriousness for the set of descriptors was slightly higher for the voluntary agencies on three versions of the form, slightly higher for public agencies on one version, and showed no difference on the remaining version. The relatively small and inconsistent nature of these differences did not seem to warrant separate consideration of the voluntary and public agency data in the successive intervals analysis.

Table 4-1 Characteristics of Professional Survey Sample
(All Forms, N = 765)

	N	%		N	%
Agency Affiliation			Social Work Experience		
Voluntary	435	57.2	1–4 years	188	24.9
Public	325	42.8	5–10 years	181	23.9
Unknown	5	—	Over 10 years	387	51.2
			Unknown	9	—
	765	100.0%		765	100.0%
Respondent's Position			Ethnicity		
Director/Administrator	275	36.5	White	645	86.2
Supervisor	236	31.3	Black	83	11.1
Caseworker	242	32.1	Hispanic	20	2.7
Unknown	12	—	Other/Unknown	17	—
	765	99.9%		765	100.0%
Education			Age		
B.A.	102	13.9	18–29	75	9.9
B.S.W.	38	5.2	30–39	311	41.1
M.A.	48	6.5	40–49	196	25.9
M.S.W.	529	72.2	50–59	133	17.6
D.S.W./Ph.D.	16	2.2	60 and Over	41	5.4
Other/Unknown	32	—	Unknown	9	—
	765	100.0%		765	99.9%

Sample Size

The sample sizes obtained for the successive intervals analysis compare favorably with recommendations in the literature. Although Thurstone and Chave's original scaling work (1929) was based on 300 judges, subsequent research has shown that results using around 50 judges are highly reliable (Edwards 1982). A recent derivation of a health status index used only 31 professionals (Blischke et al. 1975). The present study had between 129 and 172 respondents on each version of the form, enough to subdivide reliably should differences in response patterns by agency auspices or respondent's position have required this.

Comparison of Survey Forms

The use of multiple survey forms may affect the subsequent successive intervals analyses, since it creates the possibility that respondents on different forms may use different reference points in rating seriousness. This result would invalidate pooling the different samples for analysis. To reduce this possibility, we attempted to equalize the distributions of presumed seriousness by assigning vignettes randomly to the different forms, as noted previously.

The procedure was not entirely successful. The main problem is that one version of the form has significantly fewer descriptors ranked at "2" on the scales and more ranked at "3," suggesting a disproportionate number of more serious descriptors on that form.[11] This sample can validly be pooled with the others only if the seriousness ratings on the form actually reflect the apparently greater seriousness of descriptors on the form.

To examine this issue, the ratings over all vignettes were averaged for each respondent,

Table 4-2   Response Rates on Primary Professional Survey, by Form Version,
Agency Auspices, and Respondent's Position
(Excludes Supplemental Form)

Form Version	Number of Vignettes	N of Forms Sent	N of Forms Returned	% Returned
"A"	40	214	129	60.3
"B"	40	211	156	73.9
"C"	39	214	172	80.3
"D"	35	222	146	65.7
Total	154	861	603	70.0

Agency Auspices	N of Agencies Sampled	N of Agencies Responding	% Responding	N of Forms Sent	N of Forms Returned	% Returned
Voluntary	80	65	81.3	511	365	71.4
Public	35	30	85.7	350	238	68.0
Total	115	95	82.6	861	603	70.0

Respondent's Position	N of Forms Sent	N of Forms Returned	% Returned
Director/Administrator	365	236	64.7
Supervisor	248	186	75.0
Caseworker	248	174	70.2
Total	861	596[a]	70.0

[a] Respondent's position unknown on seven forms.

and a heuristic average rating of seriousness over all respondents was then computed for each version of the survey form.[12] This average rating of seriousness was definitely higher for the form with the presumably more serious vignettes. The consistency of this result indicates that pooling the responses from all five survey forms is justifiable for the purpose of the successive intervals analysis.

Preliminary Item Analysis

The findings in previous sections indicate that it is probably valid to pool the survey data without regard to the version of the form used or the characteristics of the respondents. Successive intervals analysis requires that the vignette response distributions for the pooled data also meet several additional assumptions. This section examines these issues.

Table 4-3   Distribution of Median Ratings for Descriptors on Professional Survey (All Forms)

Ratings	Number of Descriptors	% of Descriptors
Under 2.0	12	7.3
2.01–3.0	30	18.2
3.01–4.0	18	10.9
4.01–5.0	24	14.5
5.01–6.0	23	13.9
6.01–7.0	23	13.9
7.01–8.0	17	10.3
8.01 and over	18	10.9
Total	165	99.9%

The median value of the responses on the nine-point rating scale was calculated for each vignette. Table 4-3 presents the grouped distribution of these medians for the vignettes included in the final successive intervals analysis. The vignette medians are well distributed across the rating categories, as is desirable for successive intervals scaling. This result is also expected from the construction of the Child Well-Being Scales because each scale is intended to encompass a wide range of seriousness. Although there are slightly higher proportions of responses in the middle categories, there did not seem to be a strong reluctance by respondents to use the end categories, in contrast to what was found for health status preferences (Patrick et al. 1973: 19–20). This means that a satisfactory number of width estimates for the end intervals is available for the successive intervals analysis.

Response distributions for individual vignettes resembled nonmonotonic trace lines, a basic requirement of successive intervals scaling (Nunnally 1978: 77–79). (A nonmonotone distribution is an ascending and then descending unimodal curve.) This result indicates that the probability of a descriptor eliciting a response is highest for the rating category correlated with the descriptor's location on the attribute continuum of seriousness, and that the probabilities decrease in both directions away from that category. This situation would result if the seriousness of the descriptors were being defined in a desirably narrow and mutually exclusive manner.

Vignettes with medians in the middle scale categories had fairly symmetrical distributions, though usually flatter (platykurtic) than those for the normal curve (coefficients of kurtosis ranged from 0 to −1). Vignettes with medians near the scale extremes were skewed due to the presumed truncation of responses that is typical for category ratings.

The quartile deviation, appropriate for ordinal data, was calculated as a measure of dispersion of the vignette response distributions. This is defined as half the distance between the first and third quartiles; that is, between the points below which 25% and 75% of the responses fall (Blalock 1972: 79). It represents one-half of the range covered by the middle half of the cases for an individual vignette. The mean of the quartile deviations for the entire set of vignettes used in the final successive intervals analysis is 1.17.

The standard deviation of the distribution of quartile deviations is the statistic of interest. This standard deviation may be taken as measuring the degree of homogeneity of the vignette response distributions; that is, the degree to which ratings agree more for some vignettes than for others. The standard deviation of the quartile deviations (0.30) is small compared to the range of the quartile deviations (1.33), indicating that the degree of agreement on ratings among the vignettes is similar. The finding indicates that the successive intervals requirement of (approximately) equal standard deviations for item distributions on the hypothesized attribute continuum is met by this data set.

Inter-rater agreement on the seriousness of descriptors need not be very high in an absolute sense, however, for appropriate use of successive intervals scaling. Each vignette is undoubtedly eliciting a variety of unique reactions from respondents as they place the situation described in a fuller case context based on their own experiences. The reason for obtaining many and varied respondents in the survey is that the median rating for any descriptor will then be a summary measure across many possible contexts. As a result, the seriousness scores derived are more likely to be generalizable.[13]

Computation of Seriousness Scores

The successive intervals analysis was performed twice. First the analysis was performed on the primary survey data, which led to the revision of several scales (see next section). These revisions were the basis of the supplemental survey. The second and final successive intervals analysis included the revised scales and yielded the final set of seriousness scores shown in table 3-1.

The computational procedures follwed Edwards' (1982) least squares approach. The details need not be repeated here. Step-by-step examples may be found there as well as in Blischke et al. (1975). In brief, the sizes of successive intervals on the seriousness continuum were estimated by averaging. Then the seriousness scores of the descriptors were defined as the medians of their cumulative frequency distributions on that continuum.

The results of the analysis place all descriptors on a seriousness scale ranging from 1 (most serious) to 100 (least serious) and expressed in cental units (hundredths). Note that the conceptual range of seriousness encompassed by the scale is limited to the range encompassed by the individual descriptors. For example, a descriptor representing a situation more serious than any used in the survey (perhaps a child's death) could conceivably be constructed, but would fall conceptually below the lower numerical limit of the present seriousness scale.

As mentioned previously, the most positive descriptors for each scale (defining "adequacy" or lack of problems on that dimension) were not included in the survey. These were assigned a score of 100, the numerical ceiling of the derived seriousness scale. Operationally, this is equivalent to assuming that all respondents would have categorized these descriptors in the first interval (that is, category "1") on the nine-point rating scale, had they been included in the survey.

Criterion-Related Validity

The seriousness scores derived for the levels of the Child Well-Being Scales may be used as a criterion against which to assess the validity of the scales. The seriousness scores should rank the levels of each scale in the hypothesized order; that is, level 5 should be most serious, level 4 next most serious, and so on. This would confirm that appropriate conceptual distinctions in seriousness had been made in developing the scales. (Refer to table 3-1.)

The scales included in the primary survey had seriousness scores computed for each scale level. Satisfactory results were obtained for 30 out of the 41 scales; their seriousness scores changed monotonically from one level to the next. For 11 scales, there was at least one reversal in the progression of seriousness scores across the scale levels. The causes of this were determined, and suitable revisions were then made in the scale descriptors.[14] Also, two new scales, Sexual Abuse—Other Adult and Continuity of Parenting—were added at this time, based on social workers' recommendations during the field tests of the instrument.

The supplemental survey was conducted to validate these modifications and to provide seriousness scores for the revised (and new) scale descriptors. The successive intervals analysis was repeated in its entirety. About one-fourth of the descriptors from the primary survey were replaced by descriptors newly developed for the supplemental survey. The hypothesized ranking of the scale levels was confirmed visually now for all scales, except for the two Sexual Abuse scales.

In addition to visual inspection of scores for ordinality, a statistical test determined whether significant differences existed among the seriousness scores of the different levels for a given scale. The multiple comparisons for each scale were made by the Honestly-Significant-Difference (HSD) method (Namboodiri et al. 1975: 236). The seriousness scores met the HSD criterion at the $p = .05$ level (two-tailed test), except for the Sexual Abuse and Locking-Out scales. These discrepancies were handled as follows:

On the Sexual Abuse-Parent scale, the differences in seriousness scores between "harassment," "exhibitionism," and "molestation" (levels 3, 4, and 5) were not statistically significant (the range of these scores was 2.8). Consequently, the mean of the three scores was assigned to each of these descriptors.

The obtained difference (2.0) between the seriousness scores for levels 4 and 5 on the Sexual Abuse-Other Adult scale was not statistically significant; again, the mean score of these two levels was assigned to both. Despite the identical seriousness of some descriptors, it was decided to retain them as separate on the Sexual Abuse scales for informational purposes. Finally, no significant difference was found between levels 3 and 4 of Locking-Out, so again their mean score was assigned to each.

Generally, a difference in seriousness scores of at least 3.0 (computed from unrounded figures) between any two levels of a scale is required for HSD significance in these data. As can be seen from inspection of table 3-1, this condition holds for all scales except those discussed above.

Clearly some scales are closer than others to the "ideal," which would be seriousness scores changing in approximately equal increments and traversing the entire range of the continuum from 1 to 100. Nutrition/Diet is a good, though not perfect, scale in this sense. Supervision of Younger Children is not as good, because levels 2 and 3 are separated by only three units. A descriptor for level 3 scoring about 58 would have been ideal.

Several general observations can be made about the final set of seriousness scores. First, the scales vary greatly in the perceived seriousness of the most negative descriptors. Highest seriousness (1) was found for level 6 of Abusive Physical Discipline (involving life-threatening or permanently disabling injuries). Lowest seriousness (64) for the base of a scale was for level 4 of Security of Residence (involving actual or imminent loss of a family's residence). Second, there is large variation in the seriousness scores for any given level of the scales. For example, scores for level 3 range from 12 to 85 among the set of scales. These facts demonstrate the necessity of deriving the seriousness scores; the level of a scale is not a particularly good indication of seriousness across the various scales.

Some patterns in the seriousness scores may be due to the substantive nature of the dimensions themselves. For example, Abusive Physical Discipline of any kind is apparently regarded as quite serious by professionals, even if there is no, or only superficial, physical injury. One can speculate that it is the intention or recklessness of such excessive or inappropriate discipline and the constant potential for more serious injury that account for the high perceived seriousness of levels 3 to 6.

Possibly additional improvements could be made in the content of these scales. This analysis, however, supports their validity as indicators of the seriousness of a wide spectrum of situations detrimental to children's welfare.

Validity of the Criterion

The seriousness scores, derived from professionals' judgments of seriousness on a rating scale, have been treated as a criterion for the validity of the Child Well-Being Scales. The survey incorporated a test to help support the logic of using the scores in this way. In addition to rating vignettes on the nine-point scale, respondents were asked to "recommend one of the following five possible community responses" to the situation represented by each vignette:

1. *Community involvement should be avoided.* This situation is best left to the family itself for solution. The community should not become involved.

2. *Community involvement is desirable, but only on a voluntary basis.* The family should be encouraged to seek outside help, and efforts to reach out to such families should be supported. But the family should not be forced or required to acccept outside help.

3. *The community should intervene in some way, even if the family doesn't want outside help.* The child(ren) should be allowed to remain in the home. *The child(ren) should be removed only if the situation gets worse or something worse happens.*

4. *The community should intervene in some way, even if the family doesn't want outside help.* The child(ren) should be allowed to remain in the home for now. *The child(ren) should be removed only if the situation doesn't improve soon, or if the same thing happens again.*

5. *The community should intervene by removing the child(ren) from the home immediately, at least on a temporary basis.*

These "recommended community responses" incorporate two concepts of increasing community intervention in family life—voluntary vs. mandatory service, and in-home vs. foster care services. We hypothesize that, as the actual or potential harm to a child's well-being increases, the resulting level of intervention to protect the child will also increase. In other words, the seriousness of a child's situation is an important factor in determining the level of community response. The correlation between a descriptor's seriousness rating and the recommended community response can therefore be considered a test of the former's construct validity.[15]

Pearson correlations were computed between the seriousness ratings (1 through 9) and the recommended community responses (1 through 5) for each vignette on all survey forms. The average correlation taken over all five forms was .63. This indicates that, as a descriptor's seriousness rating increases, the intensity of community intervention that respondents recommend also generally increases.[16] There may be an item-to-item carryover effect contributing to this correlation, since responses on the two variables for each vignette were paired on the survey forms. This could have only been avoided, however, through a more complex and in this case impractical research design. Given this limitation, the results do support the use of the seriousness scores as a criterion measure of validity for the Child Well-Being Scales.

Constructing a Composite Child Well-Being Score (CWBS)

Constructing a composite score by arithmetically combining ratings of the individual child well-being scales would not be valid, because these ratings ("1," "2," "3," and so on) are not numbers representing interval-level measurement. In addition, combining data from different scales can only be valid if measurement is on an attribute common to all scales. Derivation of the seriousness scores addresses both these issues.

The seriousness scores obtained through the method of successive intervals may be interpreted as true interval-level numbers. For example, it is correct to say that the differences in seriousness between scores of 20 and 40, and between 40 and 60, are the same. Adding or averaging the scores is therefore mathematically justifiable.[17]

The seriousness scores also serve as a common unit of measurement for the entire set of scales. The child well-being data were scaled on a single dimension, "seriousness for the welfare of the child." Consequently, seriousness scores for different individual scales have the same intrinsic meaning and may be combined.

A straightforward composite score can be defined as follows:

$$CWBS = SUM/N$$

where SUM = Sum of the seriousness scores on scales rated (from table 3-1)
N = Number of scales rated

This total Child Well-Being Score (CWBS) ranges from 1 to 100.

The interpretation of the CWBS is subject to certain limitations, that must be carefully considered.

First, the averaging procedure results in a composite score that can no longer be interpreted in terms of the original seriousness continuum. This is because the unit of analysis has changed from a single dimension of a case to a multidimensional representation of a complete case situation. This may be seen, for instance, by comparing the meaning of a seriousness score of 44 (level 3) on Physical Health Care with the meaning of a CWBS score of 44.

There is a descriptor associated with the health care score that "explains" the meaning of the score. No such descriptor is associated with the CWBS score of 44. The interpretation of CWBS scores must be limited to saying that a score of 44 is less serious than a score of 43 or any lower score. But many different combinations of seriousness scores on the scales could average out to a CWBS score of 44.

Second, forming a linear composite score (as by adding or averaging) implies that the combined seriousness of multiple problems is correctly represented as the sum of the seriousness scores of the individual problems. When various problems exist together, however, their seriousness may instead "interact"—may be mutually reinforcing. The methodology employed to derive the seriousness scores did not take such possible interactions into account. The case vignettes in the survey were presented individually to respondents, not in combination with each other. The perceived seriousness of various combinations was not rated by respondents. Consequently, the CWBS may be to some degree inaccurate in scoring the seriousness of such combinations of descriptors in relation to the individual scale descriptors.

This limitation was recognized in designing the study, but it could not be easily overcome. Combinations of vignettes might have been presented to respondents to rate, but the number of such combinations, even empirically likely ones, is enormous. The method used was impractical to extend in that way. As a result, the CWBS is best viewed conservatively as a heuristic index that *retains the information* contained in the seriousness scoring of individual scales, but does not take into account possible interaction effects between the seriousness scores. With this limitation understood, the CWBS may be treated as an interval-level measurement scale for the sake of analytical convenience.

Third, the possible choices of how to handle missing data in composite scoring should be examined. The CWBS computation is equivalent to assigning the mean score of the rated scales to the unrated (unknown) scales, thus avoiding a forced correlation between the composite scores and the amount of missing data. Use of the formula, however, is recommended only when information is available on most of the scales. When most scales cannot be rated, it may be misleading to assign the average score for the known scales to the unknown scales. The fewer scales requiring score estimation, the more valid the CWBS is likely to be for a case.

Making an alternative assumption that a family is "adequate" ($= 100$) on the unrated (unknown) scales seems unsatisfactory, as that would lead composite scores to be correlated with the number of rated scales. Of course, requiring instead that all scales be scored is unrealistic, because as a practical matter some information may not be available. (Using a cutoff point of 50% missing data might be reasonable.)

The CWBS is "self-weighting," in the sense that the contribution of each scale to the composite score depends on the seriousness of each scale's descriptors. For example, Nutrition/Diet has more potential to depress the CWBS than Clothing, because of the lower numerical seriousness scores of descriptors for the former (refer to table 3-1). On the other hand, the CWBS is sensitive to the number of individual scales in different problem areas. For example, adding or deleting dimensions pertaining to emotional care of children would change, at least implicitly, the interpretation of the composite scores.

Finally, the CWBS as defined is not the only plausible way of forming a composite score. Different methods may be chosen for different evaluative purposes. For instance, a subset of dimensions with some common conceptual element, such as housing conditions or emotional care, may be combined into an overall index, or multivariate analysis might indicate the existence of broader concepts measured by groups of scales (see next section). Whether any particular composite is useful depends on the evaluation design. In addition, averaging scores of scales may not always be the preferred choice for an analysis. For example, for some purposes it may be more useful to represent a family's status by their lowest (most serious) score on any scale. This method might be reasonable if the service objective is to bring the family up to some uniform minimum standard on every dimension of concern. The most important point is that the CWBS, as defined, is not the only plausible way to summarize the child well-being information.

Trait Validity

Introduction

The Child Well-Being Scales were developed as single-item measures of different dimensions pertinent to the needs of children. No assumptions were made about whether or how these dimensions might be related empirically in a population of cases. It is possible, however, that groups of scales might be intercorrelated, revealing interpretable higher-order constructs. Such constructs would then be said to have trait validity, and could assist in further understanding the meaning of the child well-being data as a whole. To address this issue, an exploratory factor analysis was conducted on child well-being scale data collected for a current service population.

Description of Sample

The sample consisted of 240 families who had completed the intake process and been newly accepted for services and who had at least one child residing at home. This intake sample was selected during 1981 at three public agencies: Texas Department of Human Resources (Dallas, $N = 69$, and Nacogdoches/Lufkin, $N = 16$), Hennepin County (Minnesota) Community Services Department ($N = 53$), and Dade County (Florida) Department of Youth and Family Development ($N = 102$). The Texas and Hennepin cases were referred for child protective services; Dade serves multiproblem families at risk of involvement with the protective service or juvenile justice systems. Sampling was either random or systematic (that is, every nth eligible case), depending on the site. Both methods yielded representative samples of the intake populations, with the one exception that sexual abuse cases were deliberately oversampled in Dallas.

The scales were completed by the intake worker at the time the case was selected for the study. The instructions were to describe the family situation at the time of referral to the agency. The demographic characteristics of the sample are given in appendix 1. Scale frequencies are presented in table 3-2.[18]

The 41 scales used in this study were identical to those used for the primary survey of professionals. Thus some of the scales appearing are the versions before final revisions to the instrument were made (cf. note 14).

The analysis relied on data collected at intake because the patterns of problems that might be found would not have been influenced by the effects of subsequent service intervention.

Results of Factor Analysis

The factor analysis was conducted on the metric seriousness scores previously derived for the Child Well-Being Scales. Averaging children's scores was used to obtain a single score for those scales measuring individual children. Common factors were obtained by principal factoring with iteration to estimate the communalities, followed by orthogonal rotation using the varimax criterion. Pairwise deletion was used in computing the correlation matrix, since all families had some missing data. Bivariate correlations were computed on an average of 185 cases. The factor analysis involves about five times as many cases as variables, which is usually considered satisfactory to yield stable factors.

The results are given in table 4-4. A distinct factor structure was found, best represented by a rotated three-factor solution accounting for 43% of the common variance of the individual scales. Applying the Scree-Test indicated that factor extraction should stop at three, since the rate of decrease in eigenvalues leveled off after that (Kim and Mueller 1978:44). In addition, factors beyond the third had only small loadings and thus were not

Table 4-4   Factor Analysis of Child Well-Being Scales—Factor Loadings for Terminal Solution (Intake Data, N = 240)

	Factor 1: Household Adequacy	Factor 2: Parental Disposition	Factor 3: Child Performance	Communality
Scales Assigned to Factors				
Nutrition/Diet	74*	16	−08	59
Clothing	71*	21	−03	52
Personal Hygiene	79*	06	12	64
Household Furnishings	74*	07	06	59
Overcrowding	60*	05	21	40
Household Sanitation	76*	16	08	58
Security of Residence	51*	−04	11	28
Availability of Utilities	58*	11	03	34
Physical Safety in Home	71*	41	03	52
Money Management	72*	31	−05	62
Mental Health Care	17	50*	19	32
Parental Capacity for Child Care	26	62*	10	46
Parental Recognition of Problems	22	58*	18	41
Parental Motivation to Solve Problems	35	65*	20	60
Parental Cooperation with Case Planning/Services	30	50*	12	36
Acceptance of/Affection for Children	11	50*	40	43
Approval of Children	09	64*	17	44
Expectations of Children	36	69*	17	63
Consistency of Discipline	23	50*	36	44
Teaching/Stimulating Children	52	56*	29	66
Protection from Abuse	23	69*	−04	53
Abusive Physical Discipline	05	57*	−09	34
Threat of Abuse	−11	54*	03	31
Children's Family Relations	05	57*	44	50
Adequacy of Education	33	02	55*	41
Academic Performance	09	04	66*	45
School Attendance	15	01	59*	37
Children's Misconduct	−24	42	63*	64
Scales Not Assigned				
Physical Health Care	44	16	08	22
Supervision of Children	41	40	31	43
Arrangement for Substitute Child Care	48	30	−05	32
Parental Relations	24	48	09	30

Table 4-4 (Continued)

	Factor 1: Household Adequacy	Factor 2: Parental Disposition	Factor 3: Child Performance	Communality
Scales Not Assigned				
Support for Principal Caretaker	29	09	19	13
Availability/Accessibility of Services	35	03	09	42
Deliberate Deprivation of Food/Water	12	16	18	33
Physical Confinement or Restriction	−03	49	−13	42
Deliberate "Locking-Out"	−09	22	18	26
Sexual Abuse	−06	16	−17	29
Economic Exploitation	16	33	−10	40
Coping Behavior of Children	−04	32	47	51
Children's Disabling Conditions	17	21	28	37
Eigenvalue	10.7	4.3	2.7	
% of Variance	26.2	10.4	6.5	

Notes:

Method used was principal factoring with varimax rotation.

Average number of cases used to compute correlations was 185.

Decimal points are omitted from table.

Eigenvalue and percentage of variance are for initial (unrotated) solution.

Asterisks (*) denote variables assigned to factors.

Some revisions were made to the scales after the analysis was conducted. Therefore some current scales relating to child supervision, continuity of parenting, and sexual abuse do not appear. See the text of this chapter for further details.

readily interpretable. A scale was assigned to a factor if its loading was at least .50 on that factor. This is a conservative criterion, since loadings of .30 to .40 are typically used in psychometric research. The three terminal factors are labeled Household Adequacy (HA), Parental Disposition (PD), and Child Performance (CP).

Household Adequacy, defined by 10 scales, appears to involve the most basic needs of daily life—food, shelter, clothing, and cleanliness. To find these aspects of a child's living situation associated is perhaps no surprise. The common link may be economic, perhaps insufficient family income, or noting that Money Management loads on this factor, poor use of available resources by parents.

The second factor, Parental Disposition, represents a somewhat more complex concept. It involves 14 scales measuring parental capacity for child care, interactions with the children, understanding of problems and motivation to solve them, and emotional care of the children. The common element may be attitudinal or dispositional—a positive force, concern, and self-control characterizing the parent in his or her relations with others.

Child Performance, the third factor, is defined by four scales, three measuring educational status and performance, and one measuring delinquent behavior. This factor seems to represent poor academic achievement accompanied by aggressive nonconformity.

In addition to helping understand what concepts the Child Well-Being Scales are measuring, the results of the factor analysis can also assist in developing reliable composite scoring procedures. This subject is discussed in the next chapter.

Notes

1. The term "scale" is used here, but this should not be taken to mean that the psychometric characteristics of the measures were already established. Doing so was the goal of the work described in this chapter.

2. Criterion-related and trait validity are defined in chapter 2.

3. The original scale Supervision of Children was subsequently replaced by two supervision scales, for younger and teenage children (see below).

4. An "ordinal scale" (or "ordinal level of measurement") means that the scale rank-orders cases on the attribute of interest; that is, we can say only that one score is higher than another, but not how much higher.

5. An "interval scale" (or "interval level of measurement") means that the relative distance between any two scores on the scale is known. Given a unit of measurement, we can say that the difference between two scores is x units, or that one difference is y times as large as another (Blalock 1972:18).

6. The rating format, and also the use of the term "welfare" instead of "well-being," follow Giovannoni and Bacerra's (1979) study of professional and community definitions of abuse and neglect. We originally hoped to be able to make some comparisons, but, unfortunately, substantial differences in the composition of the case vignettes between their study and ours make that very difficult.

7. A different rating format could have been devised to include them. This might have had some statistical advantage, though at the expense of increasing the number of vignettes requiring inclusion in the survey.

8. If this were not true, it might prevent pooling the different samples to derive a common scale of seriousness by the successive intervals method.

9. Examining the seriousness ratings of items as sequenced on the survey forms for patterns (for example, monotonicity, lag correlations) revealed no obvious sequencing effects in the data.

10. A more detailed statistical explanation of the method of successive intervals appears in Edwards (1982) and Torgerson (1958).

11. This result might have been avoided by modifying the random assignment of vignettes through quota assignments tied to scale levels.

12. It is termed "heuristic" because formally it is incorrect to compute averages of these rank-order ratings. But the procedure is convenient for this analysis, which aims only to identify grossly divergent patterns of responses.

13. The goodness-of-fit of the scaling model to the observed data (that is, the response distributions) can be assessed by comparing the theoretical cumulative response distributions derived from the scale values and interval widths with the observed cumulative distributions (Edwards 1982). Essentially, this means reversing the procedure used to compute the interval widths and scale values. The procedure involves subtracting the scale value of each vignette (in Z-units) from the cumulative interval width to obtain a matrix of theoretical normal deviates. The theoretical cumulative proportions corresponding to these theoretical normal deviates are then obtained by referring to a table of the normal curve. Subtracting the respective theoretical and observed cumulative proportions for each rating category, summing the absolute values of these differences, and dividing by the total number of differences summed, gives the desired goodness-of-fit measure. This absolute average deviation is .019, which is quite small and similar to results typically obtained in successive intervals scaling. This result increases our confidence that the set of assumptions underlying the successive intervals model has been met, though it is not a guarantee (Torgerson 1958:241–245). We have, however, already offered some more direct evidence in the preceding section that several individual assumptions required by the method of successive intervals have been met.

14. Revisions were made in the following scales: Personal Hygiene, Household Sanitation, Availability of Utilities, Mental Health Care, Supervision of Children, Arrangements for Substitute Child

Care, Parental Recognition of Problems, Availability/Accessibility of Services, Sexual Abuse, Academic Performance, School Attendance.

15. Construct validity involves examining correlations between the measure of the construct of interest and measures of other constructs that would be expected to relate to it, if it were measuring the intended concept.

16. The average level of intervention recommended for each case situation, though of interest for other purposes, is not at issue here.

17. It would be incorrect, however, to say that a score of 20 is half as desirable (or twice as serious) as a score of 40. This would imply that the seriousness scale has a "rational zero" and that therefore scores on the scale could be validly divided. This is not true; zero on the present scale is a relative, not an absolute, reference point for the attribute of seriousness.

18. The scale distributions are skewed. Normality is not a required assumption for the factor analysis model, however, although it is for certain associated significance tests (O'Muircheartaigh and Payne 1977:92).

5

Reliability of the
Child Well-Being Scales

Introduction

Reliability refers to whether a measure gives accurate and consistent results under a variety of different circumstances. The following types of reliability were assessed for the Child Well-Being Scales:

- Stability
- Inter-rater agreement
- Alternate forms equivalence
- Internal consistency

In addition, confidence intervals were computed where appropriate.
Reliability was determined for:

- Individual scale ratings
- Individual scale seriousness scores
- Composite seriousness scores
- Difference scores for independent composites
- Change scores for composites

Not all types of reliability could be determined for each type of score, however.

The version of the Child Well-Being Scales used is that prior to final revisions based on successive intervals analysis as described in chapter 4. The great majority of scales remained unchanged, so that as a practical matter the reliability results can be considered indicative of the current instrument's psychometric characteristics.

The reliability statistics are offered not only to support the credibility of the scales, but also as a means for statistically adjusting research results to take measurement unreliability into account. The analysis assumes that the validity of the scales—that they are measuring what is intended—has already been satisfactorily demonstrated (see chapter 4).

Reliability of Ratings for Individual Scales

This section considers the reliability of the ratings made by social workers on the individual Child Well-Being Scales. The reliability of the seriousness scores assigned to those ratings is considered in the subsequent section.

Stability of Classification

The stability of the child well-being ratings (classifications) made by workers was determined by comparing the results of repeated completions of the scales on a set of families. This technique addresses what is often termed "test-retest" reliability. An additional objective was to compare the effects of both different cases and different workers on the stability of classification. A fully crossed design with two replications would have been desirable for this (Namboodiri et al. 1975:330). This would have entailed repeated measurements by staff on several of their own cases as well as on the cases of other staff members. The second condition was impossible to meet because only one worker is assigned to and familiar with a family at any given time. With some effort it was possible, however, to set up a simpler nested design with individual workers performing repeated measurements on between two and 10 of their own cases.

Description of Repeated Measures Data

The repeated measures data set consists of 86 families for whom the Child Well-Being Scales were completed twice by the same worker at a 2-week interval. The cases for repeated measurement were obtained from two source samples. Thirty-five families came from cases open 5 to 6 months at three agencies (Texas, Hennepin, and Dade), and 51 from two intensive services projects at Spence-Chapin and the Foundling Hospital in New York. All families had at least one child residing at home. The forms were completed by six workers from the public and seven from the voluntary agencies. The two voluntary agency projects participated only in the repeated measures study, so that we were able to arrange a larger number of repeat forms than proved possible at the public agencies. The 51 cases represent the majority of the families in the two projects.

The repeated measures cases were not randomly chosen; inclusion depended primarily on the willingness of the individual staff members to complete repeat forms on as many cases as time permitted. The table in the appendix indicates, however, that the demographic characteristics of the repeated measures families and the more representatively selected intake families are similar, except on ethnicity, where the proportion of white mothers was less for the former.

Results of Analysis

Agreement between the two sets of ratings on a given scale is measured by Cohen's kappa (K) (Light 1975). Kappa takes a value of 0 when the observed agreement is equal to the agreement expected by chance, and a maximum value of 1 when complete agreement exists. Chance agreement is defined as the proportion of identical responses expected even when the two response distributions are statistically independent (uncorrelated). Thus kappa is a more conservative method of reporting agreement than simply computing the proportion of all responses that are identical at the two completion times.

The results are given in table 5-1. The first column shows the number of cases entering each computation. A case was included only if the given scale was assessed on both occasions (that is, "unknown" and "not applicable" were excluded). For scales rated on individual children, each child is treated as a separate case, so that the number of cases in these computations may exceed 86. The values of kappa are moderately high, ranging from a low of .37 (Consistency of Discipline) to a high of .83 (Physical Safety in Home). The mean value of kappa taken over all scales is .65, with a standard deviation of .12.

It is also possible to examine whether the degree of response agreement depends on the *initial* rating of a case. Kappa may be modified to give a measure of conditional agreement (Light 1975). When the initial rating was "1" ("adequate"), the mean amount of agreement between the first and second ratings taken over all indices was $K_1 = .76$. When the initial rating was "2" or more, indicating some level of problem, the result was $K_2 = .57$. This result suggests that ratings of adequacy are being slightly more reliably measured than ratings of problems on these scales. Possibly workers are more confident about the absence or presence of a problem than they are about the specific level of an identified problem.[1]

Worker Effect on Stability of Classification

Since most workers in the repeated measures data set completed schedules on more than one case, it is possible to determine whether the identity of the worker affects reliability for the child well-being ratings. An average kappa was computed over all child well-being ratings for an individual family in the data set. An intraclass correlation (r_c) was then computed between the individual workers as "classes" and these kappas for each case. The analysis compares the similarity of the kappas among workers relative to the total observed variability of kappa (Namboodiri et al. 1975).

The results are presented in table 5-2. Only workers with four or more cases are represented, in order to obtain reasonably stable mean kappa values. The intraclass correlation is essentially zero, indicating there is no relationship between the identities of individual workers and the stability of classification on the Child Well-Being Scales.

The number of child well-being schedules completed by an individual worker was uncorrelated with kappa. Of course, the maximum number of cases per worker in this sample was 10, so that we do not know how experience with a large: number of cases might affect

Table 5-1 Stability of Individual Child Well-Being Scales
(Repeated Measures Data)

Scale Name	No. of Cases[a]	Kappa	Intraclass Correlation	Standard Error
Physical Health Care	85	.79	.79	8.5
Nutrition/Diet	83	.67	.83	5.6
Clothing	85	.72	.88	4.6
Personal Hygiene	84	.81	.87	5.5
Household Furnishings	71	.76	.90	4.5
Overcrowding	81	.79	.87	5.8
Household Sanitation	71	.59	.72	9.7
Security of Residence	83	.68	.91	2.0
Availability of Utilities	82	.81	.84	7.9
Physical Safety in Home	69	.83	.94	7.0
Mental Health Care	78	.49	.61	16.0
Supervision of Children	80	.70	.81	11.4
Arrangements for Substitute Child Care	83	.71	.78	8.1
Money Management	82	.76	.92	4.3
Parental Capacity for Child Care	86	.82	.88	7.8
Parental Relations	25	.53	.72	10.3
Parental Recognition of Problems	85	.62	.70	12.5
Parental Motivation to Solve Problems	84	.54	.64	11.6
Parental Cooperation with Case Planning/Services	82	.75	.87	7.7
Support for Principal Caretaker	85	.62	.71	5.9
Availability/Accessibility of Services	85	.68	.77	6.9
Acceptance of/Affection for Children	81	.61	.81	10.3
Approval of Children	72	.65	.76	5.4
Expectations of Children	84	.61	.78	6.8
Consistency of Discipline	74	.37	.62	7.6
Teaching/Stimulating Children	80	.71	.78	6.3
Abusive Physical Discipline	177	.41	.74	9.6
Deliberate Deprivation of Food/Water	174	.62	.49	4.9
Physical Confinement or Restriction	169	.57	•	•
Deliberate "Locking-Out"	163	.85	.66	4.5
Sexual Abuse	179	•	•	•
Threat of Abuse	175	.57	.70	11.0
Economic Exploitation	147	•	•	•
Protection from Abuse	4	•	•	•
Adequacy of Education	135	.55	.70	8.7
Academic Performance	125	.42	.64	7.6
School Attendance	131	.70	.73	8.7
Children's Family Relations	165	.56	.84	7.4
Children's Misconduct	162	.57	.68	11.4
Coping Behavior of Children	162	.58	.75	8.0
Children's Disabling Conditions	175	.62	.64	10.2
Mean		.65	.75	
Standard Deviation		.12	.15	
Minimum		.37	.49	
Maximum		.85	.94	

•Too little variance in responses at both completions did not allow computation of stable statistics.

[a] The number of cases for the child-specific scales, beginning with Abusive Physical Discipline, is the total number of children rated.

Note: Some revisions were made to the Child Well-Being Scales after this analysis was conducted. Therefore some current scales relating to child supervision, continuity of parenting, and sexual abuse do not appear. See chapter 4 for further details.

Table 5-2   Social Worker Effect on Stability of Classification
(Repeated Measures Data)

					Worker No.				
	1	2	3	4	5	6	7	8	9
No. of Cases	10	10	8	8	7	4	4	4	4
Mean Kappa	.64	.72	.67	.66	.61	.70	.81	.74	.59
SD of Kappa	.12	.08	.09	.04	.12	.08	.02	.04	.14
Intraclass correlation = .04									

reliability. Normally, additional practice leads to higher reliability on standardized instruments; however, carelessness could set in too and reduce reliability. Reliability on the scales when used as a routine assessment or evaluation tool might depend as much on the agency context and the attitudes of staff members towards the process as on the inherent characteristics of the instrument.

As usual for repeat measurements, the amount of time between repeated completions of the scales affected stability. Kappa coefficients were somewhat higher when time between completions was less (Pearson $r = -.26$). This correlation is not high enough to cause problems in interpreting the repeated measures results.

Inter-Rater Agreement on Classification

Inter-rater reliability considers the degree to which different raters using the same instrument at the same time obtain equivalent results. Essentially this assesses differences due to variation in the administration method of an instrument.

For this analysis, the Child Well-Being Scales were completed for 32 families, both by their workers and their workers' supervisors. The families were obtained from the population of cases open 5 to 6 months at three public agencies (Texas, Hennepin, and Dade). The families are not a random sample since completion of duplicate schedules depended on the availability of supervisor time.

Using workers and their supervisors for assessing inter-rater reliability has limitations, because the pairs of ratings cannot be considered entirely independent. The supervisors for the most part were relying not on independent observations of the families, but rather on information communicated by the workers through case records and case conferences. Nevertheless it seems useful to compare worker and supervisor ratings, if only to determine whether their shared information about a family can be translated into consistent responses on the Child Well-Being Scales.

Response agreement was measured again by kappa. Because of the limited sample size, responses on all scales were combined to yield an overall coefficient. The result was $K = .60$, a moderately high level of agreement. The conditional coefficients were dissimilar. K_1, signifying the degree of worker/supervisor agreement when caseworkers gave a rating of "1" ("adequate"), was .85. K_2, signifying the degree of agreement when workers gave a rating of "2" or greater (below adequate), was .55. This result may be due to disagreements about what constitutes a problem, but it may also represent the presumably lesser knowledge supervisors have about problems in individual families.

Alternate Forms Equivalence

Another type of reliability for the Child Well-Being Scales can be examined by making comparisons with information contained in agency case records. These comparisons may be thought of as a test of "alternate forms equivalence." Child well-being ratings are a structured method of recording problem information, while case record narratives are a relatively unstructured alternative method; results using the two methods should be reasonably consistent.[2]

Paired child well-being schedules (completed at intake) and case record intake studies were compared for 48 families. The same worker usually completed both. This information was a convenience sample obtained from the Texas and Baltimore County agencies.

To make the comparisons, the case record intakes were coded by the authors using Child Well-Being Scale categories. It was determined that the case records had insufficient detail to allow reliable coding of severity levels for each problem (scale) type. Consequently, the records were coded as either "some stated problem" or "no stated problem" for each Child Well-Being Scale. One difficulty in interpreting the case records was that, when no problem in a given area was stated, it was unclear whether the caseworker had ruled out that problem, or whether the intake studies were simply incomplete for some reason (for example, lack of time, space, attention, perceived importance). This is why the term "no stated problem" is used. This ambiguity could depress the coefficients of equivalence.

The reliability of the authors' coding of the intake studies themselves was not examined. This coding, however, was done "blind"; the child well-being schedules were not inspected prior to the coding.

The number of cases was too small to permit reliability analysis for individual scales, so only the average results for all scales are presented. Kappa was used as the measure of agreement on problem ratings.

The results were: $K = .72$; $K_1 = .66$, $K_2 = .82$. The conditional coefficient K_1 measures the degree of agreement between the Child Well-Being Scales and the case records, given a rating of adequate ("no problem") on the scales. Similarly, K_2 measures this degree of agreement, given a below-adequate rating ("some problem") on the scales. The fact that K_1 is substantially lower than K_2 is probably attributable to the ambiguity referred to above; that is, the unclear meaning of not finding a given problem stated in the case record. Overall, the analysis does seem to support the reliability of the Child Well-Being Scales; problems as stated in the records are generally consistent with those rated on the scales.

Reliability of Seriousness Scores for Individual Scales

Stability of Scale Scores

The analysis of reliability can be extended by observing that not all disagreements on ratings are equally important. The results of the successive intervals scaling show that some adjacent scale levels are much closer in perceived seriousness than are others. For instance, on Acceptance of/Affection for Children, ratings of 1 and 2 constitute greater disagreement than rankings of 3 and 4. The seriousness score difference between levels 1 and 2 is 30, but between levels 3 and 4 is only 10 (refer to table 3-1).

The intraclass correlation coefficient (r_c) can be used as a measure of response agreement that takes into account the differences in seriousness scores between scale levels. To do this the scale levels were assigned the seriousness scores derived through the successive intervals analysis. (For the scales scored on individual children, an average was computed for the family.) The intraclass correlation is essentially a product-moment correlation within classes of a categorized variable. In computing r_c here, the "classes" are defined as the individual families, and the entries are the two seriousness scores from repeated measurement. The repeated measurement data were used. The possible values of r_c for this design range between 1 (highest agreement) to -1 (lowest agreement). In this analysis, the intraclass correlation is directly comparable to kappa, since $r_c = 0$ means that the observed agreement on paired seriousness scores is equal to that expected when the classes are independent of (uncorrelated with) the scores (Fleiss and Cohen 1973).[3]

As shown in table 5-1, the values of r_c for the seriousness scores are generally higher than the values of kappa for the corresponding ratings. This results from taking into account the magnitude of disagreement between responses as represented by differences in seriousness scores. For example, on Acceptance of/Affection for Children, r_c (.81) is considerably higher than kappa (.61). This reflects the fact that most of the disagreements were between the lower two levels of the scale, whose seriousness scores are fairly similar. Disagreements here do little damage to scale reliability as measured by r_c, since their effect on scoring is relatively small. The mean intraclass correlation over all scales was .75.

For the scales scored on individual children, using an average score for the family might mask changes in the scoring of individuals, despite the average score remaining stable. Computing a weighted intraclass correlation based on paired measurements for individual children, however, yielded statistics virtually identical to those using the average scores. Thus, for the sake of convenience, average family scores are used for these scales hereafter.

Confidence Intervals for Individual Scales

In using the Child Well-Being Scales to assess the problems of individual families, it is important to know the confidence that can be placed in any family's obtained (that is, observed) score. Specifically, how far is any given family's obtained score from the "true" score expected under perfectly reliable measurement? The precision of measurement for any observation is given by the standard error of measurement, which depends both on the reliability of a scale and on the observed dispersion of scale scores.[4] The standard error can be used to place statistical confidence intervals around individual obtained sources.

Standard errors were computed for each scale from the repeated measures data (refer to table 5-1). The intraclass correlation (r_c) instead of the usual Pearson correlation (r) served as the reliability estimate in the calculation. Because r_c takes into account any differences in means as well as in the ordering of scores between repeated measurements, it is a more conservative estimate of reliability than r.[5] These standard errors were than used to compute confidence intervals for the Child Well-Being Scale scores obtained for the intake cases, which data were previously described (chapter 4). This illustrates how potential users would calculate confidence intervals for their own data.

The standard error of measurement is normally assumed to be a fixed characteristic of an instrument, whereas the standard deviation and reliability of obtained scores vary from one sample to the next (Nunnally 1978:241). This assumption is usually justified unless the scale means are very different between samples. To justify generalizing the standard errors, individual Child Well-Being Scale means were compared for the repeated measures data and the intake data. Scale-by-scale inspection showed no large differences. Thus it was considered satisfactory to apply the standard error estimates from the repeated measures data to the intake data.

Because confidence intervals based on the standard error are centered on estimated true scores, not obtained scores, estimated true scores must first be calculated for each intake case. This calculation involved computing scale reliabilities for the intake data and then using these reliabilities to adjust the obtained scores for regression to the mean, yielding expected true scores.[6]

Ninety-five percent confidence intervals (which range from $+2$ to -2 standard errors from the true score) were computed for each family on each scale. The "95% confidence interval" is interpreted to mean that, if the measurement were repeated a large number of times, 95% of the intervals computed would contain the actual (not estimated) true score. The confidence intervals are symmetric around the estimated true score, but asymmetric around the obtained score. For example, obtained scores below the scale mean are always systematically biased downward; thus the confidence interval around such obtained scores extends farther upward than downward. The opposite is true for obtained scores above the scale.

Reliabilities and 95% confidence intervals around obtained scores for individual Child Well-Being Scales are given in table 5-3.[7,8] On the unitary (single rating) scales, the possible obtained scores are simply the values of the scale anchor points. On the scales averaged for children, each of which can range from 0 to 100, confidence intervals were computed for several illustrative locations on each scale: 100, 75, 50, 25. Note that the asymmetry of the confidence intervals increases as scale scores become lower, because unreliability always biases lower values increasingly downward.

The results indicate that, for the unitary scales, the 95% confidence interval for a given scale level often includes at least the next *higher* scale level, but the 95% interval only rarely includes the next *lower* scale level. On the averaged scales, which have a more continuous range of scores, the 95% confidence intervals span roughly one-third of the possible range.

Standards of Reliability

What are the implications of the reliability analysis for assessing individual families? Generally, a family's score on one of these scales cannot be considered an "exact" measurement, because there is a greater than negligible chance that a repeat measurement would yield a different result, usually a higher scale score. Clearly, no assessment of, or decision about, an individual family should be predicated solely on the basis of one of these individual scale scores. Nunnally (1978:246) believes that reliability of .90 is the minimum tolerable, and .95 the standard desirable, when important decisions about individuals are to be made on the basis of test scores. Reliabilities of the individual Child Well-Being Scales, though quite high for what are in essence individual items on an instrument, are generally lower than this. Individual scales, however, can help identify a family's probable range of seriousness scores for specific problem areas, or can help rule out a variety of specific problems as a focus of casework.

Rarely do individual items on a social measurement instrument have reliabilities high enough to warrant inferences being made about single cases. Fortunately, less stringent standards of reliability may be applied to instruments used in the analysis of aggregate data

Table 5-3   95% Confidence Intervals for Individual Child Well-Being Scales

Scale Name	Level of Scale					
	1	2	3	4	5	6
Physical Health Care	100→82	99←81→66	70←44→36	52←22		
Nutrition/Diet	100→88	85←71→63	67←50→44	50←32→28	41←22→19	29←9
Clothing	100→90	96←83→78	89←74→71	69←46→46		
Personal Hygiene	100→88	95←82→71	72←53→50	60←39→37	49←31	
Household Furnishings	100→90	98←88→81	78←64→60	69←54		
Overcrowding	100→87	97←82→74	81←62→58	72←51		
Household Sanitation	100→78	92←71→58	73←38→35	59←21→19	57←18	
Security of Residence	100→98	98←94→90	78←71→70	70←64		
Physical Safety in Home	100→85	74←44→36	52←31→25	47←25→19	43←20	
Money Management	100→91	99←90→82	78←66→61	65←52		
Parental Capacity for Child Care	100→83	81←63→50	67←48→36	36←13		
Parental Motivation to Solve Problems	100→71	96←70→50	90←62→44	83←50→36	70←31	
Parental Cooperation with Case Planning/Services	100→82	78←59→47	74←54→43	67←46		
Support for Principal Caretaker	100→87	100←96→84	98←85→75	89←73→66	83←67→60	75←56
Acceptance of/Affection for Children	100→76	94←70→53	75←45→34	67←35		
Approval of Children	100→87	90←78→69	86←72→64	78←63		
Expectations of Children	100→84	95←80→68	83←65→56	68←47		
Consistency of Discipline·	100→82	100←85→70	89←70→59	76←53		
Teaching/Stimulating Children	100→85	97←84→72	86←70→61	62←41		
Abusive Physical Discipline	100→79	91←75→53	73←50→35	48←25		
Deliberate Deprivation of Food/Water	100→90	91←75→71	72←50→50	53←25		
Deliberate Locking-Out	100→90	89←75→71	66←50→48	44←25		
Threat of Abuse	100→75	100←75→58	89←50→45	74←25		
Adequacy of Education	100→81	97←75→63	85←50→49	·		
Academic Performance	100→80	99←75→69	84←50→50	·		
School Attendance	100→81	97←75→63	78←50→43	·		
Children's Family Relations	100→83	92←75→63	72←50→43	·		
Children's Misconduct	100→73	99←75→54	80←50→36	60←25		
Coping Behavior of Children	100→81	91←75→59	72←50→40	·		
Children's Disabling Conditions	100→76	96←75→55	91←50→50	·		

·Base of scale is larger than 25.

Note: Some Child Well-Being Scales do not appear in the table (cf. note 8).

(grouped cases). Program evaluation deals mainly with scores for groups of clients and with comparisons among groups. Reliability of .50 has been considered acceptable for such studies (Helmstadter 1964), and reliability of .80 is usually considered excellent. Problems posed by measurement unreliability in applied research, and methods of dealing with them, are discussed in a later section. The point made here is that the reliabilities of the individual Child Well-Being Scales seem quite satisfactory for program evaluation purposes.

It would also be possible to compute reliabilities and confidence intervals for change scores on each scale, for example, for changes between intake and follow-up scores. The reliability of a change score, however, depends on, and is generally lower than, the averaged reliability of the scores entering the difference (Nunnally 1978:248–249). Since the individ-

**Table 5-4   Correlations Between Composite Scales
(Intake Data)**

	CWBS	HA	PD
Child Well-Being Score (CWBS)	1.00		
Household Adequacy (HA)	.70	1.00	
Parental Disposition (PD)	.88	.42	1.00
Child Performance (CP)	.46	.09	.31

ual scales are not entirely precise even for single observations, use of change scores to assess individual families on individual scales is not the best approach to take, given the stringent standards of confidence being recommended.

The next step examines how composite measures might be formed from the individual Child Well-Being Scales and how to determine the reliabilities of such composite scales. If the reliabilities are high enough, then the composites may be used to track case change for individual clients. The total Child Well-Being Score, computed by averaging all individual scale scores, is one such composite measure already described (chapter 4).

Reliability of Composite Scales

Description and Intercorrelations of Composite Scales

The results of the factor analysis reported in chapter 4 can be used as a basis for data reduction, specifically, to construct additional composite scales useful in summarizing the child well-being data. The advantage of a factor scale is that it is usually more reliable than an arbitrarily formed composite of identical item length.[9] This fact is due to the higher average inter-item correlation and (when used) to the differential item weighting of factor scales.

Three factor-based scales were created from the individual scales that were found to load on the respective factors (see chapter 4). These scales are termed Household Adequacy (HA), Parental Disposition (PD), and Child Performance (CP). The term "factor-based" indicates that the individual scales were equally weighted in computing the sum. It was decided to ignore the observed differential factor loadings among the scales assigned to each factor, since it is unlikely that these loadings could be exactly replicated. One reason is that several of the individual scales underwent revision subsequent to this analysis. In addition, sampling errors, possible nonrandom measurement error, and possible minor factors not extracted in the analysis always affect the observed pattern of factor loadings. A conservative stance in exploratory factor analysis, therefore, is to ignore differential loadings (Kim and Mueller 1978).

The construction of the Child Well-Being Score (CWBS), a composite of all individual scales, was described in chapter 4.

The correlations among the composite scales is given in table 5-4. There are moderate correlations between HA and PD and between PD and CP; HA and CP are essentially uncorrelated. Both HA and PD are highly correlated with the CWBS. In fact, PD and CWBS are close to being redundant, with 77% common variance, despite the fact that PD incorpo-

Table 5-5   Internal Consistency of Composite Scales
(Intake Data)

	No. of Individual Scales	Mean	Standard Deviation	Mean Inter-Item Correlation	Internal Consistency (Alpha)
Child Well-Being Score (CWBS)	41	82.5	14.8	.18	.89
Household Adequacy (HA)	10	91.4	15.5	.44	.88
Parental Disposition (PD)	14	72.8	22.7	.33	.86
Child Performance (CP)	4	81.2	23.1	.29	.53

rates only 34% of the individual scales. A partial explanation of this may be that the 14 PD-loading scales tend to have considerably larger score dispersions than the other scales. Consequently, a disproportionate amount of the variance in the CWBS is being contributed by these 14 scales, leading to the observed high correlation between PD and CWBS.

Internal Consistency of Composite Scales

Reliability of the factor-based scores is measured by Cronbach's alpha, an internal consistency coefficient. Internal consistency is appropriate here because the individual scales assigned to a factor may be considered as multiple measures of a higher-order construct. Although the CWBS is not being conceptualized as a unidimensional measure, internal consistency is computed anyway, strictly for comparative purposes. The results are presented in table 5-5.

The major factors, Household Adequacy and Parental Disposition, have coefficients above .80. Child Performance is considerably less reliable (.53), which may be due to the smaller number of individual scales defining this factor. The mean inter-item correlation for CP is only slightly less than that for PD, but the latter has 14 constituent scales. Scale reliability of .50 has been suggested as the minimum necessary when data are to be grouped (Helmstadter 1964). Using this criterion, all three factor-based scores may be considered useful for program evaluation work.

Stability and Inter-Rater Reliability

Stability estimates can be made from the repeated measures data for the CWBS and the three factor-based scales. The results are given in table 5-6. The stability estimate for the CWBS ($r_c = .96$) is high enough to suggest its potential usefulness in assessing individual families. The factor-based scales HA ($r_c = .82$) and PD ($r_c = .92$) are each more stable than the average individual scale (refer to table 5-1). CP, however, does not improve on the stability of the average individual scale.

Inter-rater reliability of the CWBS and factor-based scales was calculated for the Worker/Supervisor data. The results were (r_c): CWBS (.85), PD (.79), HA (.94), and CP (.48). Except for HA, these coefficients are less than those for stability. The coefficient for CP is rather low, but otherwise the analysis supports the adequate reliability of the composite scales.

Table 5-6   Stability of Composite Scales
(Repeated Measures Data)

	Mean[*]	Standard Deviation[*]	Intraclass Correlation	Standard Error
Child Well-Being Score (CWBS)	79.9	12.0	.96	2.5
Household Adequacy (HA)	84.9	14.1	.82	5.9
Parental Disposition (PD)	69.7	17.9	.92	5.0
Child Performance (CP)	79.5	21.6	.71	11.5

[*]Mean and standard deviation are for first completion of the instrument.

Confidence Intervals for Composite Scales

As in the case of the individual scales, the standard errors of the composite scales can be estimated from their reliabilities and can then be used to place confidence intervals around obtained composite scores. To do this for the intake data we have available two estimates of reliability for the factor-based scales—internal consistency coefficients from the factor analysis of the intake data and stability coefficients from the repeated measures data. (For the CWBS, internal consistency has no psychometric rationale, and thus the stability coefficient must be preferred.)

Which reliability estimates for the factor-based scales should be used? Short-term stability coefficients have the advantage of avoiding "shared irrelevance" (correlated errors) that may occur at a single completion of an instrument (Cronbach and Furby 1970). In our case, the advantage of using the stability coefficients for the factor-based scales is less clear, since they are not entirely derived from the same cases to which they would be applied, whereas the internal consistency coefficients are. Actually, the choice matters little for HA and PD, since the alternative estimates of reliability are similar. There may be some advantage in using the same type of reliability coefficient derived in the same manner for all individual and composite scales. Thus, the stability coefficients from the repeated measures data were chosen to serve as the reliability estimates for the computation of confidence intervals.

This decision seems reasonable except for CP. Here there is a considerable discrepancy between the two reliability estimates, and in an unexpected direction, since internal consistency is usually considered an upper bound for reliability. The result may be partly due to the necessity of pairwise deletion to handle missing data in computing the coefficients. In any event, the stability coefficient is also used for CP for the sake of uniformity.[10]

Ninety-five percent confidence intervals for the four composite scales are given in table 5-7. The intervals are drawn around four illustrative obtained scores: 100, 80, 60, 40. Again, expected true scores were calculated for each obtained score to serve as the midpoint of each confidence interval. The CWBS clearly gives the most precise measurement of a family's status at a given point in time. It is evident that even very high reliability cannot yield highly precise measurement for individual cases if the dispersion of scores within the reliability sample is relatively large. (Of course, with less score dispersion a high reliability may not be attainable.) Nevertheless, the level of precision achieved by the CWBS compares favorably with the best standardized instruments in other fields, such as individual psychological testing.

Table 5-7 95% Confidence Intervals for Composite Scales
(Intake Data)

		Illustrative Intervals		
Child Well-Being Score (CWBS)	100→94	85←80→75	66←60→56	46←40→36
Household Adequacy (HA)	100→87	94←80→70	77←60→44	56←40→32
Parental Disposition (PD)	100→89	90←80→70	71←60→51	52←40→32
Child Performance (CP)	100→72	100←80→57	88←60→42	73←40→27

Note: Reliabilities for the intake data derived from standard errors for the Repeated Measures data (refer to table 5-6) are: CWBS (.97), HA (.85), PD (.95), CP (.75).

Confidence Intervals for Differences of Composites (Independent Cases)

In addition to the confidence that can be placed in any individual family's composite score, it can be useful to know the confidence one can place in the observed *difference* of composite scores between two separate families. In particular, how close can two observed scores be before one should conclude that there probably is no *actual* difference between the families on the given scale? The size of the confidence interval for independent (uncorrelated) scores on a scale is determined by the standard error of the differences between such scores.[11] The smallest observed difference whose 95% confidence interval does *not* include the value of zero is then defined as the smallest discriminable difference between two scores on the scale. As before, the confidence interval is centered on the expected true difference score (note 6), since obtained differences above an assumed mean difference of zero are biased upward by measurement error, and obtained differences below zero are biased downward.

The result of the calculations is given in table 5-8. (Standard deviations from the intake data were used to compute the standard errors.) On the CWBS, families differing by at least 7.2 points may be considered as being actually different on the scale, at 95% confidence. The other "smallest significant differences" are interpreted similarly.

Note that these results differ from those that would have been (wrongly) inferred by inspecting the "overlap" in the confidence intervals for individual scores (table 5-7.) The HA and PD scales are moderately discriminating within their 100-point ranges, but the best CP can do is to discriminate scores in the top half vs. the bottom half of the scale. These results are useful for answering any questions about whether a given family's problems are more or less severe than another's; this can assist in such tasks as "balancing" caseloads when families are assigned to staff.

Reliability of Changes Over Time for Composite Scales

Description of Follow-up Sample

Change scores are the basis of outcome measurement on the Child Well-Being Scales. To assess change score reliability, the intake sample families (described in chapter 4) were

**Table 5-8   Smallest Significant Difference at 95% Confidence for
Independent (Uncorrelated) Scores on Composite Scales
(Intake Data)**

	Reliability (Uncorrelated Differences)	Standard Error (Uncorrelated Differences)	Smallest Significant Difference (95% Confidence)
Child Well-Being Score (CWBS)	.97	3.5	± 7.2
Household Adequacy (HA)	.85	8.3	±19.5
Parental Disposition (PD)	.95	7.1	±14.9
Child Performance (CP)	.75	16.1	±42.9

followed up an average of 5 to 6 months from the date of agency referral. Linear change scores for the composite scales were formed by subtracting intake scores from follow-up scores for each case. Thus positive change scores indicate improvement, negative scores deterioration. Table 5-9 gives the means and standard deviations of the change score distributions for each composite scale.

Sample attrition could affect the generalizability of the subsequent reliability analysis. Fortunately, it was possible to obtain follow-up information on 80% of the families in the intake sample. Demographic comparison of families followed up with those not followed up shows the groups to be similar (see appendix). The total Child Well-Being Scores at intake were also similar for the cases followed up vs. those not followed up (83 vs. 78, respectively).* Consequently, the change score distribution for the study is probably free of any substantial nonresponse bias.

Confidence Intervals for Change Scores

The reliabilities of the change scores for the composite scales can be computed from the reliabilities of the respective composite scores at intake and follow-up and from their variances and covariances.[12] The standard error of each change score can then be calculated (see note 4). Both of these statistics are presented in table 5-9.

Change scores for CWBS and PD have excellent reliability, though lower than the reliabilities for the respective single measures. (This is generally the case for dependent or correlated data.) Consequently, the standard errors of the change scores are relatively small in comparison with their standard deviations, which is desirable. The composite scales HA and CP are much less adequate in this respect. One can conclude that CWBS and PD may be useful in assessing changes on a case-by-case basis, whereas HA and CP should only be used with aggregate (grouped) data.

These statistics may be used to compute confidence intervals for obtained change scores and to draw some conclusions about true changes for cases in the intake sample. Of greatest interest is the determination of the upper and lower 95% confidence limits for obtained change scores of zero. Cases falling above or below these limits may be considered as actually having changed positively or negatively, respectively.[13]

The last part of table 5-9 indicates the result of this analysis of change. On the CWBS,

*However, the difference is statistically significant ($p<.05$, two-tailed test).

Table 5-9 Reliability and Confidence Intervals for Change Scores for Composite Scales (Intake/Follow-up Data)

		Change Scores			95% Confidence Interval for "No Change"		Results	
	Total No. of Cases	Mean	SD	R	SE	Upper Limit	Lower Limit	% Positive Change	% Negative Change
Child Well-Being Score	192	4.4	12.8	.94	3.0	6.3	− 5.7	44.6	20.7
Household Adequacy	189	4.6	11.1	.70	6.1	13.6	− 10.8	34.9	0
Parental Disposition	192	3.9	21.6	.91	6.6	13.6	− 12.9	38.1	27.0
Child Performance	182	8.2	21.1	.56	13.9	31.5	− 24.3	23.1	0

45% of the sample display reliable positive change, while 21% display deterioration. Our best estimate for the remaining 34% of families is that no overall change occurred. The factor-based scales help to provide some idea of how changes were distributed among different dimensions of child well-being. Reliable changes on Household Adequacy and Child Performance were uniformly positive, while on Parental Disposition more than 25% of the families show negative change. (Since HA and CP are not extremely reliable, relatively small but perhaps frequent negative changes are doubtless difficult to detect.)

The analysis has focused on the null hypothesis of "no change," but analogous computations may be made to determine reliable, specific degrees of change for this sample. To make this worthwhile, however, some standards of desirable or expected amount of change should be established or derived. One way to derive such standards empirically would be to examine the change scores of cases eligible for closure or of cases otherwise considered successful by agencies using an independent criterion.

Ceiling Effects—Change Scores

The possibility of "ceiling" or "floor" effect (a type of instrumentation effect) must be considered in analyzing and interpreting the change scores. A ceiling (or floor) effect occurs when a measurement instrument is unable to register scores above (or below) a certain limit (Huitema 1980: 345–346); in this case, possible amounts of obtained change are constrained by the defined upper and lower boundaries of the scales (100 and 0). For example, a family scoring 85 at intake can change positively no more than 15 units and negatively no more than 85 units. As a practical matter, only ceiling effects need be discussed, since a family's composite scores are unlikely to be so low that a floor effect would occur.

Failing to consider ceiling effects can adversely affect the interpretation of evaluation results. For instance, consider two service programs being compared; the average pre-service CWBS of families in the first is 80, in the second, 90. Suppose that all clients attain scores of 100 at follow-up. The average change score for the first program would be about 20, for the second about 10. It would be misleading to conclude that the first program is "more effective" than the second; the most that can be said is that each program achieved the maximum possible gain for its clients.

Ceiling effects can be taken into account by restricting comparisons to groups of clients at similar pre-service score levels, or groups of clients for whom total possible change, summed over all clients in the group, is the same. The best approach to take will depend on the particular problem at hand.

The possibility of a ceiling effect does not mean that it will be very frequent or important. For the intake cases, only 8% ($N = 15$) of the families with follow-up data obtained their maximum possible CWBS change score. (Users of the scales should determine the apparent amount of ceiling effect in their own evaluations and consider whether compensation for it is required.)

Reliability Considerations in Analyzing Grouped Scores

Until now the discussion of reliability has been limited to determining errors in measurement on the Child Well-Being Scales for *individual* cases (families). Criteria were developed for interpreting a family's score at a single point in time, for comparing scores of two different families, and for comparing the scores of the same family between two points in time (change scores). The results may be applied directly to assessing the status and progress of individual families in "single-subject" evaluations, which are becoming frequent in social work (Kratochwill 1978; Reid and Smith 1981: chapter 5). Program evaluation, in contrast, usually deals with scores for groups of clients and with comparisons between groups. What are the implications of the preceding reliability findings for the analysis of grouped data?

Unreliability, in the sense of random measurement error, can affect the magnitudes of observed correlations, decisions in inferential statistics, and estimation of treatment (program) effects in nonequivalent group designs. Each issue will be briefly considered in turn as it applies to the Child Well-Being Scales.

Random measurement error in variables tends to reduce the correlations observed between them. Using reliability theory it is possible to predict the amount of that reduction, which forms the basis of the "correction for attenuation" found in the psychometric literature (Lemke and Wiersma 1976: 122–123; Nunnally 1978:219).[14] It is possible in principle to correct the correlation between a child well-being score (individual or composite) and another variable in a research study by using the reliability estimates of both measures. If a reliability estimate is available only for a child well-being score, then the correlation may be corrected for this alone, with the reliability of the other variable placed equal to "1" in the formula. In a multivariate analysis, most convenient would be to correct each bivariate correlation, and then perform the analysis on the matrix of intercorrelations (rather than on the raw scores).

Of course, when some of the other variables are categorical rather than continuous, an ad hoc strategy for analyzing may have to be devised. Also, the suggestion is not appropriate in an evaluation study where child well-being change scores have been obtained (see below).

The same kind of adjustment can be made to correct tests of statistical significance for measurement unreliability. Since variances are inflated by a factor of $1/R_{xx}$ by unreliability, observed variances may be multiplied by the reliability coefficient (R_{xx}) and then entered into the computing formulas in the normal way.

While sound in principle, the "correction for attenuation" has a poor reputation in the psychometric literature, and deservedly so. For several reasons it often works poorly in practical applications. Its adequacy depends on the accuracy of the reliability estimates and, in multivariate analysis, on the availability of *equally* accurate reliability estimates for all variables. Since adequate and/or equal accuracy is rare, using corrections for unreliability in empirical work has often resulted in analytical distortions.

The usual practice in evaluative research has been to offer some evidence for the reliability of the measures being used, without making actual numerical adjustments for degrees of unreliability. This practice is usually viewed as an appropriately conservative strategy, since in much research the only effect of random error is to reduce the precision of measurement. This loss of precision is conceptualized as a reduction in the power of inferential statistics; that is, an increase of "type 2" error in hypothesis testing. It renders more difficult the rejection of null hypotheses or the detection of correlations in the data, but in most situations will not create "positive" findings where none exist.

The reliability estimates for the Child Well-Being Scales are based on fairly large samples; their use as correction factors in statistical formulas would appear justified under certain circumstances. The most important requirement is that such corrections not be made in an arbitrary manner. Consistency can be most likely achieved in studies with few variables where an adequate estimate exists of each variable's reliability. When there are several variables of unknown reliability, it may be preferable to make no corrections at all. Since the reliabilities of the composite scales are quite high, there should be no concern about imprecision from this source. In the case of most individual scales, findings will be affected by unreliability, but probably less so than by other variables in the study. In such situations it is the pattern of findings, rather than the magnitude or statistical significance of any single correlation, that should be the focus of concern.

In evaluation designs with "before" and "after" scores, random measurement error can result in biased estimates of mean change for initially nonequivalent groups. This problem (essentially one of statistical regression to the mean) and alternative proposed solutions for it have been extensively discussed in the psychometric literature (for overviews, see Huitema 1980; Cook and Campbell 1979; Campbell and Boruch 1975). Adjustment for statistical regression is usually desirable in order to help avoid misleading inferences in program evaluations. A likely result of ignoring measurement error in "before" scores is that any positive effects of services would be underestimated, or that services could even appear to be harmful.

Although regression to the mean is a well-known source of statistical artifact, it is rarely explicitly considered in evaluation studies because adequate reliability estimates for measures are generally not available. For that reason also, except in educational psychology, methods of dealing with the problem are often unfamiliar to investigators. A detailed discussion of these methods is not practical here, and the reader is referred to the excellent sources above. One adjustment method that would be useful to an evaluator in many typical situations is outlined, however: the technique is true-score analysis of covariance (ANCOVA) (Huitema 1980:311–316).

True-score ANCOVA is useful in evaluation designs when treatment groups have been formed on the basis of unknown (or incompletely known) selection factors. This type of situation is quite common in field evaluations. For example, clients might be allowed to volunteer for a certain program (self-selection), or workers might recommend some clients for a certain service. The evaluation strategy might be to obtain "before treatment" and "after treatment" Child Well-Being Scores for two groups of clients, those in the program (or receiving the service), and those who are not. For an analysis of covariance, the "after" score is defined as the dependent variable, the group assignment as the treatment variable, and the "before" score as the covariate. The analysis is likely to lead to a biased estimate of treatment effect because of statistical regression to the mean; that is, the "after" scores of the clients in each group will tend to regress to their group mean on "before" scores because of measurement unreliability.

True-score ANCOVA corrects this source of bias by regressing each "before" score toward its group mean to produce an adjusted "before" score. The adjusted "before" score then enters the regular ANCOVA calculation. (The procedure assumes that measurement error in "before" scores is uncorrelated with true scores or with measurement error in "after" scores.) The result is an estimate of treatment effect corrected for unreliability in "before" scores.

Measurement error in the "after" scores will reduce the power of the statistical significance test for treatment effect but will not bias the estimate of the treatment effect. This test can also be corrected for unreliability (see above), but not doing so would only give a conservative result (rather than a misleading result).

True-score ANCOVA can be extended to the case of multiple covariates (Huitema 1980:318–321).

The use of the Child Well-Being Scales in program evaluation must conform to accepted principles of research design and statistical analysis. Because of the availability of firm reliability estimates, an opportunity is presented for more sophisticated evaluation than is usually possible. The evaluator is not obligated to make direct use of the reliability information, but doing so could lead to more realistic study conclusions. With this opportunity also comes a burden—the need to achieve a working familiarity with nonequivalent group evaluation designs.

Notes

1. Similar results were reported by Filstead et al. (1982:570) for reliability of mental health rating scales.

2. Some might consider this an examination of convergent validity, but since both the scales and the case record are completed by the same worker, there is low methods variance; that is, there are not actually two independent measures of the family.

3. Note that this application of the intraclass correlation differs from that in the previous section on "worker effect."

4. The formula from classical reliability theory is:
$$SE = SD \times (1-R)^{1/2}$$
where SE = standard error of measurement
SD = standard deviation
R = reliability coefficient

5. Differences in mean scores for the scales between repeated administrations were negligible. Thus, using r_c or r would give equivalent results. If large observed differences in mean scores had been found, this result might have indicated the occurrence of actual change, thereby violating the assumption of no change, which is required for using a stability coefficient as a reliability estimate.

6. The formula for computing scale reliability for the intake data is:
$$R = 1 - (SE)^2/(SD)^2,$$
where R = scale reliability
SE = standard error of measurement (from repeated measures data)
SD = standard deviation (from intake data)
The formula for computing the true scores is:
$$T = R \times (0 - M) + M,$$

where T = expected (estimated) true score on scale
R = scale reliability (from previous formula)
O = obtained score on scale
M = mean scale score

7. The obtained scores used in the computations are the seriousness scores for the descriptor levels (refer to table 3-1).

As an example, the steps in computing the confidence intervals for the Parental Capacity for Child Care scale are as follows:

$$SE = 7.8 \text{ (from table 5-1)}$$
$$M = 82.9 \text{ (for intake data)}$$
$$SD = 23.3 \text{ (for intake data)}$$

The reliability of parental capacity for child care for the intake data is (see note 6):

$$R = 1 - (7.8)^2/ (23.3)^2 = .89$$

The true scores for each scale level (1 to 4) corresponding to the seriousness scores are (see note 6):

$$T_1 = .89 \times (100 - 82.9) + 82.9 = 98.1$$
$$T_2 = .89 \times (63 - 82.9) + 82.9 = 65.2$$
$$T_3 = .89 \times (48 - 82.9) + 82.9 = 51.8$$
$$T_4 = .89 \times (13 - 82.9) + 82.9 = 20.7$$

The 95% confidence intervals are ($\pm 2 \times SE$) = ($\pm 2 \times 7.8$) = + 15.6 around each of these true scores. That is:

$$(98.1 \pm 15.6) (65.2 \pm 15.6)(51.8 \pm 15.6) (20.7 \pm 15.6)$$

Rounding off after the computation yields:

$$(100\leftarrow98\rightarrow83) (81\leftarrow65\rightarrow50) (67\leftarrow52\rightarrow36) (36\leftarrow21)$$

The boundaries of these confidence intervals are the figures found in table 5-3; however, table 5-3 follows convention in locating them around obtained scores, which are the seriousness scores for each scale level.

8. Confidence intervals are not computed for all Child Well-Being Scales. Seven scales were substantially revised subsequent to the reliability study, yielding new seriousness scores, so that computation of confidence intervals here would not be meaningful. These were Availability of Utilities, Mental Health Care, Supervision of Children, Arrangements for Substitute Child Care, Parental Recognition of Problems, Availability/Accessibility of Services, and Sexual Abuse. Intervals could not be computed for four scales due to statistical considerations such as small number of cases or too little variance in responses (refer to table 5-1). Those were: Parental Relations, Physical Confinement, Economic Exploitation, and Protection from Abuse.

9. Of course, any arbitrary set of individual scales can legitimately be formed into a linear combination because all are measured on the same metric of seriousness. The total Child Well-Being Score is such a combination.

10. Other decisions might also be reasonable. Averaging all available estimates of reliability has been suggested (Cook and Campbell 1979:191), or a range of results could be computed using each of the different reliability estimates (Huitema 1980:313).

11. The general formula for the variance of a difference score is (Nunnally 1978:153):

$$SD_d^2 = SD_1^2 + SD_2^2 - (2 \times R_{12} \times SD_1 \times SD_2)$$

where SD_d = standard deviation of differences
SD_1 = standard deviation of first set of scores
SD_2 = standard deviation of second set of scores
R_{12} = correlation between first and second set of scores (which is negative for differences)

For random pairs of scores drawn from a single score distribution, R_{12} = O and $SD_1 = SD_2 = SD$. Therefore, the formula reduces to:

$$SD_d = SD \times (2)^{1/2}$$

Substituting into the general formula for the standard error (note 4), the standard error of uncorrelated score differences may be expressed as:

$$SE_d = SD \times (2 - 2 \times R_d)^{1/2}$$

where R_d = reliability of differences of uncorrelated scores.

The value of R_d in this case is identical to the reliability of individual scale scores (Lemke and Wiersma 1976:102).

12. There are several equivalent formulas for the reliability of a difference (R_d). The one used for the present analysis is (Nunnally 1978:248):

$$R_d = 1 - (VAR_1 + VAR_F - R_1 \times VAR_1 - R_F \times VAR_F)/VAR_d$$

where VAR_1, R_1 = variance and reliability of intake scores, respectively

VAR_F, R_F = variance and reliability of follow-up scores, respectively

VAR_d = variance of the difference scores

13. Using the true score formula in note 6 and statistics from table 5-9, the expected true change score associated with an obtained change score of zero on CWBS is:

$$T = .94 \times (0-4.4) + 4.4 = 0.3$$

The 95% confidence interval for this score is $2 \times SE = 2 \times (3.0) = 6.0$. Thus the upper limit of the confidence interval is $6.0 + 0.3 = 6.3$, and the lower limit is $0.3 - 6.0 = -5.7$.

14. The key idea is that random measurement error introduces variance into an observed score distribution beyond that attributable to the variance of true scores. The definitional formula for the reliability coefficient (R_{xx}) is:

$$R_{xx} = VAR_t/VAR_x$$

where VAR_t = variance of true scores

VAR_x = variance of obtained scores

When there is no unreliability ($R_{xx} = 1$), the variances of true and observed scores are identical. When unreliability exists ($O < R_{xx} < 1$), the variance of obtained scores is larger than that of true scores by a factor of $1/R_{xx}$. It can be shown that the "corrected" correlation for two unreliable variables is (Nunnally 1978:219–220):

$$\overline{R}_{12} = R_{12}/(R_{11})^{1/2} (R_{22})^{1/2}$$

where $\overline{R}_{12}$ = corrected correlation between variables 1 and 2

R_{12} = observed correlation

R_{11} = reliability of variable 1

R_{22} = reliability of variable 2

6

The Parent Outcome Interview

Description

The Parent Outcome Interview is an evaluation instrument designed to obtain the client's assessment of agency services and case outcomes in child welfare cases. Parents are interviewed only once, preferably at the conclusion of service. Information on family problems at referral and on service delivery is obtained through retrospective questioning.

The interview consists of 11 sections in a modular format. These are:

1. Referral Situation
2. Out-of-Home Placement
3. Housing and Economic Conditions
4. Physical Child Care
5. Discipline and Emotional Care of Children
6. Children's Academic Adjustment
7. Children's Conduct
8. Children's Symptomatic Behavior
9. Victimization of Children

10. Parental Coping

11. Relationship with Social Worker

Sections 3 through 10, which ask about problems, services, and changes in eight specific content areas of concern in child welfare, have a uniform format consisting of a mix of structured and semistructured questions.

Each section leads off with a detailed checklist of problems; clients are asked whether they had each of these problems at the time of referral to the agency and whether they have the problem now. The next major question in each section asks the client to rate problem change between referral and the interview, by selecting one of five responses ("a lot better" through "a lot worse"). As a follow-up, clients are asked to describe the reasoning behind their ratings. The checklist is intended to indicate relative changes in the types and numbers of problems between referral and the interview. The rating is intended to indicate changes in the degree of the problems in each content area. Together, the questions constitute the method of measuring case change for each problem content area.

Asking clients to describe the basis of their change rating has two purposes. First, it can help to verify that clients understand the meaning of their rating. Second, it can point to possible differences between clients and service providers in their definitions of case improvement (or deterioration).

The third main question in each section asks clients to describe the services received, if any, in response to the past or present problems mentioned. The fourth main question asks clients to try to identify possible connections between change reported and services received. The wording of the latter question is contingent on how clients rated change and whether they received services for the problems identified. The logic is as follows:

- If problems are rated "better" and services were received, clients are asked whether the improvement is attributable to the service(s).
- If problems are rated the "same" or "worse" and services were received, clients are asked why the services were apparently ineffective.
- If problems are rated "better" and no services were received, clients are asked about how the stated improvement occurred.
- If problems are rated "the same" or "worse" and no services were received, clients are asked why no improvement occurred, and whether services had been requested by or offered to them.

Finally, parents who report at least one present problem are asked to describe what kind of additional agency service they might still want.

The Referral Situation section, which leads off the interview, has a structure similar to that of the problem-specific sections, with two exceptions. This section asks clients to describe, in their own words, the problem that precipitated (that is, was immediately responsible for) the family's contact with the agency. Because of the wide variety of such possible problems, as well as the wish to obtain the client's "definition of the situation," no referral problem checklist is used. The remaining questions, keyed to the referral problem described by the client, follow the format of the problem-specific sections, as just described. The Referral Situation section ends with a global question on satisfaction with the agency, followed by a request for explanation of the client's response.

The second section, Out-of-Home Placement, is intended to determine parents' perceptions of why their children were placed, what might have been done to prevent placement, the circumstances of children's return home, or the conditions that would make return home possible. If no children had been placed, the only question to be asked is whether the parent sees a need for foster care for any child.

The last section is titled Relationship with Social Worker and begins with a list of structured response questions about the worker's interaction with the client. Many of the questions are adaptations of items appearing on Schulman's (1978) index of social worker skills. Others are based on protective service clients' descriptions of what satisfied and dissatisfied them about their workers (Magura 1982). If the case had been closed before the interview, several questions explore the closing circumstances. A global question on satisfaction with the worker is then asked, with a request for explanation of the response. The section concludes with several questions about the amount of in-person contact with the worker and the parent's agreement with the worker's activities.

Scoring

Ratings of problem change and satisfaction with services are obtained through structured response questions; these may be used directly for presentation. A purely heuristic, but reliable, summary measure of change based on client ratings may be constructed by assigning numerical values to each response (that is, "a lot better" = 5 to "a lot worse" = 1), summing the change ratings for each problem-specific area, and dividing by the total number of areas rated (a maximum of eight). These Average Change scores range from 1 (lowest) to 5 (highest) for the family.[1]

Presentation of interview results can be facilitated by using the codes that were developed from the field test interviewing. Codes are available for client descriptions of change in the problem-specific sections (see chapter 7). Of course, users are also encouraged to develop coding formats tailored to their own client populations.

A reliable measure of the client's Relationship with Social Worker may be constructed by summing the numerical values of the responses on the 17 items in that section and dividing by the number of items rated. To create a scale with origin at zero, the item responses are recoded "always" = 3, "usually" = 2, "sometimes" = 1, and "never" = 0. The possible scale scores thus range on a continuum from 0 to 3.

Administration

The Parent Outcome Interview is designed as an in-person interview with the principal caretaker of the children. The preferred interviewer is an agency employee with previous interviewing experience who is knowledgeable about child welfare. An agency's research department or evaluation unit, if one exists, would be a suitable auspice for the study. The interview is not intended to be administered by workers to their own clients.

The modular format of the Parent Outcome Interview provides a great deal of flexibility in administration. A "short" interview may be constructed of three sections—Referral Situation (Section 1), Out-of-Home Placement (Section 2), and Relationship with Social Worker (Section 11). If only specific types of problems are at issue, either for all agency clients or for particular clients, then those problem-specific sections may be added to the interview. Use of different sections of the interview for different clients, however, may also make it difficult to aggregate interview results for a client population. Thus, administration of the complete interview is recommended whenever possible. The advantage of the problem-specific sections is that coverage of all important types of problems is ensured. Field test experience indicates that a less directive format, such as that used in Referral Situation, will not pick up all the problem information elicited by more structured questions.

In the field tests, the interview consisted of 16 sections and required an average of 2 hours to administer to clients. Clients were paid between $12 and $15 per interview in the field tests, depending on the site. It is likely that remuneration would be necessary routinely to obtain clients' participation, unless the agency makes such participation a condition of service. Remuneration could also be viewed simply as equitable.

The authors strongly recommend that client participation be voluntary, that informed consent be obtained (as in any other research study), and that confidentiality be maintained. Detailed instructions for implementing a client-based evaluation study are available in Beck and Jones (1980) and Millar and Millar (1981). Federal guidelines for the protection of human subjects should be reviewed before undertaking such a study (US DHHS 1983).

Reliability and Validity

These subjects are completely discussed in chapter 7.

Sensitivity to Change

If we hypothesize that the receipt of agency services has some effect, however small, on case outcomes, then an observed relationship between services received and ratings of change can be interpreted as evidence of the latter's construct validity. To examine this for the normative sample (see Norms), numbers of services received by families in each problem-specific area were cross-tabulated with clients' change ratings for the respective areas. Gamma was computed to indicate the strength of the relationship, ranging from a high of .57 for Living Conditions to a low of .20 for Children's Conduct; the mean gamma for all areas was .35.[2] This indicates a moderate tendency toward positive change ratings when more services have been received. In addition, the correlation between the Average Change score and total number of services received by the family was $r = .30$. (For more details on this analysis, see chapter 7.)

Norms

The normative sample consists of 250 families receiving child welfare services whose cases had been open between 5 and 6 months at the time of the interview and who had at least one child residing at home. The sample was drawn during 1981 from three public social services agencies in Texas, Minnesota, and Florida. In 90% of the cases, the person interviewed was the mother or maternal figure. Sample demographics appear in the appendix.

Client ratings of change for each problem-specific area are given in table 7-5. Despite some differences in how the areas are defined on the final version of the interview, these results can provide a benchmark for comparison with later studies. The distributions of client descriptions of improvement for each area are given in table 7-6.

The mean Average Change score was 3.6, with standard deviation of 0.6. The mean Relationship with Social Worker score was 1.9, with standard deviation of 0.8. Additional statistics of interest for the normative sample may be found in chapter 7.

It is important to emphasize that the study agencies were chosen to maximize the diversity of case situations, not to yield a representative national sample of child welfare cases. Consequently, the percentage of the total sample with a given referral problem may not be meaningful. The changes for clients in the various separate problem areas, however, are likely to be generalizable to other clients *with such problems in similar agency contexts.*

Completeness/Response Rates

The initial contact with clients in the normative sample on behalf of the CWLA was made by introductory letter from each agency, explaining the purpose and voluntary nature of the study. Local project coordinators at two of the agencies made follow-up efforts to contact clients who did not respond to the initial request; one agency did not approve additional contact attempts. On this basis, parent interviews were arranged and completed in 35% of the families eligible for the study. The most frequent reason that interviews were not completed was inability to obtain a response from the client (53%), followed by direct refusals (33%). Some of the former probably involve "passive" refusals to participate, as well as cases where apparently clients were rarely at home. (For a complete breakdown, refer to table 7-1.)

A test for nonresponse bias was built into the study by comparing subsamples of interviewed and noninterviewed cases on Child Well-Being Scores, an independent measure obtained from workers (see chapter 3); no statistically significant differences were found. (For complete details, see chapter 7.)

Regarding completeness, no important difficulties were encountered in getting clients to respond to individual questions. Only two interviews had to be terminated prematurely during the field tests because of client restiveness or time complaints. Clients generally appeared to understand the questions as worded and to give appropriate answers.

Discussion and Recommendations

Obtaining feedback from clients on case outcomes and satisfaction with services is often desired in program evaluation. The Parent Outcome Interview is tailored for child welfare service evaluation and its feasibility has been demonstrated in several public agency settings. Because in-person client interviews do require greater investment of time by the agency than other evaluation methods, the interview may be most suitable for routine use only on a sampling basis or for periodic special studies. Substantive analysis of the field test interviews has shown that the results can be useful in understanding the client's perspective and in pointing to needed areas of service improvement (Magura and Moses 1984).

Since low response rates are always a potential problem, it is important to note that bias due to nonresponse was not found in the field tests. The consistency and honesty of clients' responses seemed satisfactory (see Chapter 7). Convergent validity of the client change ratings, as determined by comparison with Child Well-Being Scale change scores obtained from social workers, was unsatisfactory, however. This result requires additional investigation to explain, although similar findings have been reported in the social services evaluation literature. Potential users should probably use the Parent Outcome Interview in conjunction with alternative client outcome measures, so that appropriate comparisons can be made, and possibly divergent results explained.

Source

The text of the Parent Outcome Interview follows in this chapter. Prospective users are granted permission to reproduce or retype the text for non-profit research and evaluation purposes only. (Field versions of the interview should include space to record client answers.)

The
Parent Outcome Interview

Stephen Magura
and
Beth Silverman Moses

Complete documentation on the Parent Outcome Interview is given in Stephen Magura and Beth Silverman Moses, *Outcome Measures for Child Welfare Services.* Washington, D.C.: Child Welfare League of America, 1986.

Development of the Parent Outcome Interview was funded by Grant No. 90-CW-2041 from the Administration for Children, Youth and Families, Office of Human Development, Department of Health and Human Services, Washington, D.C.

Child Welfare League of America, Inc.
Washington, D.C.

Parent Outcome Interview

Face Sheet

FAMILY IDENTIFIER: DATE CASE OPENED:

NAME OF INTERVIEWER: DATE CASE CLOSED:

PERSON INTERVIEWED: HOUSEHOLD COMPOSITION: *

DATE OF INTERVIEW:

	Name	Relationship to Interviewee	Age	Sex	Ethnicity
Primary Caretaker					
Secondary Caretaker					
Other Adult					

	Name	Age	Sex	Where Living
First Child				
Second Child				
Third Child				
Fourth Child				
Fifth Child				
Sixth Child				
Seventh Child				
Eighth Child				

*This information should be obtained prior to the interview, e.g., from case records. If necessary, obtain any missing (or updated) information from the client.

Section 1   Referral Situation

1. How did you first happen to talk with a social worker from AGENCY? *Or* What was the reason you were referred?
   Probes: In your opinion, how did PROBLEM MENTIONED come about? What do you think caused this situation? Was it something out of your control?

2. Did you agree with the worker about this problem or about your situation?
   Probes: Did the worker tell you that a problem(s) existed that you did not agree with? Did you and the worker disagree about what happened or what caused it?

Ask either questions 3–3c or questions 4–4c. If reason for referral was an INCIDENT, ask question 3. If reason for referral was a SITUATION, ask question 4.

3. Since you first talked to someone from AGENCY, how often has REFERRAL INCIDENT happened again?
   Read responses 1–4 only.
   1. Not at all *Ask 3a.*
   2. Less often than before *Ask 3b.*
   3. About the same as before or *Ask 3b.*
   4. More often than before *Ask 3c.*

   | 8. Other *Have client explain.* |
   | 9. Not sure |

   3a. Why do you feel that INCIDENT MENTIONED hasn't happened again?
   3b. What needs to be changed (improved) to prevent REFERRAL INCIDENT from happening again (*or*, continuing to happen)?
   3c. Why do you think REFERRAL INCIDENT happens more often now?

4. Overall, how is (are) the REFERRAL PROBLEM(s) for your family now as compared with when you first talked with someone from AGENCY? Would you say it's
   Read responses 1–5 only:
   1. A lot better now *Ask 4a.*
   2. A little better now *Ask 4a.*
   3. About the same now *Ask 4b.*
   4. A little worse now, or *Ask 4c.*
   5. A lot worse now *Ask 4c.*

   | 8. Other *Have client explain.* |
   | 9. Not sure |

   4a. What do you feel is the most important way that REFERRAL PROBLEM is better now?
   4b. What do you feel is the most important way that REFERRAL PROBLEM still needs to be improved?
   4c. What do you feel is worse now about REFERRAL PROBLEM?

5. Did you receive any counseling or other services to help you with REASON FOR REFERRAL?
   Have client describe service(s) received.

Consider client's responses to questions 3, 4, and 5—see table; then ask one *question only from 6a–6d.*

Rating (Q.3 or 4)	Services (Q.5)	
	Received	Not Received
Better/Not Happening	Ask 6a	Ask 6c
Same/Worse– Still Happening	Ask 6b	Ask 6d

6a. *If referral problem(s) better or not happening and service received, ask:*
   Do you think IMPROVEMENT MENTIONED would have happened without your caseworker's help?

6b. *If referral problem(s) same, or worse, or still happening, and service received, ask:*
   Why do you think SERVICE(S) MENTIONED didn't help to improve (*or,* change) PROBLEM(S) MENTIONED? (Why didn't SERVICE(S) RECEIVED make a difference? What do you think should have been done instead?)

6c. *If referral problem(s) better or not happening and no service received, ask:*
   Why do you think IMPROVEMENT MENTIONED happened? (What happened to change things?)

6d. *If referral problem(s) same, or worse, or still happening, and no service received, ask:*
   What do you think is the reason that PROBLEM(S) MENTIONED has not improved (*or,* gotten better)? (Why didn't you mention it to your caseworker? Did you ask for any service or for any help from your caseworker? What did your caseworker say?)

7. Overall, how satisfied are you with the services you received or what your caseworker did? Are you
   Read responses 1–5 only:
   1. Very satisfied *Ask 7a.*
   2. Somewhat satisfied *Ask 7a.*
   3. Somewhat dissatisfied *Ask 7b.*
   4. Very dissatisfied, or *Ask 7b.*
   5. No particular feeling *Ask 7a.*

   > 8. Other *Have client explain.*
   > 9. Not sure

   7a. What did you like most about the agency? (What do you think helped you the most?) *Ask 8.*
   7b. What didn't you like about the agency? (What were you unhappy with about the agency?) *Ask 8a.*

8. Was there anything you didn't like about the agency? (What were you unhappy with?)
   8a. Was there anything you did like about the agency?

Section 2   Out-of-Home Placement

1. Since you first talked to someone from AGENCY, have any of your children been placed?

If no child placed, skip to question 6.
   1a. Are any of your children still in placement or have they been returned home?

2. As you see it, how did it come about that your child(ren) was (were) placed?

3. What do you think might have prevented your child(ren) being placed?
   Probes: What could AGENCY have done differently? What could you have done differently? Did your caseworker try to find some other answer to the problem?

4. *If at least one child has returned home, ask:*
   In your view, what made it possible for CHILD to return home?

5. *If at least one child has not returned home, ask:*
   Do you feel your CHILD(REN) should be returned home to you now? (What do you think make it possible for CHILD(REN) to return?)

6. Do you feel that any of your children should be placed in foster care for any reason? Do you think things would be better if one of your children was placed in foster care?
   If yes, ask:
   Have you asked the worker about placement? What did he/she say?

This new series of questions deals with your housing and economic situation.

1. When you first talked to someone from AGENCY, did you have any problems with
   Read first question:
   If answer is yes, ask: Is this still a problem for you?
   If answer is no, ask: Is this a problem now for you?
   Repeat for each question 1b–1j

	Yes, at Referral	Yes, Still or Now
a. Your kitchen appliances, that is, refrigerator, stove, sink, or in the bathroom with the shower, tub, or toilet?	1	1
b. Overcrowding in your home, that is, not enough space for everyone to sleep, live, and have some privacy?	1	1
c. An unsafe or dangerous conditon in your home that could hurt someone?	1	1
d. Not having enough furnishings like chairs, tables, a crib, mattresses, blankets, sheets, pots, or dishes?	1	1
e. The building or neighborhood being unsafe because of a lot of crime or illegal things going on?	1	1
f. Rats coming into your home?	1	1
g. Being forced to move out of your home?	1	1
h. Running out of money before the next check comes?	1	1
i. The building (or the house) being rundown and neglected?	1	1
j. Any other problems with your housing that I haven't mentioned? *Have client explain.*	1	1

2. When you first talked to someone from AGENCY, did you have enough money
   Read first question:
   If answer is yes, ask: Is this still a problem for you?
   If answer is no, ask: Is this now a problem for you?
   Repeat for each question 2b–2g.

	Yes, at Referral	Yes, Still or Now
a. To pay your rent?	1	1
b. To pay your electric and heating bills?	1	1
c. To buy food for your family?	1	1
d. To see a doctor or buy medicine?	1	1
e. To buy needed clothes for your children?	1	1
f. To pay someone to watch your children?	1	1
g. To pay for something I haven't mentioned? *Have client explain.*	1	1

If no to all questions 1a–1j and 2a–2g, skip to section 4.

3. Overall, how would you say your housing and economic situation is now as compared with when you first talked to someone from AGENCY? Are they
   Read responses 1–5 only:
   1. A lot better now *Ask 3a.*

2. A little better now *Ask 3a.*
3. About the same *Ask 3b.*
4. A little worse now, or *Ask 3c.*
5. A lot worse now *Ask 3c.*

> 8. Other *Have client explain.*
> 9. Not sure

3a. What do you feel is the most important way that your housing or economic situation is better now?
3b. What do you feel is the most important way that your housing or economic situation still needs to be improved?
3c. What do you feel is worse now about your housing or economic situation?

4. Did you and your caseworker discuss PROBLEM(S) MENTIONED? Did you receive any counseling or other services to help you with PROBLEM(S) MENTIONED?
Have client describe services received.

Consider client's responses to questions 3 and 4—see table; then select one question only from 5a–5d.

Rating (Q.3)	Services (Q.4)	
	Received	Not Received
Better	Ask 5a	Ask 5c
Same/Worse	Ask 5b	Ask 5d

5a. *If better and service received, ask:*
Do you think SERVICE(S) RECEIVED was the reason for IMPROVEMENT MENTIONED? (Do you think IMPROVEMENT MENTIONED would have happened without your caseworker's help?)
5b. *If problem(s) same, or worse, and service received, ask:*
Why do you think SERVICE(S) RECEIVED didn't help to improve (or change) PROBLEM(S) MENTIONED? (Why didn't SERVICE(S) RECEIVED make a difference? What do you think should have been done instead?)
5c. *If problem better and no service received, ask:*
Why do you think the IMPROVEMENT MENTIONED happened? (What happened to change things?)
5d. *If problem same, or worse, and no service received, ask:*
What do you think is the reason that PROBLEM(S) MENTIONED has not improved (or gotten better)? (Why didn't you mention it to your caseworker? Did you ask for any service or your caseworker to do something? What did your caseworker say?)

6. *If client has any problem "still or now" (see Q.1), ask:*
Is there anything else you would like your caseworker to do to help you with PROBLEM MENTIONED?

Section 4 Physical Child Care

Parents often worry that their children's needs are not always met. I'd like to ask some questions about how your children are faring.

1. When you first talked to someone from AGENCY
   Read first question:
   If answer is yes, ask: Has this happened *again?* (*or,* Is this still a problem?)
   If answer is no, ask: Has this happened *recently?* (*or,* Is this a problem now?)
   Repeat for each question 1b–1h.

	Yes, At Referral	Yes, Happened Again or Recently
a. Were your children hungry sometimes because you had trouble preparing meals?	1	1
b. Were your children getting rashes, lice, or skin conditions because they were not bathed or washed?	1	1
c. Were you worried about leaving your children alone when you had to go out?	1	1
d. Had any of your children gotten hurt in any way while they were in someone else's care?	1	1
e. Were your children playing in places they shouldn't be or playing with dangerous things?	1	1
f. Were you unable to take your children to see a doctor when they were sick or had an accident?	1	1
g. Were you unable to take your children to the dentist when they were having trouble with their teeth?	1	1
h. Any other concerns about your children's physical needs that I haven't mentioned?	1	1

If no to all questions 1a–1h, skip to section 5.

2. Think about your children's physical needs. Overall, how are these needs being met now as compared with when you first talked to someone from AGENCY. Would you say
   Read responses 1–5 only.
   1. A lot better now *Ask 2a.*
   2. A little better now *Ask 2a.*
   3. About the same *Ask 2b.*
   4. A little worse now, or *Ask 2c.*
   5. A lot worse now *Ask 2c.*

   > 8. Other *Have client explain.*
   > 9. Not sure

   2a. What has been the most important improvement in your children's physical needs?
   2b. What is the most important physical need of your children that should still be improved?
   2c. In what way are your children's physical needs worse now?

3. Did you and your caseworker discuss PROBLEM(S) OR INCIDENT(S) MENTIONED? Did you receive any counseling or any other services to help you with PROBLEM(S) OR INCIDENT(S) MENTIONED? *Have client describe service(s) received.*

210

Consider client's responses to questions 2 and 3—see table; then ask one question only from 4a–4d.

Rating (Q.2)	Services (Q.3)	
	Received	Not Received
Better	Ask 4a	Ask 4c
Same/Worse	Ask 4b	Ask 4d

4a. *If problem(s) better and service received, ask:*
Do you think SERVICE(S) MENTIONED was the reason for IMPROVEMENT MENTIONED? (Do you think IMPROVEMENT MENTIONED would have happened without your caseworker's help)?

4b. *If problem(s) same, or worse, and service received, ask:*
Why do you think SERVICE(S) MENTIONED didn't help to improve (or, change) PROBLEM(S) MENTIONED? (Why didn't SERVICE(S) RECEIVED make a difference? What do you think should have been done instead?)

4c. *If problem(s) better and no service received, ask:*
Why do you think IMPROVEMENT MENTIONED happened? (What happened to change things?)

4d. *If problem(s) same, or worse, and no service received, ask:*
What do you think is the reason that PROBLEM(S) MENTIONED has not improved (or, gotten better)? (Why didn't you mention it to your caseworker? Did you ask for any service or for any help from your caseworker? What did your caseworker say?)

5. *If client has any problem "still or now" (see Q.1), ask:*
Is there anything *else* you would like your caseworker to do to help you with PROBLEM(S) MENTIONED?

Raising children is not always easy, so we are asking about problems that sometimes come up in training children or in relating to them.

1. When you first talked to someone from AGENCY
   Read first question:
   If answer is yes, ask: Is this *still* happening? (*or,* Has this happened again?)
   If answer is no, ask: Is this happening *now*? (*or,* Has this happened since you first talked to someone from AGENCY?)
   Repeat for each question 1b–1l.

	Yes, At Referral	Yes, Again or Now
a. Did your children get on your nerves so much that you sometimes lost your temper with them?	1	1
b. Did you find that hitting your children was the best way to get them to listen?	1	1
c. Did you sometimes feel uncomfortable when one of your children wanted to be hugged or held a lot?	1	1
d. Did you sometimes find yourself blaming your children for things that were not really their fault?	1	1
e. Did you sometimes hit your children harder than you should have?	1	1
f. Did you sometimes expect your children to do things that they really couldn't do?	1	1
g. Did things sometimes get out of control when you were punishing your children?	1	1
h. Did you sometimes say things to your children that you regretted later on?	1	1
i. Did people complain about the way you punished your children?	1	1
j. Did you sometimes feel that your children were taking up too much of your time, that they kept you from doing the things you really wanted to do?	1	1
k. Had any of your children been hurt in some way while they were being punished?	1	1
l. Were there any other problems in relating to your children that I haven't mentioned? *Have client explain.*	1	1

If no to all questions 1a–1l, skip to section 6.

2. Since you first talked to someone from the AGENCY, do you feel there's been a change in how well you're training your children and relating to them? Do you feel things are
   Read responses 1–5 only:
   1. A lot better now *Ask 2a.*
   2. A little better now *Ask 2a.*
   3. About the same now as before *Ask 2b.*
   4. A little worse now, or *Ask 2c.*
   5. A lot worse now *Ask 2c.*

> 8. Other *Have client explain.*
> 9. Not sure

2a. What is the most important way that the training of your children is better?

2b. What still needs to be improved about your children's training?

2c. What is worse about your children's training?

3. Did you and your caseworker discuss PROBLEM(S) MENTIONED? Did you receive any counseling or other service to help you with PROBLEM(S) MENTIONED? *Have client describe service(s) received.*

Consider client's responses to questions 2 and 3—see table; then ask one question only from 4a–4d.

	Services (Q.3)	
Rating (Q.2)	Received	Not Received
Better	Ask 4a	Ask 4c
Same/Worse	Ask 4b	Ask 4d

4a. *If problem(s) better and service received, ask:*
Do you think SERVICE(S) MENTIONED was the reason for IMPROVEMENT MENTIONED? (Do you think IMPROVEMENT MENTIONED would have happened without your caseworker's help)?

4b. *If problem(s) same, or worse, and service received, ask:*
Why do you think SERVICE(S) MENTIONED didn't help to improve (or, change) PROBLEM(S) MENTIONED? (Why didn't SERVICE(S) RECEIVED make a difference? What do you think should have been done instead?)

4c. *If problem(s) better and no service received, ask:*
Why do you think IMPROVEMENT MENTIONED happened? (What happened to change things?)

4d. *If problem(s) same, or worse, and no service received, ask:*
What do you think is the reason that PROBLEM(S) MENTIONED has not improved (or, gotten better)? (Why didn't you mention it to your caseworker? Did you ask for any service or for any help from your caseworker? What did your caseworker say?)

5. *If client has any problem "still or now" (see Q.1), ask:*
Is there anything *else* you would like your caseworker to do to help you with PROBLEM(S) MENTIONED?

Section 6   Children's Academic Adjustment

Now I'd like to ask about problems children sometimes have related to school.

1. When you first talked with someone from AGENCY, were any of your children
   Read first question:
   If answer is yes, ask: Is this still a problem for any of your children?
   If answer is no, ask: Is this a problem now for any of your children?
   Repeat for each question 1b–1i.

	Yes, At Referral	Yes, Still or Now
a. Not enrolled in school (if of school age)?	1	1
b. Having difficulty keeping up with their school work?	1	1
c. Failing any classes?	1	1
d. Not attending school or cutting classes?	1	1
e. Causing trouble in school?	1	1
f. Being temporarily suspended from school?	1	1
g. Being expelled from school or involuntarily transferred?	1	1
h. Being complained about to you by their teachers?	1	1
i. Getting ready to drop out of school?	1	1

If no to all questions 1a–1i, skip to section 7.

2. Overall, how are your children's grades and behavior in school now as compared with when you first talked to someone from AGENCY? Would you say these things are
   Read responses 1–5 only:
   1. A lot better now *Ask 2a.*
   2. A little better now *Ask 2b.*
   3. About the same *Ask 2b.*
   4. A little worse now, or *Ask 2c.*
   5. A lot worse now *Ask 2c.*

> 8. Other *Have client explain.*
> 9. Not sure

   2a. What do you feel is the most important way that your children are doing better in school?
   2b. In what way do you feel your children's work or behavior in school needs to be improved?
   2c. In what way are your children's problems in school worse now?

3. Did you and your caseworker discuss PROBLEM(S) MENTIONED? Did you receive any counseling or any other services to help you with PROBLEM(S) MENTIONED? *Have client describe service(s) received.*

Consider client's responses to questions 2 and 3—see table; then ask one question only from 4a–4d.

Rating (Q.2)	Services (Q.3) Received	Not Received
Better	Ask 4a	Ask 4c
Same/Worse	Ask 4b	Ask 4d

214

4a. *If problem(s) better and service received, ask:*
Do you think SERVICE(S) MENTIONED was the reason for IMPROVEMENT MENTIONED? (Do you think IMPROVEMENT MENTIONED would have happened without your caseworker's help)?

4b. *If problem(s) same, or worse, and service received, ask:*
Why do you think SERVICE(S) MENTIONED didn't help to improve (*or,* change) PROBLEM(S) MENTIONED? (Why didn't SERVICE(S) RECEIVED make a difference? What do you think should have been done instead?)

4c. *If problem(s) better and no service received, ask:*
Why do you think IMPROVEMENT MENTIONED happened? (What happened to change things?)

4d. *If problem(s) same, or worse, and no service received, ask:*
What do you think is the reason that PROBLEM(S) MENTIONED has not improved (*or,* gotten better)? (Why didn't you mention it to your caseworker? Did you ask for any service or for any help from your caseworker? What did your caseworker say?)

5. *If client has any problem "still or now" (see Q.1), ask:*
Is there anything *else* you would like your caseworker to do to help you with PROBLEM(S) MENTIONED?

Section 7   Children's Conduct

Ask section only if family has school-age children. If none, skip to section 8.

Now I'd like to ask some questions about your children's conduct.

1. When you first talked to someone from AGENCY, were any of your children
   Read first question:
   If answer is yes, ask: Is this *still* a problem for any of your children?
   If answer is no, ask: Is this a problem *now* for any of your children?
   Repeat for each question 1b–1l.

	Yes, At Referral	Yes, Still or Now
a. Breaking and busting things on purpose?	1	1
b. Hitting or fighting with other children?	1	1
c. Lying and not listening to you?	1	1
d. Stealing or copping things?	1	1

Ask families with children ages 10 and up.

f. Hanging around with friends you disapprove of?	1	1
g. Running away from home?	1	1
h. Beating up or assaulting people?	1	1
i. Being picked up or arrested by the police?	1	1
j. Appearing in family or juvenile court?	1	1

Ask only families with teenagers.

k. Getting drunk or using drugs?	1	1
l. Having sex or "sleeping around"?	1	1

If no to all questions 1a–1l, skip to section 8.

2. Since you first talked with someone from AGENCY, have there been any changes in your child(ren)'s behavior? Would you say their behavior is
   Read responses 1–5 only:
   1. A lot better now *Ask 2a.*
   2. A little better now *Ask 2a.*
   3. About the same *Ask 2b.*
   4. A little worse now, or *Ask 2c.*
   5. A lot worse now *Ask 2c.*

   > 8. Other *Have client explain.*
   > 9. Don't know, not sure

   2a. What is the most important way your children's behavior is better now?
   2b. In what way does your children's behavior still need to be improved?
   2c. In what way is your children's behavior worse now?

3. Did you and your caseworker discuss PROBLEM(S) MENTIONED? Did you receive any counseling or any other services to help you with PROBLEM(S) MENTIONED?

216

Consider client's responses to questions 2 and 3—see table; then ask one question only from 4a–4d.

	Services (Q.3)	
Rating (Q.2)	Received	Not Received
Better	Ask 4a	Ask 4c
Same/Worse	Ask 4b	Ask 4d

4a. *If problem(s) better and service received, ask:*
Do you think SERVICE(S) MENTIONED was the reason for IMPROVEMENT MENTIONED? (Do you think IMPROVEMENT MENTIONED would have happened without your caseworker's help)?

4b. *If problem(s) same, or worse, and service received, ask:*
Why do you think SERVICE(S) MENTIONED didn't help to improve (*or,* change) PROBLEM(S) MENTIONED? (Why didn't SERVICE(S) RECEIVED make a difference? What do you think should have been done instead?)

4c. *If problem(s) better and no service received, ask:*
Why do you think IMPROVEMENT MENTIONED happened? (What happened to change things?)

4d. *If problem(s) same, or worse, and no service received, ask:*
What do you think is the reason that PROBLEM(S) MENTIONED has not improved (*or,* gotten better)? (Why didn't you mention it to your caseworker? Did you ask for any service or for any help from your caseworker? What did your caseworker say?)

5. *If client has any problem "still or now" (see Q.1), ask:*
Is there anything *else* you would like your caseworker to do to help you with PROBLEM(S) MENTIONED?

Section 8   Children's Symptomatic Behavior

Ask section only if family has at least one child over age three. If none, skip to section 9.

Now I'd like to ask about some nervous difficulties children could have in growing up.

1. When you first talked to someone from AGENCY, were any of your children
   Read first question:
   If answer is yes, ask: Is this still a problem for any of the children? (Is the child still having this problem?)
   If answer is no, ask: Is this a problem *now* for any of your children?
   Repeat for each question 1b–1j.

	Yes, At Referral	Yes, Still or Now
a. Anxious, afraid, or tense a lot of the time?	1	1
b. Depressed, sad, or withdrawn a lot of the time?	1	1
c. Restless or fidgety a lot of the time?	1	1
d. Being confused or not remembering things a lot of the time?	1	1
e. Sluggish or sleeping a lot of the time?	1	1
f. Getting moody suddenly a lot of the time?	1	1
g. Complaining about aches and pains a lot?	1	1
h. Wetting or soiling the bed a lot?	1	1
i. Having nightmares a lot of the time?	1	1
j. Talking about wanting to die, or saying they'd rather be dead?	1	1

If no to all questions 1a–1j, skip to section 9.

2. Does PROBLEM(s) MENTIONED interfere with his/her school work or attendance, or his/her relationship with friends?

3. Since you first talked to someone from AGENCY, have your child(ren)'s nervous difficulties
   Read responses 1–5 only:
   1. Gotten a lot better *Ask 3a.*
   2. Gotten a little better *Ask 3a.*
   3. Stayed about the same *Ask 3b.*
   4. Gotten a little worse, or *Ask 3c.*
   5. Gotten a lot worse *Ask 3c.*

   > 8. Other *Have client explain.*
   > 9. Don't know, not sure

   3a. In what way are your children's nervous problems better now?
   3b. In what way do your children's nervous problem(s) still need to be improved?
   3c. In what way are your children's nervous problems worse now?

4. Did you and your caseworker discuss PROBLEM(s) MENTIONED? Did you receive any counseling or any other services to help you with PROBLEM(s) MENTIONED? *Have client describe service(s) received.*

Consider client's responses to questions 3 and 4—see table; then ask one question only from 5a–5d.

Rating (Q.3)	Services (Q.4) Received	Not Received
Better	Ask 5a	Ask 5c
Same/Worse	Ask 5b	Ask 5d

5a. *If problem(s) better and service received, ask:*
Do you think SERVICE(S) MENTIONED was the reason for IMPROVEMENT MENTIONED? (Do you think IMPROVEMENT MENTIONED would have happened without your caseworker's help)?

5b. *If problem(s) same, or worse, and service received, ask:*
Why do you think SERVICE(S) MENTIONED didn't help to improve (*or*, change) PROBLEM(S) MENTIONED? (Why didn't SERVICE(S) RECEIVED make a difference? What do you think should have been done instead?)

5c. *If problem(s) better and no service received, ask:*
Why do you think IMPROVEMENT MENTIONED happened? (What happened to change things?)

5d. *If problem(s) same, or worse, and no service received, ask:*
What do you think is the reason that PROBLEM(S) MENTIONED has not improved (*or*, gotten better)? (Why didn't you mention it to your caseworker? Did you ask for any service or for any help from your caseworker? What did your caseworker say?)

6. *If children have any problem "still or now" (see Q.1), ask:*
Is there anything *else* you would like your caseworker to do to help with PROBLEM(S) MENTIONED?

Now I'd like to ask whether any of your children have had any experience where someone bothered or mistreated them.

1. At the time you first talked to someone from AGENCY, had any of your children
   Read first question:
   If answer is yes, ask: Has this happened again?
   If answer is no, ask: Has this happened recently? (Has this happened since you first talked to someone from AGENCY?)
   Repeat for each question 1b–1f.

	Yes, At Referral	Yes, Happened Again or Recently
a. Had things taken from them or stolen?	1	1
b. Been attacked or beaten up?	1	1
c. Been threatened by anyone?	1	1
d. Been made to do work for which they were too young, or that was no good for them?	1	1
e. Been forced to do something against the law?	1	1
f. Been molested or taken advantage of sexually by an adult?	1	1

If no to all questions 1a–1f, skip to section 10.

2. *If yes to any questions 1a–1f, ask:*
   Was (were) your child(ren) hurt or injured in some way? What kind of injury was it? How serious was the injury?
   2a. Who did this to your child(ren)? (Who was responsible?)

3. Since you first talked with someone from AGENCY, has there been a change in how safe your children are from being hurt or threatened by other people? Do you think that your children are
   Read responses 1–5 only:
   1. A lot safer now *Ask 3a.*
   2. A little safer now *Ask 3a.*
   3. About the same *Ask 3b.*
   4. A little less safe now, or *Ask 3c.*
   5. A lot less safe now *Ask 3c.*

   > 8. Other *Have client explain.*
   > 9. Not sure

   3a. What is the most important way that your children are safer now? (*or,* Why do you feel that INCIDENT MENTIONED won't happen again?)
   3b. What is the most important way your children's safety still needs to be improved? (*or,* What needs to be done to prevent INCIDENT MENTIONED from happening again?)
   3c. What is worse now about your children's safety? (How are they less safe now? Or, Why do you think that INCIDENT MENTIONED could happen again?)

4. Did you and your caseworker discuss INCIDENT MENTIONED? Did you receive any counseling or any other services to help you with INCIDENT(s) MENTIONED?

Consider client's responses to questions 3 and 4—see table; then ask one question only from 5a–5d.

	Services (Q.4)	
Rating (Q.3)	Received	Not Received
Safer	Ask 5a	Ask 5c
Same or Less Safe	Ask 5b	Ask 5d

5a. *If safer and service received, ask:*
Do you think SERVICE(S) RECEIVED was the reason for IMPROVEMENT MENTIONED? (Do you think IMPROVEMENT MENTIONED would have happened without your caseworker's help?)

5b. *If safety same or less, and service received, ask:*
Why do you think SERVICE(S) RECEIVED didn't help to improve (*or*, change) PROBLEM(S) MENTIONED? (Why didn't SERVICE(S) RECEIVED make a difference? What do you think should have been done instead?)

5c. *If safer and no services received, ask:*
Why do you think IMPROVEMENT MENTIONED happened? (What happened to change things?)

5d. *If safety same or less, and no service received, ask:*
What do you think is the reason that your children's safety has not improved (*or*, gotten better)? (Why didn't you mention it to your caseworker? Did you ask for any service or for your caseworker to do something? What did your caseworker say?)

6. *If any incidents happened again or recently (see Q.1), ask:*
Is there anything else you would like your caseworker to do to help you prevent INCIDENT(S) MENTIONED from happening again?

Section 10   Parental Coping

All people sometimes have personal difficulties in their lives. I'm going to read a list of common difficulties and I'd like you to tell me whether any describe your situation.

1. When you first talked to someone from AGENCY, were you
   Read first question:
   If answer is yes, ask: Are you *still* having this difficulty?
   If answer is no, ask: Are you *now* having this difficulty?
   Repeat for each question 1b–1i.

	Yes, At Referral	Yes, Still or Now
a. Having any health problems that limited what you could do?	1	1
b. Having trouble with drinking too much or using drugs?	1	1
c. Feeling depressed or "blue"?	1	1
d. Overwhelmed with work and no one to help you?	1	1
e. Having a lot of fights and arguments with your husband (or the person you're living with)?	1	1
f. Feeling nervous, tense, or worried?	1	1
g. Getting yourself into some trouble with the law?	1	1
h. Hating yourself or wanting to just give up?	1	1
i. Feeling lonely or out of touch with people?	1	1

If no to questions 1a–1i, skip to section 11.

2. You mentioned PROBLEM(S) MENTIONED. Right now, is this at all affecting your ability to run your house or to take care of your children? In what way?

3. Since you first talked to someone from AGENCY, have there been any changes in your personal life or personal difficulties? Are things
   Read responses 1–5 only:
   1. A lot better now *Ask 3a.*
   2. A little better now *Ask 3a.*
   3. About the same *Ask 3b.*
   4. A little worse, now or *Ask 3c.*
   5. A lot worse now *Ask 3c.*

   > 8. Other *Have client explain.*
   > 9. Not sure

   3a. What's the most important thing in your personal life that has changed for the better?
   3b. What's the most important change in your personal life that you would like to see?
   3c. What's the most important thing that has gotten worse?

4. Did you and your caseworker discuss PROBLEM(S) MENTIONED? Did you receive any counseling or any other services to help you with PROBLEM(S) MENTIONED?

Consider client's responses to questions 3 and 4—see table; then ask one question only from 5a–5d.

| | Services (Q.4) | |
Rating (Q.3)	Received	Not Received
Better	Ask 5a	Ask 5c
Same/Worse	Ask 5b	Ask 5d

5a. *If problem better and service received, ask:*
Do you think SERVICE(S) RECEIVED was the reason for IMPROVEMENT MENTIONED? (Do you think IMPROVEMENT MENTIONED would have happened without your caseworker's help?)

5b. *If no improvement or worse and service received, ask:*
Why do you think SERVICE(S) RECEIVED didn't help to improve (*or,* change) PROBLEM(S) MENTIONED? (Why didn't SERVICE(S) RECEIVED make a difference? What do you think should have been done instead?)

5c. *If problem and no services received ask:*
Why do you think the IMPROVEMENT MENTIONED happened? (What happened to change things?)

5d. *If no improvement or worse and no services received ask:*
What do you think is the reason that PROBLEM(S) MENTIONED has (have) not improved (*or,* gotten better)? (Why didn't you mention it to your caseworker? Did you ask for any service or for your caseworker to do something? What did your caseworker say?)

6. *If client has any problem "still or now" (see Q.1), ask:*
Is there anything else you would like your caseworker to do to help you with PROBLEM(S) MENTIONED?

Section 11 Relationship with Social Worker

Now I'd like to find out some more about how you and your caseworker(s) got along together. I'll read a list of questions and you can answer "always," "usually," "sometimes," or "never."

If more than one worker, ask about current worker or the one assigned longest.

	Always	Usually	Sometimes	Never
1. Did your caseworker explain to you what she/he was trying to do and why she/he was doing it?	4	3	2	1
2. Did your caseworker give you confidence that headway or progress could be made on your problems?	4	3	2	1
3. Did (*or*, does) your caseworker ask for your opinions, about your problems, and about the kinds of help you want(ed)?	4	3	2	1
4. Did (*or*, does) your caseworker try to help you understand better your own feelings and behavior?	4	3	2	1
5. Do you feel your caseworker cared (*or*, cares) about you or was (*or*, is) concerned about you as a person?	4	3	2	1
6. Did (*or*, does) your caseworker fight for you or stick up for you with other agencies or other people? *Leave blank if not applicable.*	4	3	2	1
7. Do you feel that your caseworker was (*or*, is) easy to talk to?	4	3	2	1
8. Do you feel that your caseworker understood (*or*, understands) your opinions, even if she/he didn't (*or*, doesn't) always agree with you?	4	3	2	1
9. Do you have the feeling that you could (*or*, can) depend on or rely on your caseworker when you ran (*or*, run) into a problem?	4	3	2	1
10. Do you feel that your caseworker knew what she/he was doing, that she/he was organized?	4	3	2	1
11. Did your caseworker help you to talk about subjects that were not easy to talk about?	4	3	2	1
12. Did (*or*, does) your caseworker make you feel that everything wrong was your own fault?	4	3	2	1
13. Did your caseworker let you know when she/he thought you weren't working hard enough on your problems?	4	3	2	1
14. Did (*or*, does) your caseworker help you to see your good points as well as your problems?	4	3	2	1
15. Did (*or*, does) your caseworker visit you regularly and keep in touch with you?	4	3	2	1
16. Was (*or*, is) your caseworker available when you want(ed) or need(ed) her/him?	4	3	2	1
17. Do you feel your caseworker was (*or*, is) open or "straight" with you?	4	3	2	1

Ask only if case is closed:
You can answer the next two questions "yes," "no," or "not sure."

	Yes	No	Not Sure
18. Before your case closed, did your caseworker talk to you about what you had done together, about what you had accomplished?	1	2	3
19. Did you agree with the decision to close your case?	1	2	3

20. *If answered no or not sure to Q. 19, ask:*
    Why didn't you agree?

21. In general, how satisfied are you with the way you and your caseworker got along together? Are you
    Read responses 1–5 only:
    1. Very satisfied *Ask 21a.*
    2. Somewhat satisfied *Ask 21a.*
    3. Somewhat dissatisfied *Ask 21b.*
    4. Very dissatisfied, or *Ask 21b.*
    5. No particular feeling about it *Ask 21a.*

> 8. Other *Have client explain.*
> 9. Not sure

    21a. What did you like the most about your caseworker? *Ask Q.22.*
    21b. What didn't you like about your caseworker? *Ask Q.23.*

22. Was there anything about your caseworker that you didn't like? (What were you unhappy with?)
    Go to Q. 24.

23. Was there anything about your caseworker that you especially liked? (What was that?)

24. About how often did you see your caseworker? Was it
    Read responses 1–5 only:
    1. Several times a week
    2. About once a week
    3. About once every two weeks
    4. About once a month, or
    5. Less than once a month

> 0. Never
> 8. Other
> 9. Don't know, not sure

25. Do you feel you talked to your worker about the most important things? (*or*, the right things?)
    (What else did you want to talk about with your worker?)

26. Was there anything else you wanted your caseworker to do but, he/she didn't do? (What was that?)

27. Did your caseworker do anything you objected to, were against, or didn't want done? (What was that?)

Notes

1. This associanistic procedure is unfortunately not very sophisticated; it treats the change ratings as equal-interval measures and assigns equal weight to changes in each of the separate problem areas. See chapter 7 for details on reliability.

2. The Living Conditions section in the pilot interview is similar to the Housing and Economic Conditions section in the final version. See chapter 7 for further details.

7

Reliability and Validity of the Parent Outcome Interview

Introduction

The Parent Outcome Interview was pretested, revised, and then used in a large sample reliability and validity pilot study.

Pretest Results

The initial draft of the Parent Outcome Interview was pretested at two public agencies, the Baltimore County Department of Social Services and the Baltimore City Department of Social Services. Forty-four interviews were conducted with a convenience sample of parents where families were receiving child protective services. Interviews were conducted by agency social workers working as part-time researchers for the Child Welfare League. (Social workers did not interview their own clients.)

Three methods were used to analyze the interview process: an Interviewer Debriefing

Form, tape recording of some interviews, and content analysis of client responses. The debriefing form completed for each case asked whether the interviewer found the instructions, content, length, and format of the schedule satisfactory; whether the client understood each question, seemed to be threatened by any question, had to have questions repeated, had difficulty choosing responses, seemed accurate or truthful, and so forth. At one site, where permitted by agency and client, 10 interviews were tape recorded; this allowed a more direct inspection of the interview process. Content analysis of client answers was done in order to suggest how the interview questions might be improved.

Interviewers had some difficulty in writing down clients' responses since about half the questions required narrative answers. Some interviewers were more skilled than others in summarizing answers. The tape recordings indicated that significant parts of clients' answers were sometimes omitted, and that interesting probes were sometimes foregone in order to expedite the interview process. Thus, two important objectives for the final interview schedule were a decrease in the number of open-ended items and an overall reduction in the length of the interview.

The pretest indicated that the workers varied widely in their research interviewing (as opposed to casework interviewing) skills, and that consequently better selection and/or additional training for this task should be provided. Greater emphasis would have to be placed on training in the differences between casework and research interviewing.

The pretest also resulted in the rewording of some question "stems" and in changing item sequencing to improve interview flow. Open-ended response formats, however, were usually retained because one goal of the field work was to develop response categories based on clients' narrative answers to questions. The interview was revised on the basis of the pretest. A detailed study of the interview's reliability and validity, using a large sample of families, was then conducted with another group of agencies.

Final versus Pilot Version of the Interview

The Parent Outcome Interview was revised for a final time after the reliability and validity pilot study. The principal changes were: a further consolidation of individual sections, some alteration in question sequencing, increased structuring of some questions, increased uniformity in the section formats, and improved focusing of content. Although this may sound extensive, most of the interview content and the methods of assessing case change have remained quite similar. The main changes are described here, to aid in understanding the data presented in this chapter.

The pilot study interview had an Initial Case Exploration section that was broader in scope than the present Referral Situation section, which is restricted to assessment of change in presenting problem(s) only. The number of problem-specific sections on the pilot version was 12, in contrast to eight on the final version. Certain sections were found to be fairly redundant, prompting clients to remark that problems just discussed were being asked about again. Some redundance was also attributable to overlap in the services provided for families with multiple problems. These considerations led to three revisions: Economic Circumstances and Living Conditions were consolidated into a single Housing and Economic Conditions section; Children's Health Care, Physical Child Care, and Supervision of Children were consolidated into a new Physical Child Care section; and Disciplinary Behavior and Emotional Care of Children were consolidated into Discipline and Emotional Care of Children. In addition, the former Sexual Abuse section was generalized to a more inclusive Victimization of Children section.

The problem questions for each section on the pilot version were less structured and uniform than those appearing on the final version as a problem checklist. Thus it is not possible to do "before" and "after" comparisons of specific problems for the pilot interviews, although it could be done for the final version of the schedule.

Design for Reliability and Validity Study

Sample Selection

The Parent Outcome Interview sample for the reliability and validity study consisted of 250 families receiving child welfare services whose cases had been active between 5 and 6 months at the time of the interview. This seemed a reasonable time at which to assess case progress and also ensured a sufficient number of cases for the study.[1] Families had to have at least one child at home to be eligible for the interview. Sampling on these criteria was done during 1981 at three agencies: Texas Department of Human Resources (Dallas, $N = 74$, and Nacogdoches/Lufkin, $N = 29$); Hennepin County (Minnesota) Department of Community Services ($N = 51$); and Dade County (Florida) Deaprtment of Youth and Family Development ($N = 96$). In Dallas, sexual abuse cases were intentionally oversampled to allow individual analysis of this important category. Parents were contacted to participate until the desired quota of cases for the study was obtained. In 90% of the cases the person interviewed was the mother or maternal figure. (Sample demographics are given in the appendix.)

Sample Attrition

Interviews were conducted with 35% of the parents eligible for the study. A detailed analysis of reasons for interview noncompletion was possible for Dade and Nacogdoches; the results are presented in table 7-1.

The ability to generalize the findings on reliability and validity may depend on how well the interviewed cases represent all cases eligible for the study. In particular, is there any indication that interviewed families differed from the noninterviewed in the seriousness of their problems or in the amount of problem change that took place since referral?

The possibility of nonresponse bias was examined as follows. The Child Well-Being Scales were completed at intake and at the time of the interview on 61 interviewed families. The scales were also completed at intake and at 5 to 6 months after referral on 138 families for whom an interview could not be obtained.[2] No statistically significant differences ($p > .05$, two-tailed test), were found between interviewed and noninterviewed cases on mean Child Well-Being Scores at intake (82.3 versus 82.6, respectively) or on change in Child Well-Being Scores between intake and follow-up (6.3 versus 3.6, respectively). This suggests that the interviewed cases are typical of the case populations at these agencies.

Reliability of the Parent Outcome Interview

Equivalence of Change Ratings versus Descriptions of Change

In this and the next section we examine whether changing the format of the interview questions affects clients' responses. Clearly, the interview would not be very useful if its results

Table 7-1   Reasons for Noncompletion of Interviews[a]

Reason	%
Direct refusal (total)	33
Declined—no reason given	20
Too busy	8
Dissatisfied with agency	3
Illness in family	2
Unable to obtain response (total)	53
Phone not answered, no one at home, and/or follow-up letter answered	41
Message left with family member at home, no response	12
Unable to locate client (moved, etc.)	8
Client did not complete arrangements	4
Unknown	2
Total	100
(N)	(184)

[a] Information from Dade and Nacogdoches only.

depended largely on *how* questions were being asked, rather than on *what* was being asked. In other words, we are interested in the equivalence of alternate forms of asking the same question, a reliability issue. The analysis focuses specifically on the equivalence of alternate questions on case change, this being the most important aspect of the interview.

The interview obtains information on clients' perception of case change in two different ways: fixed-response ratings of change, and narrative descriptions of change. The two questions were linked; a change rating was obtained and then followed with a request for a description:

| "Better" | → | "What things are better now?" | → | "Is there anything else you wish was better?" (Explain) |
| "Worse" | → | "What things are worse now?" | | |

There were two types of change ratings. The first was a global rating: "Overall, how are things for your family now as compared with when you first talked to someone from (the agency)? Are things: a lot better, a little better, about the same, a little worse, or a lot worse?" The second was a rating for each of 12 problem-specific areas, for example: "How are your living conditions now as compared with when you first talked to someone from (THE AGENCY): a lot better, a little better, about the same, a little worse, or, a lot worse?"

The analysis for the global change rating is given in table 7-2. Of those responding "a lot better," 90% were able to describe some concrete problem improvement (excluding "optimism"), and of those responding "a little better," 82% were able to do so. Only 10 clients responded "worse," nine of whom described an example of problem deterioration. Note that a considerably higher percentage of clients responding "a lot better" said their referral problem was resolved (52%) than did those responding "a little better" (26%), which suggests that clients are making a meaningful distinction between the terms "a lot" and "a little."

Table 7-2   Analysis of Item Equivalence: Global
Change Rating vs. Descriptions of Change

Type of Change Described	Global Change Rating		
	A Lot Better (%)	A Little Better (%)	Worse (%)
Referral problem resolved, or has not recurred, and no threat of recurrence	52	26	0
Referral problem still exists, but lessened in frequency or intensity	23	34	0
No change in referral problem, but client more optimistic about progress	3	8	10
Improvement in some other problem (not referral problem)	15	22	0
No improvement described	7	10	90[a]
Totals	100	100	100
(N)	(99)	(82)	(10)

[a] Deterioration was described in these instances.

A similar analysis for the 12 problem-specific ratings of change is given in table 7-3. Again, the great majority of clients are able to describe problem improvement (or deterioration) to support their ratings of change. Also, in almost every comparison, clients responding "a lot better" are able to describe improvements more frequently than clients responding "a little better."[3]

These findings indicate that clients are quite consistent in responding to inquiries on problem change. Different ways of asking the question yield largely compatible results. Of course this fact does not necessarily mean that clients' responses are valid; that is, that such changes have actually occurred. Clients may be consistently misperceiving or misrepresenting their situations.

A related equivalence analysis compared ratings of change with clients' descriptions of additional change possibly needed; the results are presented in table 7-4.[4] Between 19% (School Adjustment and Children's Conduct) and 47% (Financial Situation) of clients responding "a lot better" for problem-specific areas believe additional improvements are still needed in those areas. This result indicates that ratings of "a lot better" do not necessarily reflect the resolution of all problems or the absence of a desire for further progress. This is important to keep in mind in interpreting any client interview results.

Equivalence of Global versus Problem-Specific Change Ratings

The pilot interview attempted to determine the equivalence of two different approaches to rating case change. One may be termed the "whole-case" approach, the other the "problem-specific" approach. The Initial Case Exploration section of the pilot interview was based on the whole-case idea. The section was relatively unstructured; clients were asked to describe their family's situation at the time of contact with the agency (including but not

Table 7-3   Analysis of Item Equivalence: Percentage of Clients Giving Each
Change Rating Who Described Improvement or Deterioration to
Support Their Rating, by Problem Area

	Rating of Change			
	Responding "A Lot Better" Who Describe Improvement % (N)	Responding "A Little Better" Who Describe Improvement % (N)	Responding "A Little Worse" Who Describe Deterioration % (N)	Responding "A Lot Worse" Who Describe Deterioration % (N)
Discipline of Children	98 (46)	91 (49)	89 (8)	100 (1)
Supervision of Children	96 (25)	91 (22)	100 (4)	—
Living Conditions	94 (26)	71 (12)	100 (5)	100 (2)
Financial Situation	92 (36)	a	96 (25)	a
Physical Child Care	100 (22)	100 (18)	100 (2)	—
Child Health Care	93 (28)	100 (11)	100 (1)	—
Emotional Child Care	97 (50)	84 (46)	67 (3)	100 (1)
School Adjustment	91 (54)	82 (29)	67 (3)	100 (6)
Children's Conduct	98 (52)	87 (53)	100 (12)	100 (9)
Symptomatic Behavior	85 (26)	80 (49)	100 (7)	100 (6)
Sexual Abuse	100 (19)	60 (10)	50 (2)[b]	—
Parental Coping	96 (39)	87 (40)	33 (4)	83 (4)

[a] The only rating choices were "better," "the same," or "worse."

[b] Deterioration described was not sexual reabuse.

Notes: N is the total number of clients giving each rating.

The problem areas listed are from the pilot interview.

The relationship between the pilot and final interviews is explained in the introduction to this chapter.

limited to the presenting problems leading to referral), to rate change in their family's overall situation between referral and the present, and to describe what had (or had not) changed. The problem-specific approach asked clients about problems and change in problems in 12 separate content areas. The potential advantage of the whole-case approach is that key problems might be focused on immediately and the outcome of the case could be measured in a single, brief global question. If the global and problem-specific ratings yield equivalent results, then the former might be preferred because of its brevity and simplicity.

The results of the analysis are given in table 7-5. Comparing the global with the problem-specific change ratings indicates that the latter are always less positive (except for Sexual Abuse); that is, the percentage of clients responding "a lot better" for the problem-specific areas range from 15% (Symptomatic Behavior) to 36% (School Adjustment), as compared with 40% for the global rating.

In addition, an Average Change score was computed by averaging the change ratings for the specific-problem areas (that is, "a lot better" = 5 to "a lot worse" = 1). Average Change was only moderately correlated with the global change rating ($r = .41$).

These results indicate that the whole-case and problem-specific approaches to rating change cannot be considered equivalent. The whole-case approach appears to yield considerably more positive findings, and the change measures from each are not highly correlated.[5]

At least part of the explanation for these differences is that clients tended to respond to the global question on the basis of change in the problem leading to referral, as they defined it

Table 7-4   Analysis of Item Equivalence: Percentage of Clients Giving Each Change Rating Who Believe Change Still Needed, by Problem Area

	Rating of Change			
	Responding "A Lot Better" Who Believe Change Still Needed		Responding "A Little Better" Who Believe Change Still Needed	
	%	(N)	%	(N)
Discipline of Children	25	(46)	31	(49)
Supervision of Children	0	(25)	14	(22)
Living Conditions	42	(26)	50	(12)
Financial Situation	47	(36)	a	
Physical Child Care	0	(22)	0	(18)
Child Health Care	7	(28)	0	(11)
Emotional Child Care	42	(50)	39	(46)
School Adjustment	19	(54)	38	(29)
Children's Conduct	19	(51)	55	(49)
Symptomatic Behavior	0	(25)	2	(48)
Sexual Abuse	b		b	
Parental Coping	b		b	

[a] Only rating choices were "better," "the same," or "worse."

[b] Not coded or not asked.

Notes: N is the total number of clients giving each rating.

The problem areas listed are from the pilot interview; for further details, see the introduction to this chapter.

(refer to table 7-2). In other words, the global rating tended to assign greater weight to change in the problem leading to referral than to changes in other problems the family had at that time. Clients were apparently not trying, or not able, to subjectively "average" changes in all areas of their families' lives in making the global rating. Consequently, although the difference observed between the global and problem-specific change ratings may not signal inconsistency, the results do imply that a global rating alone will fail to provide a representative view of changes in all significant life areas for a family.

These findings led to a revision of the Initial Case Exploration section, which was renamed Referral Situation. Instead of trying to obtain a global change rating from clients, the section was refocused explicitly on the client's view of the problem precipitating referral and perceived change in that problem. The change in the section also serves to minimize redundancy between the content of this section and the subsequent problem-specific sections.

Reliability of Composite Change Score

It is useful to construct a summary measure of case change for the interview based on the problem-specific change ratings. This is analogous to the total Child Well-Being Score constructed from the Child Well-Being Scale ratings.

The 12 problem-specific change ratings were moderately intercorrelated ($r = .31$). This indicates that the change ratings possess some common element. It may be systematic

Table 7-5   Client Ratings of Change by Problem Area
(N = 250)

	% of Clients with Each Problem at Referral[a]	% of Clients Giving Each Rating of Change[b]				
		A Lot Better	A Little Better	Same, No Improvement	A Little Worse	A Lot Worse
Global Rating	—	40	33	20	2	2
Discipline of Children	59	32	33	29	5	1
Supervision of Children	40	25	22	48	4	1
Living Conditions	49	21	11	62	4	2
Financial Situation	66	19	c	66	c	15
Physical Child Care	50	18	14	66	2	0
Child Health Care	56	20	9	69	1	1
Emotional Child Care	76	26	24	47	2	1
School Adjustment	60	36	20	38	2	4
Children's Conduct	77	27	25	37	6	5
Symptomatic Behavior	65	15	30	47	4	4
Sexual Abuse	13[d]	60	31	3	0	6
Parental Coping	67	23	24	49	2	2

[a] Percentages for change ratings based on clients who stated having a given problem at referral.

[b] For global rating, 3% gave "other" responses. For problem-specific ratings, other responses and non-responses were negligible.

[c] Only rating choices were "better," "the same," or "worse."

[d] Sexual abuse cases were oversampled; this is *not representative* of agencies' caseloads.

Note: The problem areas listed are from the pilot interview; for further details, see the introduction to this chapter.

response bias, in that there may be an item "carryover effect" from one rating to the next. In refutation of this, other analysis in this chapter shows that clients' narrative descriptions of change nearly always supported their ratings of change. If there is some systematic bias in clients' change ratings, it occurred with very few contradictions in the course of a 2-hour interview.

Other than response bias, the positive correlation between change ratings may be attributable to the fact that problems in the different areas are actually aspects of the same situation, or that they are causally related to each other. (Indeed, this observation led to the consolidation of certain sections of the interview, as described earlier.) It may also be that services have a positive effect not only on the problems to which they are explicitly addressed, but on other problems as well. Explaining the correlations among change ratings in this way justifies constructing a composite measure of change.

The method selected was to average the problem-specific change ratings to yield an Average Change score. This procedure treats the change ratings as equal interval measures and gives equal weight to change in each of the problem areas. The internal consistency of this measure based on 12 change ratings was alpha = .84. The internal consistency of an Average Change score based on the current eight problem areas can also be estimated. Assuming that the average intercorrelation remains the same (r = .31), the result is alpha = .78.[6]

Reliability of Relationship with Social Worker Scale

An index of Relationship with Social Worker was constructed by averaging the ratings of the first 17 items in that section of the interview. To create an index with origin at zero, the responses were recoded "always" = 3, "usually" = 2, "sometimes" = 1, and "never" = 0. The measure thus ranges from 3 (most positive) to 0 (least positive). The mean intercorrelation of the items was $r = .43$ and the internal consistency of the scale was alpha = .93.

An alternative measure of the quality of the client-social worker relationship was a global question on the client's satisfaction with the social worker: "In general, how satisfied are you with the way you and your social worker got along together?" The responses were recoded as follows: "very satistifed" = 5, "somewhat satisfied" = 4, "no particular feeling" = 3, "somewhat dissatisfied" = 2, and "very dissatisfied" = 1. The correlation between the relationship scale and the global satisfaction item can be considered an equivalence coefficient; this was $r = .60$. This result indicates that positive relationship scores are quite highly associated with general satisfaction, as would be expected for reliable measurement.

The format of the items comprising the Relationship with Social Worker scale makes them potentially susceptible to an "acquiescent response set," defined as any tendency to agree with questions irrespective of their content (Selltiz et al. 1976: 165–166). The usual strategy to compensate for this tendency is to vary the directionality of a set of items. For example, items are constructed so that a high score on the attribute being measured can be obtained only if the respondent agrees with half the items and disagrees with the other half. On the present scale, the directionality of 16 of the items is the same, in that positive responses are signified by "always."

Analogous questions constructed with reverse directionality were considered awkward in view of the frequency assessments required by the fixed responses. Alternative responses using (for example) an "agree-disagree" format would have allowed mixed directionality, but at the expense of logical compatibility between the question stems and the fixed responses.

One question with reverse directionality was included, however, to help signal the presence of any acquiescent response bias: "Did your social worker make you feel that everything wrong was your own fault?" If clients are tending to respond "always" to the questions irrespective of their content, then answers to this question should be positively correlated with answers to the other questions. The mean correlation between this question and the other 16 questions was found to be negative ($r = -.26$). This shows that clients were internally consistent in responding to the reversed "fault" item. In fact, the correlation might have been more strongly negative if responses to the "fault" item had not been so highly skewed—82% of the responses were "never."

Validity of the Parent Outcome Interview

Face Validity of Descriptions of Change

Clients' narrative descriptions of perceived changes in the various problem areas were categorized using content analysis; the results are given in table 7-6. This helps to clarify the bases of clients' change ratings. The descriptions generally seem to reflect what child welfare

Table 7-6   Client Descriptions of Improvement by Problem Area

	% of Clients[a]
Discipline of Children	
More effective control by using alternative or modified disciplinary techniques	17
Less discipline required because children's conduct improved	30
Parent more at ease in administering discipline	29
Increased understanding of or communication with children	29
Supervision of Children	
Improved awareness or alertness regarding children's activities or whereabouts	39
Decreased supervision responsibilities (e.g., receiving more familial help)	18
Increased capacity to supervise (e.g., being home more or drinking less)	25
Improved responsiveness of children to supervision	25
Living Conditions	
Moved to new residence	61
Improvement made in current residence	20
Financial Situation	
Increased income (or reduced expenses)	61
Improved budgeting skills	52
Physical Child Care	
Improvement on all problems mentioned	55
Improvement on some problems only	45
Child Health Care	
All health care obtained	67
Some health care obtained but more required	28
School Adjustment	
Conduct in school	37
Grades	27
Attendance	25
"Academic" behavior (e.g., studying)	14
New school/class/teacher	13
Receiving specialized instruction	8
Children's Conduct	
No recurrence of problem(s)	26
Problem(s) not as frequent or intense	65
Other	10
Children's Symptomatic Behavior	
No recurrence of symptoms	10
Symptom(s) not as frequent or intense	75
Other	13
Emotional Child Care	
More patience and understanding of children or improved control of frustrations	65
Children more responsive, more mature, or less troublesome	20
Parent has increased contact with children	16
Parent has more support from others to relieve stress or assist in child care	8

Table 7-6   (Continued)

Parental Coping	% of Clients[a]
Positive change in mental attitude (e.g., more optimistic, feels more capable, resolved internal conflicts, accepts self, different perspective on life)	57
Better relations with family and others (e.g., less conflict, more communication)	23
More support from others or someone to talk to	11
Believes that problems are being worked on and will be resolved	11
Fewer personal responsibilities or demands from others	7
Sexual Abuse	
Person responsible removed from household and/or contact with person severed	37
Child in foster care or otherwise out of the home	27
Child receiving adequate supervision now	17
Other descriptions	19

[a] Percentages are based on number of clients responding "a lot" or "a little better" in each problem area. More than one description could be given; thus percentages may sum to more than 100%.

Note: The problem areas listed are from the pilot interview; for further details, see the introduction to this chapter.

professionals would regard as substantive improvements, although the study did not formally examine this. (There were too few descriptions of deterioration for a content analysis.)

Considering the types of change reported by clients may help an agency to assess whether a program or service is helping clients in the ways intended and may identify differences between agencies and clients in their definitions of case improvement or deterioration. There is some evidence for child and family services that clients' and workers' perceptions can be discrepant (Maluccio 1979; Pelton 1982).

Construct Validity of Composite Change Score

If we hypothesize that the receipt of agency services has some effect, however small, on case outcomes, then an observed relationship between services received and ratings of change can be interpreted as evidence of the latter's construct validity. To examine this, numbers of services received by families in each problem-specific area (categorized as none, one, and two or more) were cross-tabulated with clients' change ratings for the respective areas. Gamma, a measure of association for ordinal-level data, ranged from a high of .57 for Living Conditions to a low of .20 for Children's Conduct; the mean gamma for all areas was .35. This indicates a moderate tendency toward positive change ratings when more services have been received.[7] In addition, the correlation between the Average Change score and total number of services received by the family was $r = .30$.

It is likely that these correlations would be higher if the study had a more direct measure of service intensity. "Number of services received" is only a rough indicator of service intensity, which would be better measured by the number and duration of worker-client contacts or by the number of units of service received. The Parent Outcome Interview is not designed to document services quantitatively in any detail. Nevertheless, the moderate correlations found between services and case change do support the construct validity of the change ratings.

Convergent Validity of Problem Checklists

The convergent validity of the problem checklists on the interview was examined by comparing clients' checklist responses with social workers' Child Well-Being Scale ratings. The Parent Outcome Interview and the Child Well-Being Scales represent entirely different methodologies, but they focus on similar child welfare concerns. The analysis is for 96 families who were both interviewed and had the scales completed at 5 to 6 months after case opening. The demographic characteristics of this data set (Worker/Parent Problem Comparison) are given in the appendix.[8]

Problem information is not obtained on the two instruments in the same way, so the question of how to structure the desired comparisons must be addressed. There are two possible approaches to making the two sets of problem data commensurable. One would be to record the data from each instrument according to a new, uniform format. The other would be to recode the data from one of the instruments according to the format of the other. The approach chosen was the second; specifically, the Parent Outcome Interview problem check-list data were recoded to conform to the categories of the Child Well-Being Scales. This allowed recoding to be limited to only one data set and also used the more standardized and conceptually developed coding framework.

Consequently, the Parent Outcome Interview problem checklists were reviewed to identify the existence of problems as defined by the Child Well-Being Scales. Problems were coded dichotomously for each scale type—"no problem" vs. "some problem"—because we determined that the precise level of a problem as conceptualized on the Child Well-Being Scales could not be coded with sufficient reliability from the Parent Outcome Interviews. Ratings on the worker-completed Child Well-Being Scales were similarly dichotomized for the analysis. Comparisons were of problems as they existed at the 5 to 6 month point in the case.

Kappa was used as the measure of agreement between the data from workers and clients.[9] The mean kappa, averaged over all problem types, was .62. K_1, the conditional measure of client agreement with worker ratings of "adequate" (no problem), was .58. K_2, the conditional measure of client agreement with worker ratings below adequate (some level of problem), was .73; that is, clients agree with workers more often when workers report problems than when they report no problems. This result indicates that, on average the interview is picking up more problems than are the scales.

It is important not to conclude from this that clients are necessarily more disposed to report problems than are their social workers. The nature of the interview, involving opportunities for open-end response, interviewer probes, and perhaps an even wider range of issues than the scales, could well account for the findings. Thus, if workers had been interviewed for 2 hours instead of completing the scales, it is likely that additional client problems would have been reported. In other words, it is not the source of the information as much as the mode of eliciting it that probably accounts for the results of the comparisons.

The overall level of agreement between clients and workers on problems seems encouraging and increases our confidence in the validity of both instruments. Perfect agreement, given the great difference in measurement methods and the difficulty of administering the instruments at precisely identical times, cannot be expected. In addition, there may be some disagreements between workers and clients in the definition of a problem that cannot be reduced to a simple question of "yes" or "no." The present analysis indicates that worker- and client-derived problem information is usually mutually supportive but not entirely redundant; one method is not a substitute for the other.

Convergent Validity of Change Measures

The convergent validity of the change measures from the interview was examined by comparing clients' global change rating and the Average Change score with the Child Well-Being Scales' composite change score. The analysis is for 61 families who were both interviewed 5 to 6 months after case opening *and* had the Child Well-Being Scales completed twice, at intake and at the time of the interview. The demographic characteristics of this data set (worker/Parent Outcome Comparison) are given in the appendix.

The findings are as follows: the correlation between clients' global change rating and CWBS change was $r = .09$ and that between Average Change and CWBS change was .11. These correlations are low, clearly indicating that measuring case change by the interview and by the scales yields different results.

One possible explanation of the findings is that workers and clients do not agree on the assessment of case change. This explanation finds support in the research literature, but leaves open the question of which source of information, the worker or the client, should be considered more valid, or whether both are biased in some manner. The apparently high reliability of the data from both sources, though not ruling out invalidity, certainly indicates that other possible explanations of the findings should be considered.

Above all, the consequences of using two entirely different instruments to measure change must be evaluated. Although it is true that both instruments address the same child welfare issues, there is usually no one-to-one correspondence between the various problem sections on the two instruments. This fact makes it difficult to determine whether the composite change measures from the instruments are giving similar emphasis to the different problem types and to their associated measures of change.

A more sensitive test of convergent validity would compare changes on a problem-by-problem basis. This would also help to control for differences between workers and clients on initial problem definitions, which have been shown to contribute significantly to subsequent differences in overall case outcome assessments (Mutschler and Rosen 1980).

Unfortunately, the sample size for this analysis was too small to permit a more detailed quantitative comparison of changes for specific problem types. A review of the raw data did give the impression of greater congruence between the scales and the interview for relatively homogeneous areas such as environmental problems or child behavior. At this point, however, we do not know exactly how the composite measures of change from the two instruments should be adjusted to increase their comparability. This is an important topic for further instrument development and research.

"Social Desirability" Bias

An inherent problem in interviewing on sensitive topics is the possibility that respondents might not be entirely truthful. There is always concern that respondents might be disposed to give answers that are socially acceptable or that present a favorable image of themselves. Such threats to the validity of a measure are known by the term "social desirability" bias (Selltiz et al. 1976:165–166).

It is not possible to know with certainty the extent to which such bias influenced the Parent Outcome Interview. Since clients are reporting largely on facts known only to themselves, independent verification of their responses is usually not possible, even if the

Table 7-7   Client Descriptions of Dissatisfaction With Agency/Social Worker
(N = 250)

	% of Sample[a]
Did not agree with the worker's ideas about how to handle case problems	23
Disliked the worker's attitude—perceived as condemning, pushy, threatening, impersonal, or biased	13
Believed the agency did not provide needed help with financial problems	9
Said the agency did not provide needed help with parent's mental or emotional health problems	8
Believed not enough services offered for other types of problems	9
Said the service provided did not benefit or actually hurt the family	6
Believed the worker was inexperienced or incompetent	5
Did not think their problem(s) were serious enough to justify agency involvement	3
Gave some other reason	5

[a] Some clients gave more than one reason.

Note: Citing a dissatisfaction does not mean a client was dissatisfied overall—see text.

resources were available to attempt it. For example, clients' workers are not an entirely independent source of information. Much of what workers "know" about their clients is based on client disclosures; workers too are faced with the problem of verification and the need to decide what to accept as "true."

One indication of clients' general truthfulness is simply their observed willingness to admit to problems. This attitude may be seen, first, in their descriptions of the problem that precipitated referral to the agency. These descriptions were consistent with the accepted problems of concern to child welfare agencies. The descriptions given by clients were categorized as follows: child behavior (35%), physical neglect or inadequate child care (25%), sexual abuse (13%), physical abuse (10%), and mixed (16%). Second, even clients who judged matters were "a lot better" in a given problem area tended to describe at least one remaining (or new) problem in that area. This reaction would not be expected if clients were strongly influenced by a social desirability bias.

Logically, one would not expect to find a high association between a measure of problem change and a measure of current problems, since even clients with continuing, serious problems may have experienced considerable improvement from an even worse prior situation. This circumstance was in fact the case; the mean correlation between ratings of change and numbers of current reported problems, across all problem areas, was negligible ($r = .09$).[10] This analysis is also consistent with the previous finding that many clients reporting matters "a lot better" nevertheless perceived a need for further improvement (refer to table 7-4).

Even if clients are willing to discuss their own problems with an interviewer, they may not be willing to express criticism of the agency and their worker. This unwillingness may be due to generalized anxiety or to specific fear of repercussions that even assurances of confidentiality may not completely allay. Also, clients willing to offer criticisms may still not be able to articulate them in a useful way.

In response to a global question, 70% of clients expressed at least mild overall satisfaction with the "services or help" they received from the agency.[11] Overall satisfaction with the agency and satisfaction with the worker-client relationship were highly correlated ($r = .64$). In describing their reasons for satisfaction, clients tended to reiterate some specific service they had received; a wide variety of services were mentioned favorably. The most notable finding was that 25% of clients mentioned favorable traits of, or the positive relationship developed with, their social workers.

It was possible to develop a typology of reasons for dissatisfaction; the results are given in table 7-7; 60% mentioned at least one issue. Even clients who said they were generally satisfied often mentioned a point of dissatisfaction when asked a more specific question, such as, "Was there anything you wanted your social worker to do that he or she didn't do?" These results indicate that clients are willing and able to offer concrete criticism of the agency and its staff. Certainly, in order to improve the provision of services, or at least to make them more acceptable to clients, it is important to know clients' points of satisfaction and dissatisfaction with agency efforts.[12]

A final indicator of client truthfulness is the interviewer's overall impression of client demeanor, as rated on the authors' Interviewer Debriefing Form. The results were: "completely candid/very open" (59%); "generally frank/only slightly reluctant" (32%); "somewhat hesitant and cautious about responding" (7%); and "withholding/sometimes clearly not truthful" (2%). Interviewers' commentaries supported their ratings of the clients.

Notes

1. It would have been preferable to interview clients at the time of case closing, since greatest case change might be expected by then. The period for the conduct of the interviews was, however, too short to allow waiting for many cases to close.

2. These families were part of the agency intake sample, described in chapter 4.

3. This analysis cannot determine whether the *amounts* of change considered important by clients would also be considered important by social workers.

4. This information was obtained from the question noted above, "Is there anything else you wish was better?", or its variants. This question does not appear on the final version of the interview. Instead, clients are now asked at the end of each section whether there is anything else they would like the worker to do or to help them with.

5. Note that $r = .41$ means that the two change measures have only 17% of their variance in common.

6. The formula for estimating this is given in Carmines and Zeller (1979:44).

7. Perfect positive or negative association is indicated by gamma = $\pm$ 1; no association by gamma = 0 (Blalock 1972).

8. The 96 families are a subset of the 250 interviewed families. The Child Well-Being Scales were completed by social workers on the earliest families interviewed, to allow time for analysis.

9. See chapter 5 for an explanation of the kappa coefficient.

10. A positive correlation here means that more current problems are associated with less case improvement.

11. This is now question 7 in Referral Situation. Details on reasons for satisfaction and dissatisfaction with the agency and social worker were obtained with questions similar to 7a through 8a in Referral Situation and 21a through 27 in Relationship with Social Worker.

12. Whether clients' opinions are "justified" cannot be determined through the interview process alone. The objective is for agencies to learn about clients' perception of the situation.

Appendix

Table A-1   Demographic Characteristics of Case Samples Used for Reliability and Validity Analyses

	Number of Families	Family Status (% One Parent)	Ethnicity (% Mothers White)	Number of Adults (% Two or More)	Number of Children (Mean)	Mother's Age (Mean)	Children's Age (Mean)[a]
1. Intake	240	56	59	59	2.4	33.7	9.4
Followed up	192	58	56	61	2.4	34.3	9.8
Not Followed up	48	50	73	52	2.4	31.2	7.7
2. Parent Interview	250	62	67	64	2.3	32.3	9.1
3. Worker/Parent Problem Comparison	96	65	50	59	2.5	31.7	8.5
4. Worker/Parent Outcome Comparison	61	56	55	64	2.3	32.0	8.6
5. Repeated Measures	86	70	33	53	2.3	32.8	10.1
6. Worker/Supervisor Comparison	32	63	42	47	2.7	36.8	10.3

[a] A mean age was computed for all children in each family, and then the mean of the family means was computed as the table entry.

Note: Demographic characteristics were not tabulated for the Case Record Comparison data set.

References

Abidin, R. R. The Parenting Stress—Clinical Trials. Paper presented at the meeting of the American Psychological Association, September 1979.

———. Parenting Stress Index (PSI): Clinical Interpretation of Scores for Form #5 (self-scoring). 1982a. Mimeo.

———. "Parenting Stress and Utilization of Pediatric Services." Children's Health Care 11 (Fall 1982b).

———. The Parenting Stress Index (PSI): A Review of the Research. n.d. Mimeo.

Achenbach, T. M. The Classification of Children's Psychiatric Symptoms: A Factor Analytic Study. Psychological Monographs, 1966, 80 (7, whole no. 615).

———. "The Child Behavior Profile: I. Boys Aged 6–11." Journal of Consulting and Clinical Psychology 46 (1978): 478–488.

———. "The Child Behavior Profile: An Empirically Based System for Assessing Children's Behavioral Problems and Competencies." International Journal of Mental Health 7, 3–4 (1979): 24–42.

———, and Edelbrock, C. S. "The Child Behavior Profile: II. Boys Aged 12–16 and Girls Aged 6–11 and 12–16." Journal of Consulting and Clinical Psychology 47 (1979): 223–233.

———, and Edelbrock, C. S. "The Classification of Child Psychopathology: A Review and Analysis of Empirical Efforts." Psychological Bulletin 85 (1978): 1275–1301.

———, and Edelbrock, C. S. Behavioral Problems and Competencies Reported by Parents of Normal and Disturbed Children Aged 4–16. Monograph Social Res. in Child Development, 1981, 46, #188 (University of Chicago Press, Chicago, IL).

Alderton, H. R. "The Children's Pathology Index as a Predictor of Follow-up Adjustment." Canadian Psychiatric Association Journal 15(1970): 290–294.

———. "The Residential Treatment Response of Disturbed Children Using Serial Ratings of Adjustment." Canadian Psychiatric Association Journel 17 (1972a): 294–298.

———. "A Comparison of the Residential Treatment Response of Children's Aid Society Wards and Non-Wards." Canadian Psychiatric Association Journal 17 (1972b): 291–293.

———, and Hoddinott, B. A. "The Children's Pathology Index." Canadian Psychiatric Association Journal 13 (1968): 353–361.

Alpern, G. The Developmental Profile: Review of the Instrument and Recent Research. Proceedings of the Second International Conference on Developmental Screening: 49–65. n.d. Mimeo.

Alpern, G. D., and Boll, T. J. Developmental Profile. Aspen, Colorado: Psychological Development Publications, 1972.

Alpern, G. D.; Boll, T. J.; and Shearer, M. S. The Developmental Profile II Manual. Aspen, CO: Psychological Development Publications, 1980.

American Public Welfare Association. A Report of the National Conference on Client Outcome Monitoring Procedures for Social Services. Washington, D.C.: American Public Welfare Association, 1980.

245

————. VCIS Data Gathering Instrument for Public Child Welfare Services. Final Instrument. Washington, D.C.: American Public Welfare Association, 1982.

Andreasen, N. C.; Grove, W. M.; Shapiro, R. W.; Keller M. B.; Hirschenfeld, R.M.A.; and McDonald-Scott, Patricia. "Reliability of Lifetime Diagnosis." Archives of General Psychiatry 38 (April 1981): 400–405.

Bandura, A. Social Learning Theory. New York: General Learning Press, 1971.

Barker, W. F. Emotional Development Scale for Children. Glenside, PA: Beaver College, n.d.

Barker, W. F., and Doeff, A. M. Preschool Behavior Rating Scale: Administration and Scoring Manual. New York, NY: Child Welfare League of America, 1980a.

————. Preschool Behavior Rating Scale. Methodology: How the PBRS Was Developed. New York, NY: Child Welfare League of America, 1980b.

Beck, D. F. "Patterns for University-Agency Cooperation in the Teaching of Research." Social Casework 60 (June 1979): 343–349.

Beck, D. F., and Jones, M. A. Progress on Family Problems. New York, NY: Family Service Association of America, 1973.

————. "A Look at Clientele and Services of Family Agencies." Social Casework 55 (December 1974): 589–599.

————. "Do Family Services Help? A Response." Social Service Review 50 (June 1976): 314–315.

————. How to Conduct a Client Follow-up Study. Second and enlarged edition. New York, NY: Family Service Association of America, 1980.

Benedict, W. R. Eval-u-Treat. Madison, WI: Lutheran Social Services of Wisconsin and Upper Michigan, Inc., July 1978.

Berkeley Planning Associates. Evaluation of Child Abuse and Neglect Demonstration Projects 1974–1977. Volume III. Adult Client Impact, Final Report. Berkeley, CA: Berkeley Planning Associates, 1977.

Blalock, H. M. Social Statistics (2nd edition). New York, NY: McGraw-Hill, Inc., 1972.

Blenkner, M. "Obstacles to Evaluative Research in Casework: Part II." Social Casework 31 (March 1950): 97–105.

Blischke, W. R.; Bush, J. W.; and Kaplan, R. M. "Successive Intervals Analysis of Preference Measures in a Health Status Index." Health Services Research 10 (Summer 1975): 181–198.

Bowers, E., and Bowers, R. The Elusive Unit of Service. Human Services Monograph Series. No. 1. Rockville, MD: Project Share, Aspen Systems Corporation, DHEW Contract no. HEW-100-75-0179, 1976.

Briar, Scott. "The Age of Accountability." Social Work 18 (January 1973): 2.

Burke, W. T., and Abidin, R. R. The Development of a Parenting Stress Index, Paper presented at the meeting of the American Psychological Association, August 1978.

Bush, M.; Gordon, A. C.; and LeBailley, R. "Evaluating Child Welfare Services: A Contribution From Clients." Social Services Review 51 (September 1977): 491–501.

Caldwell, Bettye M., and Bradley, Robert H. Home Observation for Measurement of the Environment. Little Rock, AR: University of Arkansas, 1978.

Campbell, D. T., and Boruch, R. F. Making the Case for Randomized Assignment to Treatments by Considering the Alternatives: Six Ways In Which Quasi-experimental Evaluations Tend to Underestimate Effects. In Evaluation and Experience: Some Critical Issues in Assessing Social Programs, edited by C. A. Bennett and A. A. Rumsdaine. New York, NY: Academic Press, 1975.

Carmines, E. G., and Zeller, R. A. "Reliability and Validity Assessment." Beverly Hills, CA: Sage Publications, Inc., 1979.

Chess, Wayne A.; Norlin, Julia M.; and Chiles, Lois S. Final Report: The Oklahoma County Child Protective Services System: Views of Clients Attending Parents Assistance Center. Norma, OK: School of Social Work, University of Oklahoma, 1982.

Child Welfare League of America. Standards for Child Protective Service. (revised edition.) New York, NY: Child Welfare League of America, Inc., 1973.

Ciarlo, J. A., and Reihman, J. The Denver Community Mental Health Questionnaire: Development of a Multi-Dimensional Program Evaluation Instrument. Denver, CO: Mental Health Systems Evaluation Project of the Northwest Denver Mental Health Center and the University of Denver, 1974.

Ciarlo, J. A.; Edwards, D. W.; Kiresuk, T. J.; Newman, F. L.; and Brown, T. R. Final Report: The Assessment of Client/Patient Outcome Techniques for Use in Mental Health Programs. Denver, CO: University of Denver, 1981.

Ciminero, Anthony R., and Drabman, Ronald S. "Current Developments in the Behavioral Assessment of Children," in Advances in Clinical Child Psychology, Vol. 1., edited by B. B. Lahey and A. E. Kazdin. New York, NY: Plenum Press, 1977.

Cohen, J. "A Coefficient of Agreement for Nominal Scales." Educational and Psycholgical Measurement 20 (1960): 37–46.

Collignon, Frederick C.; Banks, Karen; Hansen, Susan. Testing Measures of Performance for Protective Services. Berkeley, CA: Berkeley Planning Associates, 1981.

Conners, C. K. "Global Rating Scales for Childhood Psychopharmacology," in Guidelines for the Clinical Evaluation of Psychoactive Drugs in Infants and Children. HEW(FDA) 79-3055. Rockville, MD: U.S. Department of Health, Education, and Welfare, 1979.

Cook, T. D., and Campbell, D. T. Quasi-Experimentation. Chicago, IL: Rand McNally College Publishing Company, 1979.

Coombes, P.; McCormack, M.; Chipley, M.; and Archer, B. "The INCADEX Approach to Identifying Problems and Evaluating Impact in Child Protective Services." Child Welfare LVII (January 1978a): 35–44.

Coombes, P.; McCormack, M.; Chipley, M. H.; Archer, B.; and Norman, J. C. Manual for Using Abuse and Neglect Indicators and Index. Austin, TX: Region VI Resource Center on Child Abuse and Neglect, School of Social Work, University of Texas at Austin, 1978b.

Coulton, Claudia J., and Solomon, Phyllis L. "Measuring Outcomes of Intervention." Social Work Research and Abstracts 13 (Winter 1977): 3–9.

Cronbach, L. J., and Furby, L. "How We Should Measure 'Change'—or Should We?" Psychological Bulletin 74 (1970): 68–80.

Cytrynbaum, S.; Ginath, Y.; Birdwell, J.; and Brandt, L. "Goal Attainment Scaling: A Critical Review." Evaluation Quarterly 3 (February 1979): 5–40.

Davis, H. "Four Ways to Goal Attainment." Evaluation 1, 2 (1973): 43–48.

Denzin, N. K. The Research Act. New York, NY: McGraw-Hill, 1978.

Deutscher, I. "Toward Avoiding the Goal-Trap in Evaluation Research," in The Evaluation of Social Programs, edited by C. C. Abt. Beverly Hills, CA: Sage Publications, 1976.

Edelbrock, C. S., and Achenbach, T. M. "A Typology of Child Behavior Profile Patterns: Distribution and Correlates for Disturbed Children Aged 6–16." Journal of Abnormal Psychology 8, 4 (1980): 441–470.

Edwards, A. L. Techniques of Attitude Scale Construction (2nd edition). New York, NY: Irvington, 1982.

Eisen, Marvin; Donald, Cathy A.; Ware, John E.; and Brook, Robert H. Conceptualization and Measurement of Health for Children in the Health Insurance Study. Santa Monica, CA: Rand, May 1980.

Ellsworth, R. B. "Consumer Feedback in Measuring the Effectiveness of Mental Health Programs," in Handbook of Evaluation Research, Vol. 2, edited by M. Guttentag and E. L. Struening. Beverly Hills, CA: Sage Publications, 1975.

Epstein, A. S. Assessing the Child Development Information Needed by Adolescent Parents with Very Young Children. Final Report. Ypsilanti, MI: High/Scope Educational Research Foundation, January 1980.

Eric Clearinghouse on Early Childhood Education. Research Relating to Children. Bulletins 36–42. Urbana, IL: Eric Clearinghouse on Early Childhood Education, 1975–1979.

Evans, W. R. "The Behavior Problem Checklist: Data From an Inner-City Population." Psychology in the Schools 12 (1975): 301–303.

Filstead, W. J.; Shadish, W. R.; Crandell, J. S.; Altman, D. B.; Gottlieb, D. B.; and Visotsky, J. L. "Developing a Multidimensional Clinical Rating Scale." Evaluation Review 6 (August 1982): 559–576.

Fitz-Gibbons, C. T., and Morris, L. L. How to Design a Program Evaluation. Beverly Hills, CA: Sage Publications, 1978.

Fleiss, J. L., and Cohen, J. "The Equivalence of Weighted Kappa and the Intraclass Correlation Coefficient as Measures of Reliability." Educational and Psychological Measurement 33 (1973): 613–619.

Frederiksen, H., and Mulligan, R. A. The Child and His Welfare. San Francisco, CA: W. H. Freeman, 1972.

Garbarino, J.; Stocking, S. H.; and Associates. Protecting Children from Abuse and Neglect. San Francisco, CA: Jossey-Bass Publishers, 1980.

Geismar, L. L. 555 Families. A Social-Psychological Study of Young Families in Transition. New Brunswick, NJ: Transaction Books, 1973.

———. Family and Community Functioning (2nd edition). Metuchen, NJ: The Scarecrow Press, 1980.

————, and Geismar, S. Families in an Urban Mold. New York, NY: Pergamon Press, 1979.

————, and Krisberg, J. The Forgotten Neighborhood. Metuchen, NJ: The Scarecrow Press, Inc., 1967.

————; Lagay, G.; Wolock, I.; Gerhart, U. C.; and Fink, H. Early Supports for Family Life. Metuchen, NJ: Scarecrow Press, 1972.

————, and LaSorte, M. A. Understanding the Multi-Problem Family. A Conceptual Analysis and Exploration in Early Identification. New York, NY: Associated Press, 1964.

————; LaSorte, M.; and Ayres, B. "Measuring Family Disorganization." Marriage and Family Living 24, 1 (1962): 52–60.

Giovannoni, J. M., and Bacerra, R. M. Defining Child Abuse. New York, NY: Free Press, 1979.

Goldstein, J.; Solnit, A.; and Freud, A. Beyond the Best Interests of the Child. New York, NY: Free Press, 1973.

Greenblatt, B., and Bruder, G. "Note on an Experiment with Questionnaire Length." New York: State University of New York at Buffalo, 1982. Mimeo.

Guidance Associates of Delaware. Wide Range Achievement Test. Wilmington, DE: Guidance Associates of Delaware, 1965.

Hagan, H. R. "Distinctive Aspects of Child Welfare." Child Welfare XXXVI (July 1957): 1–6.

Hamilton, M. L. "Evaluation of a Parent and Child Center Program." Child Welfare LI (April 1972): 248–258.

Hargreaves, W. A.; McIntyre, M. H.; Attkisson, C. C.; and Siegel, L. M. "Outcome Measurement Instruments for Use in Mental Health Program Evaluation." In Resource Materials for Community Mental Health Program Evaluation. Part IV–Evaluating the Effectiveness of Services. U.S. Department of Health, Education, and Welfare, National Institute of Mental Health. Rockville, MD: DHEW Pub. No. (ADM) 75-222, 1975.

Hartman, B., and Wickey, J. "The Person-Oriented Record in Treatment." Social Work 23 (July 1978): 296–299.

Hatry, Harry P. "The Status of Productivity Measurement in the Public Sector." Public Administration Review 1 (January/February 1978): 28–33.

Haynes, S. N., and Wilson, C. C. Behavioral Assessment. San Francisco, CA: Jossey-Bass, 1979.

Helfer, Ray E.; McKinney, John P.; and Kempe, Ruth. "Arresting or Freezing the Developmental Process," in Child Abuse and Neglect: The Family and the Community, edited by Ray E. Helfer and C. Henry Kempe. Cambridge, MA: Ballinger, 1976.

Helmstadter, G. C. Principles of Psychological Measurement. New York, NY: Appleton-Century Crofts, 1964.

Hepner, K., and Maiden, N. C. "Growth Rate, Nutrient Intake and 'Mothering' as Determinants of Malnutrition in Disadvantaged Children." Nutrition Review 29 (1971): 219–223.

Horowitz, Bernard, and Wolock, Isabel. "Material Deprivation, Child Maltreatment, and Agency Interventions Among Poor Families," in The Social Context of Child Abuse and Neglect, edited by L. H. Pelton. New York, NY: Human Sciences Press, 1981.

Howard, G. "Response-Shift Bias: A Problem in Evaluating Interventions with Pre/Post Self Reports." Evaluation Review 4 (February 1980): 93–106.

Huitema, B. E. The Analysis of Covariance and Alternatives. New York: John Wiley & Sons, 1980.

Jenkins, S., and Norman, E. Beyond Placement. New York, NY: Columbia University Press, 1975.

Johnson, O. G. Tests and Measurements in Child Development: Handbook II (Vol. 1). San Francisco, CA: Jossey-Bass, 1976.

Jones, Mary Ann. Serving Families at Risk of Dissolution: The Evaluation. New York, NY: Human Resource Administration, 1981.

Kadushin, A. Child Welfare Services (2nd edition). New York, NY: The MacMillan Company, 1980.

————. "Child Welfare Strategy in the Coming Years: An Overview," in Child Welfare Strategy in the Coming Years. Washington, D.C.: U.S. Department of Health, Education, and Welfare, 1978.

Kahn, A. J. "Child Welfare," in Encyclopedia of Social Work (seventeenth edition). Washington, D.C.: National Association of Social Workers, Inc., 1977.

Kim, J., and Mueller, C. W. Factor Analysis. Beverly Hills, CA: Sage Publications, 1978.

Kiresuk, J., and Sherman, E. "Goal Attainment Scaling: A General Method for Evaluating Comprehensive Community Mental Health Programs." Community Mental Health Journal 4 (1968): 443–453.

Kiresuk, T., and Sherman, R. "A Reply to the Critique of Goal Attainment Scaling." Social Work Research and Abstracts 13 (Summer 1977): 9–11.

Koss, M.; Millar, A.; Hatry, H.; and Houghton, J. V. Social Services: What Happens to Clients. Washington, D.C.: Urban Institute, 1979.

Kratochwill, T. R. (ed). Single Subject Research: Strategies for Evaluating Change. New York, NY: Academic Press, 1978.

Kremer, D. Personal Communication. Michigan Department of Social Services, 1980.

Lafferty, W.; Cote, J.; Chafe, P.; Kellar, L.; and Robertson, H. The Use of the Parenting Stress Index (PSI) for the Evaluation of a Systematic Training for Effective Parenting (STEP) Programme. Ontario, Canada: Beechgrove Regional Children's Center, 1980.

Lafiosca, T. The Relationship of Parent Stress to Anxiety, Approval, Motivation, and Children's Behavior Problems. Unpublished doctoral dissertation. University of Virginia, Institute of Clinical Psychology, 1981.

Lahti, J. "A Follow-up Study of Foster Children in Permanent Placements." Social Service Review 5 (December 1982): 556–571.

Legal Action Center. "Confidentiality and Child Abuse Reporting." Of Substance: A Newsletter for the Substance Abuse Treatment Community (Winter 1983–84): 1–2.

Lemke, E., and Wiersma, W. Principles of Psychological Measurement. Chicago, IL: Rand McNally College Publishing Company, 1976.

Light, J. "Measures of Association and Agreement," in Discrete Multivariate Analysis: Theory and Practice, edited by Y. M. M. Bishop, S. E. Fineberg, and P. W. Holland. Cambridge, MA: MIT Press, 1975.

Mack, J. L. "Behavior Ratings On Recidivist and Non-recidivist Delinquent Rates." Psychological Reports 25 (1969): 260.

Magura, S. "Are Services to Prevent Foster Care Effective?" Children and Youth Services Review 3 (1981): 193–212.

———. "Clients View Outcomes of Child Protective Services." Social Casework (November 1982): 522–531.

———, and DeRubeis, R. The Effectiveness of Preventive Services for Families with Abused, Neglected and Disturbed Children: Second Year Evaluation of the Hudson County Project. Trenton, NJ: Bureau of Research, Division of Youth and Family Services, 1980.

———, and Moses, B. S. "Outcome Measurement in Child Welfare." Child Welfare LIX (December 1980): 595–606.

———, and Moses, B.S. "Clients as Evaluators in Child Protective Services." Child Welfare LXIII (March/April 1984): 99–112.

Majchrzak, A.; Schroeder, A.; Patchen, R. Assessing and Improving State Social Service Programs. Final Report. Volume I. Rockville, MD: Westat, 1982.

Maluccio, A. N. "Perspectives of Social Workers and Clients on Treatment Outcome." Social Casework 60 (July 1979): 394–401.

Marsh, E. J., and Johnston, C. "Parental Perceptions of Child Behavior Problems, Parenting Self-Esteem and Mothers' Reported Stress in Younger and Older Hyperactive and Normal Children." Journal of Consulting and Clinical Psychology 51 (1983): 86–99.

———; Johnston, C.; and Kovitz, K. "A Comparison of the Mother-child Interactions of Physically Abused and Non-abused Children During Play and Task Situations." 1982. Mimeo.

Martens, W., and Holmstrup, E. "Problem-Oriented Recording." Social Casework 55 (November 1974): 554–561.

Mayfield, D.; McLeod, G.; and Hall, P. "The Cage Questionnaire: Validation of a New Alcoholism Screening Instrument." American Journal of Psychiatry 131, 10 (October 1974): 1121–1123.

Millar, A.; Hatry, H.; and Koss, M. Monitoring the Outcomes of Social Services. Vol. II: A Review of Past Research and Test Activities. Washington, D.C.: The Urban Institute, 1977.

Millar, R., and Millar, A. (eds.). Developing Client Outcome Monitoring Systems: A Guide for State and Local Service Agencies. Washington, D.C.: The Urban League, 1981.

Miller, S. H. Children as Parents. New York, NY: Child Welfare League of America, 1983.

Michigan Department of Social Services. 1980–81 Annual Plan. Lansing, MI: Michigan Department of Social Services, 1980.

Minnesota Department of Public Welfare and Walker and Associates, Inc. Evaluation: A Total Approach. Minneapolis, MN: Minnesota Department of Public Welfare and Walker and Associates, Inc., 1984.

Mnookin, R. H. "Foster Care—In Whose Best Interest?" Harvard Educational Review XLIII, 4 (November 1973).

Mutschler, E., and Rosen A. "Evaluation of Treatment Outcome by Client and Social Worker." The Social Welfare Forum, 1979. New York, NY: Columbia University Press, 1980.

Namboodiri, N. K.; Carter, L. F.; and Blalock, H. M. Applied Multivariate Analysis and Experimental Designs. New York, NY: McGraw-Hill, Inc., 1975.

Neuman, Edward, and Turem, Jerry. "The Crisis of Accountability." Social Work 19 (January 1974): 5–16.

Nunnally, J. C. Psychometric Theory (2nd ed.). New York, NY: McGraw-Hill, 1978.

O'Muircheartaigh, C. A., and Payne, C. (eds.). Exploring Data Structures. London, England: John Wiley and Sons, 1977.

Patrick, D. L.; Bush, J. W.; and Chen, M. M. "Toward an Operational Definition of Health." Journal of Health and Social Behavior 14 (March 1973): 6–23.

Patterson, P. G. R., and Thompson, M. G. G. "Emotional Child Abuse and Neglect: An Exercise in Definition," in The Maltreatment of the School Aged Child, edited by R. Volpe, M. Breton, and J. Mitton. Lexington, MA: Lexington Books, 1980.

Pelton, L. H. "Child Abuse and Neglect and Protective Intervention in Mercer County, N.J.," in The Social Context of Child Abuse and Neglect, edited by L. H. Pelton. New York, NY: Human Sciences Press, 1981.

———. "The Client Perspective in Child Welfare Cases," in Basic Processes In Helping Relationships, edited by T. A. Wills. New York, NY: Academic Press, 1982.

Peterson, D. R. "Behavior Problems of Middle Childhood." Journal of Consulting Psychology 25 (1961): 205–209.

Phillips, M. H. The Forgotten Ones: Treatment of Single Parent Multi-problem Families in a Residential Setting. New York, NY: Henry Street Settlement, 1981.

———; Shyne, A. W.; Sherman, E. A.; and Haring, B. L. Factors Associated with Placement Decisions in Child Welfare. New York, NY: Child Welfare League of America, Inc., 1971.

Pinckney, Vergil M., and Shears, Dale. An Update of Evaluation—1974 through 1980. Lansing, MI: Michigan Department of Social Services, 1981.

Polansky, N. A.; Borgman, R. D.; DeSaix, C.; and Smith, B. J. "Two Modes of Material Immaturity and Their Consequences." Child Welfare XLIX (June 1970): 312–323.

———; Chalmers, M. A.; Buttenwieser, E.; and Williams, P. "Assessing Adequacy of Child Caring: An Urban Scale." Child Welfare LVII (1978): 439–449.

———; Chalmers, M. A.; Buttenwieser, E.; and Williams, P. Damaged Parents. Chicago, IL: University of Chicago Press, 1981.

———; Cabral, R. J.; Magura, S.; and Phillips, H. "Comparative Norms for the Childhood Level of Living Scale." Journal of Social Service Research 6 (Spring/Summer 1983): 45–55.

———; Ammons, P.; and Weathersby, B. "Is There an American Standard of Child Care?" Social Work 28 (September–October 1983): 341–346.

Project Share. The Project Share Collection 1976–1979. Rockville, MD: Project Share, 1980.

Quay, H. C., and Parsons, C. B. The Differential Behavioral Classification of the Juvenile Offender (2nd edition). Washington, D.C.: U.S. Bureau of Prisons, 1971.

Quay, H., and Peterson, D. Manual for the Behavior Problem Checklist. New Brunswick, NJ: School of Professional Psychology, Rutgers University, 1979.

Quay, H. C., and Quay, L. C. "Behavior Problems in Early Adolescence." Child Development 36 (1965): 215–220.

———; Sprague, R. C.; Schulman, H. S.; and Miller, A. L. "Some Correlates of Personality Disorder and Conduct Disorder in a Child Guidance Clinic Sample." Psychology in the Schools 3 (1966): 44–47.

Reid, J. H. Child Welfare Perspectives. New York, NY: Child Welfare League of America, Inc., 1979.

Reid, W. J. The Task-Centered System. New York, NY: Columbia University Press, 1978.

———, and Smith, A. D. Research in Social Work. New York, NY: Columbia University Press, 1981.

Rossi, P. H.; Freeman, H. E.; and Wright, S. R. Evaluation: A Systematic Approach. Beverly Hills, CA.: Sage Publications, 1979.

Rubenstein, H., and Bloch, M. H. "Helping Clients Who Are Poor: Worker and Client Perceptions of Problems, Activities, and Outcomes." Social Service Review 52 (March 1978): 69–84.

Scheirer, M. "Program Participants' Positive Perceptions: Psychological Conflict of Interest in Social Program Evaluation." Evaluation Quarterly 2 (February 1978): 53–70.

Schuerman, J. R. "Do Family Services Help? An Essay Review." Social Service Review 49 (September 1975): 363–375.

Schulman, L. "A Study of Practice Skills." Social Work 23 (July 1978): 274–281.

Seaberg, J., and Gillespie, D. "Goal Attainment Scaling: A Critique." Social Work Research and Abstracts 13 (Summer 1977): 4–8.

Selltiz, C.; Wrightsman, S.; and Cook, S. W. Research Methods in Social Relations (3rd edition). New York, NY: Holt Rinehart and Winston, 1976.

Shapiro, Deborah. Parents and Protectors: A Study in Child Abuse and Neglect. New York, NY: Child Welfare League of America, Inc., 1979.

Shyne, A. W. (ed). Use of Judgments as Data in Social Work Research. New York, NY: National Association of Social Workers, 1959.

Shyne, A. "Evaluation in Child Welfare." Child Welfare LV (January 1976): 5–18.

Shyne, A. W. "Who Are the Children? A National Overview of Services?" Social Work Research and Abstracts 16 (Spring 1980): 26–33.

Shyne, A. W., and Schroeder, A. G. National Study of Social Services to Children and Their Families. DHEW Pub. No. (OH DS) 78-30150. Rockville, MD: Westat, Inc., 1978.

Spivack, G., and Spotts, J. Devereux Child Behavior Rating Scale. Devon, PA: The Devereux Foundation, 1966.

Stein, T. Social Work Practice in Child Welfare. Englewood Cliffs, NJ: Prentice-Hall, Inc., 1981.

Straus, M. A., and Brown, B. W. Family Measurement Techniques: Abstracts of Published Instruments, 1935–1974. Revised Edition. Minneapolis, MN: University of Minnesota Press, 1978.

Stringer, T., and Marth, H. Integrated Performance Management Reporting System (IPMRS). Springfield, IL: Department of Child and Family Services, 1982.

Sundel, M., et al. Local Child Welfare Services Self-Assessment Manual. Washington, D.C.: The Urban Institute, Social Services Research Program, DHEW Contract No. 105-75-1113, 1978.

Swire, M. A., and Kavaler, F. "The Health Status of Foster Children." Child Welfare LVI (December 1977): 635–653.

Thurstone, L. L., and Chave, J. The Measurement of Attitude. Chicago, IL: University of Chicago Press, 1929.

Toby, J. "The Socialization and Control of Deviant Motivation," in Handbook of Criminology, edited by D. Glaser. New York, NY: Holt, Rinehart & Winston, Inc., 1974.

Torgerson, W. S. Theory and Methods of Scaling. New York, NY: John Wiley, 1958.

United Way of America. UWASIS: A Taxonomy of Social Goals and Human Service Programs. Alexandria, VA: United Way of America, 1976.

U.S. Department of Health and Human Services. Code of Federal Regulations—Protection of Human Subjects, Part 46. March 8, 1983.

———. Study Findings: National Study of the Incidence and Severity of Child Abuse and Neglect. DHHS Publication No. (OHDS) 81-30325, 1981.

U.S. Department of Health, Education, and Welfare, Administration for Children, Youth, and Families. Research, Demonstration, and Evaluation Studies. Fiscal Years, 1977, 1978, 1979. Washington, D.C.: U.S. Department of Health Education, and Welfare.

U.S. Department of Health, Education, and Welfare. Report to the Congress by the Comptroller General of the United States. Washington, D.C.: Social and Rehabilitation Service, Department of Health, Education, and Welfare, 1976.

U.S. Department of Health, Education, and Welfare, National Institute of Mental Health. Handbook of Psychiatric Rating Scales. 2nd edition. Washington, D.C.: DHEW Pub. No. (HSM) 73-9061, 1973.

Walker, D. K. Socioemotional Measures for Preschool and Kindergarden Children. San Francisco, CA: Jossey-Bass, 1973.

Wallace, D. "The Chemung County Evaluation of Casework Services to Dependent Multi-problem Families." Social Service Review 41 (December 1967): 349–389.

———, and Smith, J. "The Study: Methodology and Findings," in The Multiproblem Dilemma, edited by G. Brown. Methuchen, NJ: Scarecrow Press, 1968.

Ware, J.; Davis-Avery, A.; and Stewart, A. "The Measurement and Meaning of Patient Satisfaction." Health and Medical Care Services Review 1 (January/February 1978): 2–15.

Westat. Register of State Source Data. Washington, D.C.: Westat, 1980.

Zimmerman, J. L. The Relationship Between Support Systems and Stress in Families With a Handicapped Child. Unpublished doctoral dissertation, University of Virginia, 1979.

Zold, A. C., and Speer, D. C. "Follow-up Study of Child Guidance Patients by Means of The Behavior Problem Checklist." Journal of Clinical Psychology 27 (1971): 519–524.